Generis

PUBLISHING

Reporting Importance for Financial Stability

The Islamic Banking Concept

Sevgi Osman

Title: **Reporting Importance for Financial Stability**

The Islamic Banking Concept

ISBN: 979-8-89966-084-9

Author: Sevgi Osman

Cover image: www.pixabay.com

Publisher: Generis Publishing
Online orders: www.generis-publishing.com
Contact email: info@generis-publishing.com

The effects of COVID 19 on the economy and necessary measures

Sevgi Osman, VFU Assoc. Prof., PhD, sevgi.osman@vfu.bg

Varna Free University (VFU) "Chernorizets Hrabar",
Department of Economics

CONTENTS

Abstract

Periods of slowdown in economic activity and recessions are part of the process of economic development. But the current crisis is different from the usual downturns in economic activity. The protracted nature of the health crisis is affecting the global economy beyond traditional measures with potentially long-term consequences. Large developed economies, which account for 60% of global economic activity, are projected to operate below their potential output at least until 2024. Growing economic effects are increasing liquidity constraints and tightening the credit market in global financial markets as firms accumulate cash, with negative effects on economic growth. At the same time, the financial markets are doing what was expected - increased government bond issuance in the United States, Europe and other regions to cover government debt during the economic recession and increased fiscal spending to combat the effects of COVID-19. Central banks and monetary authorities in developed and emerging market economies are taking a series of interventions in financial markets, and national governments are intervening with a range of fiscal policy initiatives to stimulate their economies. But exactly what types of measures have been taken in different regions? How effective are they? What impact do they have on macroeconomic indicators and financial markets? What are the forecasts for their future impact - in the EU, and especially in Bulgaria, as the risks to Bulgaria's recovery are mostly related to the Covid-19 pandemic and its impact on the financial sector. The answers to all these questions are the subject of this report.

Key words: Covid 19, economic and financial effects, measures

1. Introduction

Unlike most previous economic recessions, in which the reason for starting this phase of the economic cycle is an imbalance in the economic structure itself, now the beginning is given by a biological threat to the social structure. This means that in the context of a viral epidemic, businesses and jobs that are economically viable will become financially vulnerable, just as businesses and jobs that do not have an economic future in terms of economic rationality are just as vulnerable. This difference requires consideration of circumstances that were not part of the economic analysis of previous crises, and here the quality of banking expertise will be very important.

The current COVID-19 crisis is different from the usual declines in economic activity, for at least two reasons. On the one hand, the crisis is not the result of internal imbalances in the economy, but is caused by external factors. On the other hand, the crisis is affecting both the supply and demand of goods and services at the same time. The crisis is having a direct impact on both the real sector and the financial sector of the economy.

The protracted nature of the health crisis is affecting the global economy beyond traditional measures with potentially lasting consequences. Economic projections reflect the continuing risks to a sustainable global recovery posed by the resumption of infectious cases and the potential inflationary pressures associated with subdued consumer demand fueled by rising personal savings. On the supply side, the shortage reflects continuing disruptions in labor markets, bottlenecks in production and the supply chain, disruptions in global energy markets and supply and transport constraints that increase inflationary pressures.

Concerns are compounded by the emergence of new disease variants and rotating pandemic hotspots that are provoking national efforts to curb infections and fully restore economic activity. Large developed economies, which account for 60% of global economic activity, are projected to operate below their potential level of production at least until 2024, indicating lower national and individual economic well-being than pre-pandemic levels. Compared to the synchronized nature of the global economic slowdown in the first half of 2020, the global economy has shown signs of a two-way recovery that began in the third quarter of 2020. Vaccinations are high but at a slower pace in emerging economies, where vaccination levels are low. Overall, developed economies have made progress in vaccinating a growing proportion of their populations, raising the prospects for sustainable economic recovery in late 2021 and 2022.

However, new variants of the COVID-19 virus and an increase in diagnoses in major developing countries economies and resistance to vaccination among some populations in developed economies raise questions about the speed and strength of economic recovery in the short term. The economic consequences of the pandemic have different effects on certain sectors of the economy, especially the services sector, and certain groups of the population, and could put at risk ongoing labor dislocations. Human costs of lost lives will have a lasting impact on global economic growth in addition to the cost of rising poverty levels and growing social unrest. Some estimates suggest that 65 million to 75 million people may be in extreme poverty in 2020, with 80 million more malnourished than pre-pandemic levels. Some estimates suggest that the downturn in world trade has dealt a particularly severe economic blow to trade-dependent emerging and emerging economies.

2. Consequences

2.1. Economic consequences of the pandemic

As infectious disease cases began to rise sharply in late February 2020, governments took unprecedented steps in March 2020 to curb the spread of the pandemic, leading to a global economic recession. The government's responses in March 2020 were exceptional in terms of the speed with which they were implemented, the wide range of fiscal and monetary policies they adopted, and the number of participating countries, often without a formal, coordinated plan. Initially, governments adopted monetary policies aimed at stabilizing financial markets and ensuring credit flow. In the second phase, governments focused their political action on fiscal measures aimed at sustaining economic growth, as they adopted quarantines and social distancing measures. In the third phase, governments shifted their policies to developing, purchasing and distributing vaccines. The economic effects of the pandemic were initially expected to be due to short-term supply problems, as factory production declined and workers were quarantined to reduce the spread of the virus through social interaction. But virus-related supply shocks have created longer-lasting and widespread demand shocks, as reduced consumer and business activity has led to lower economic growth in most countries. Almost every country experienced a decline in economic activity in the second quarter of 2020, with the exception of China, which had a growth rate of 10% compared to the previous quarter and was one of the few countries to report overall positive growth in 2020.

These growing economic effects have potentially increased liquidity constraints and tightened credit markets in global financial markets, as firms have amassed cash, with negative effects on economic growth. At the same time, financial markets took into account what was expected - increased government bond issuance in the United States, Europe and other regions to cover government debt during the economic recession and increased fiscal spending to combat the effects of COVID-19. In contrast to the financial crisis of 2008-2009, reduced consumer demand, labor market problems and reduced business activity, rather than risky trading by global banks, led to problems with corporate credit and potential insolvency.

Liquidity and credit market problems have shifted the focus of government policy from the health crisis to macroeconomic and financial markets. In essence, as businesses struggled to address labor and output issues at the firm level, national leaders sought to pursue fiscal policies to prevent sharp contractions in economic growth, and central banks adjusted monetary policies to address growing credit. market problems.

The IMF called on G20 leaders to support supportive monetary and fiscal policies to reduce the economic impact of the global recession, and in particular recommended a combination of adaptive monetary policies characterized by low interest rates and central bank programs to facilitate access to loans, fiscal support for individuals and companies and participation in a synchronized infrastructure investment program.[1]

According to IMF forecasts, the loss of global economic output between 2020 and 2025 as a result of the pandemic will amount to $ 28 trillion and 120 million jobs in the tourism industry alone. The economic recession has raised concerns about growing debt problems in emerging economies, where about 40% of banks' assets are at risk.

At the macro level, the health pandemic affects the economy through several channels. In the first place, there is an effect on the aggregate supply in case of shutdown of entire sectors of the economy, which is a prerequisite for rising unemployment. The global scale of the health crisis and its epicenter in the EU and the euro area is creating additional external pressure on broken global supply chains.

These factors for shrinking economic activity overlap with the already observed signals of a synchronized *slowdown in the global economy* from 2019, as determined by the International Monetary Fund (IMF). The complex of economic factors and consequences and especially the uncertainty about the duration of the pandemic make the unpredictable and accurate economic effect on the economy

[1] According to an IMF analysis, all other things being equal, an increase in infrastructure spending by the G20 countries by half a percent of their GDP in 2021 and 1% in 2022 by 2025 would increase global GDP by 2% in 2021. 2025, compared to growth below 1.2% for an out-of-sync approach.30.

at the macro level. The risks in the development of the current crisis can be manifested both in terms of its duration and in terms of the size of the declines in key economic indicators such as GDP (or value added of individual economic sectors), household income and employment.

Another aspect of the crisis also carries risks. In the conditions of *reduced household income* and reduced income for enterprises, it is possible to increase the share of the gray economy in order to avoid the costs of paying direct and indirect taxes and social security contributions. This will lead to a further reduction in budget revenues, hiring uncontrolled employees who will not receive social and health insurance, and companies that apply these practices will have limited opportunities to make new capital investments.

Specific risk also arises from uncertain *price dynamics*. Due to the reduction of production and the lack of sufficient financial resources for hiring new employees, as well as for new investments, it is possible that many companies, mainly producing basic necessities, will increase the prices of their products to cover accumulated losses. and accumulate fresh monetary resources. This can lead to supply-side inflation.

2.2. Consequences for individual economic activities

In fact, almost all types of services have virtually ceased operations as a result of the state of emergency. As a result of the increased number of unemployed and unpaid leave employees, household incomes are declining and will remain relatively low until the end of the state of emergency or until the start of work. During an economic crisis, household consumption tends to decline. This is understandable given the decline in income as a result of reduced production and rising unemployment. In addition, consumers' priorities are changing, and their attitudes towards the different brands and the usefulness they bring are changing. The three main trends that typically manifest themselves in consumer behavior determine the relationships between society and individual consumers, and they are already beginning to manifest themselves in the current crisis:

- There is a high sensitivity to any risks;
- Consumers are depressed and often postpone purchases of non-essential goods;
- Consumer restraint is shown and a larger share of income is saved;

- Consumption becomes more sensitive to prices and therefore less sensitive to other parameters of goods and services.

2.3. Consequences for the Financial sector

The current economic situation is radically different from the crisis of 2009. Then the problems started in the financial sector and moved to the real sector, and now the opposite direction (Congressional Research Service ,2021):

As an indicator of the economic impact of the pandemic, financial news has sometimes been a major driver of market activity. For example, the Dow Jones Industrial Average (DJIA), along with other market indices, lost a third of its value between February 14, 2022 and March 23, 2020. The index rose steadily between March and November and rose by almost three percentage points in Monday, 9 November 2020, when it was announced that a vaccine against COVID-19 had been developed (Telford, 2020). The rise in market indices reflects investors' positive assessment of effective vaccines against COVID-19, political developments in the United States, potential additional measures by governments to stimulate economic activity and the prospects for stronger economic growth in the coming years (Smith, Colby, 2020).

Following vaccine announcements, DJIA rose a total of more than 3,700 points, or nearly 14% in January 2021. In the first six months of 2021, DJIA gained 15% market value. DJIA has an upward trend in 2021, rising by more than 14% between January 4, 2021 and September 17. However, in June 2021, the index lost a quarter of the point as a whole, the first such decline since January 2021. In October, trading sessions closing lower also outperformed sessions closing higher.

By the end of January 2021, the dollar had depreciated by more than 11% from its highest level since March 2020. The development of vaccines against COVID-19 may have affected the value of the dollar in various ways. As noted above, central banks' overall policies to keep key interest rates low have also affected dollar-denominated currency developments in 2021 by reducing arbitrage capacity and limiting volatility. Despite periods of appreciation and depreciation of the dollar in 2020 and 2021, by the end of April 2021 the dollar fell by 2% compared to January 2, 2020. In part, the decision to withdraw the UK from the EU strengthened as the euro, and the pound, which tended to devalue the dollar. Between June 10, 2021 and August 20, 2021, the dollar rose by about 3.6%, almost reaching the value registered on January 2, 2020. The strengthening of the dollar is due to a number of factors, including the expected change in monetary policy. Under standard models, the depreciation of the dollar is expected to lower export prices and in turn increase demand for US exports or increase export volumes, while import volumes are expected to decline along with rising foreign currency prices against the dollar. However, GDP data for the second quarter of 2021 show that US trade prices and trade volumes tend to move in tandem.

Vaccine prospects initially signaled a possible end to business blockades, social constraints and reduced demands on politicians to implement additional fiscal and monetary policies. At the end of June 2021, various states in the United States again imposed guidelines for social distancing, which raised the prospect of delayed recovery. Prolonged recovery may increase the financial burden on small and medium-sized enterprises, which face liquidity constraints and insolvency prospects (IMF, 2020).

Differences in policy approaches between countries initially delayed a coordinated response. This lack of response may have caused long-term damage to the global economy. In some countries, the pandemic has increased the importance of public health as a matter of national security and as a national economic priority along with traditional national security issues such as terrorism, cyber attacks and the proliferation of weapons of mass destruction (FOMC Statement, 2020).

3. Measures Taken

Central banks and monetary authorities in developed and emerging market economies have undertaken a series of interventions in financial markets, and national governments have adopted a set of fiscal policy initiatives to stimulate their economies. As global economic conditions deteriorated in the first quarter of 2020, major internationally active banks tripled the amount of assets they held as loss provisions, according to the BIS (BIS, 2021). However, as economic conditions improved in the second quarter, banks began to reduce their assets and by the end of 2020 provisions for losses had returned to pre-pandemic levels. As a result of the potential damage to the global economy resulting from the pandemic, the BIS said economists could describe the pandemic as "the turning point of the 21st century". The measures taken can be systematized in the following groups:

3.1. By types

- Industrial measures

In 2020, governments adopted a number of measures, both nationally and internationally, to address the health and economic consequences of the COVID-19 pandemic. These measures include incentives to increase domestic production of vaccines, personal protective equipment (PPE) and direct government intervention to increase production in facilities that produce PPE materials. The change in the approach to the dimensions of national security of foreign investment, especially in developed economies, reflects the change in the concept of foreign investment, trade and national security.

- Government policies

On 15 April 2021, the Director-General of the WTO called on its members and vaccine manufacturers to increase production, reduce export restrictions and suspend intellectual property rights over COVID-19 vaccines in order to increase immunizations. The WHO says new COVID-19 cases have almost doubled worldwide in the past two months, approaching the highest levels of infection since the pandemic, with the largest outbreaks in India, Brazil, Poland, Turkey and some others. countries. Also on April 15, 2021, a group of 175 former world leaders and Nobel laureates called on the United States to suspend intellectual property rights over COVID-19 vaccines to facilitate the international production and distribution of vaccines, allowing developing countries to produce their own vaccines. The group warned that "... unfair access to vaccines will affect the global economy and prevent it from recovering." On April 16, the WHO announced that it would develop one or more COVID-19 technology centers to "provide appropriate technology. of interested producers "in emerging economies.

As a result of the resumption of cases, the IMF argues that developed economies need to maintain fiscal support for consumers and businesses as the most effective means of stimulating their economies. The IMF says this support is needed because the global economy is experiencing what economists call a Keynesian liquidity trap named after economist John Maynard Keynes. Theoretically, the liquidity trap exists when central banks' key interest rates are so low that they have little influence through traditional means of influencing business and consumer activity. According to the IMF, in 60% of the world economy, central banks have raised key interest rates below 1%, and in one-fifth of the world economy, interest rates have been below zero. In these circumstances, economists usually argue that adjusting fiscal policy or government taxation and spending is the more effective policy tool for boosting economic growth. The IMF concluded that "fiscal policy should play a leading role in recovery."

- Fiscal measures

Central governments in developed and emerging economies have adopted various fiscal measures to provide financial support to the health sector, households and companies, although the size and scope of programs vary by country. These measures generally include tax cuts and tax deferrals for individuals and businesses, supplements to the salaries and incomes of individuals, including extending unemployment insurance and other payments to businesses. The US Congress has approved historic fiscal spending packages, while other governments have abandoned traditional lending ceilings to boost fiscal spending to sustain economic growth. In some emerging economies, governments have reportedly adopted special programs to provide financial assistance to "informal" workers or workers outside traditional labor markets (such as the family business).

In developed economies, however, consumers have sharply increased their savings as they face limited spending opportunities and / or concerns about lost jobs, income, etc. International organizations have taken steps to provide loans and other financial assistance to countries in need. These and other actions have been described as "unprecedented", a term often used to describe pandemics and political reactions.

According to IMF estimates, measures related to government spending and revenue to maintain economic activity, adopted by September 2021, amount to 16.9 trillion dollars. The increase in government borrowing as a result of the pandemic reached 10.2% of world gross domestic product (GDP) in 2020, 7.9% in 2021 and 5.2% in 2022. Other estimates show that central banks are committing $ 17 trillion to counter the pandemic economic effects.

- Worker support programs

As part of their fiscal policy measures, governments in developed economies have strengthened existing workers' support programs and adopted new ones. The OECD categorizes the various job retention programs into six main groups, which have supported 60 million workers in developed economies (OECD,2021). Worker support programs are expected to vary from country to country, but generally include increased subsidies for existing programs. designed to support workers for lost working hours or extended wage subsidies to maintain pre - pandemic employment levels. Other programs have helped companies retain staff, making it easier for them to return to work quickly after removing pandemic restrictions (OECD, 2020).

- Monetary and prudential measures

Among central banks, the Federal Reserve has initiated emergency measures to address the economic consequences of COVID-19, which were not taken after the global financial crisis of 2008-2009. 11 developed and 28 developing economies, banks are moving fast and on a huge scale (Cantu, 2020). The BIS groups central bank measures into five categories: (1) interest rates; (2) backup policies; (3) lending operations; (4) asset purchases; and (5) foreign exchange policies, including foreign exchange swaps. In some cases, central banks have also eased capital buffers and countercyclical capital buffers adopted after the 2008-2009 financial crisis (Arnold,2020). However, in general, banks have not used their capital buffers to provide credit in their respective economies.

The five policy areas identified by the BIS are:

- Interest rates. Interest rates were reduced in most countries, except Japan and the euro area, where interest rates were zero. In many countries, monetary authorities have announced that they will maintain adaptive policies (low interest rates) for a long period of time.
- Reserve policies. With low interest rates, some central banks have also adjusted reserve requirements for commercial banks, which is changing the amount of assets that banks need to hold. Some central banks have adjusted the rate used by the central bank to pay interest on required and excess reserves. Other banks have changed the compliance requirements or the types of assets that can be reported as reserves.
- Credit operations. Central banks have adjusted credit facilities to maintain liquidity by expanding existing credit facilities or by creating new programs, which account for 60% of lending operations. In some cases, policies have targeted specific segments of the financial market, especially banks and small and medium-sized enterprises.
- Purchases of assets. Central banks in developed economies used targeted and non-targeted lending operations to support monetary policy and maintain liquidity in the financial system. These goals have been achieved by increasing the size of existing programs and by extending loan maturities. Central banks in emerging economies have expanded their existing liquidity by lowering interest rates, expanding the types of eligible collateral and increasing the number and types of eligible counterparties. The main difference between existing and new lending policies is that a large proportion of new funding goes to the private sector, including lending measures to support the flow of credit to households and non-financial corporations. In developed economies, about 40% of asset purchase programs are new facilities, while the share of new programs in

emerging economies is over 90%. In addition, asset purchases were divided almost evenly between public and private assets in developed economies

- Foreign currency. The Federal Reserve initially introduced currency swaps with five countries (Canada, the eurozone, Japan, the United Kingdom, Switzerland), followed by swap lines extended to nine other countries (Australia, Brazil, Korea) to ease pressure on the dollar.

In the early stages of the economic crisis, central banks served as lenders of last resort through large purchases of government debt and as buyers or lenders of last resort for private sector securities, activities that were previously used for extraordinary restraints. As a result of these activities, the BIS claims that central banks effectively managed the initial liquidity crisis, the first of three phases often identified with financial crises. The second and third phases, insolvency and recovery, have also been successful, but could still become dangerous if the pandemic economic crisis continues. Capital buffers have been increased since the 2008-2009 financial crisis to help banks absorb losses and remain solvent during financial crises. Some governments have ordered banks to freeze dividend payments and stop paying bonuses. In its report of 13 July 2021 to the G20 Finance Ministers and Governors, the Financial Stability Board (FSB) argued that monetary and fiscal action taken by central banks and national governments, respectively, combined with regulatory and supervisory measures, effectively manage the impact of the crisis, support the functioning of the global financial system and facilitate the financing of the real economy (Brainard, 2021).

Since the beginning of the pandemic, central banks have often adopted such policies, although not always in unison. Most central banks have followed the Federal Reserve in cutting interest rates as one of their main policy instruments to support economic activity; The ECB (Eurozone) and Japan are notable exceptions, as they cut their key interest rates to zero before the economic recession. Low interest rates had an additional, though not necessarily foreseeable, impact on foreign exchange markets, reducing arbitrage opportunities and hence exchange rate volatility. According to some analysts, the mid-summer period of 2021 was the longest in history of low volatility between the dollar and the euro.

3.2. By regions

- USA

Recognizing the growing impact of the pandemic on financial markets and economic growth, the Federal Reserve (Fed) has taken a number of steps to promote economic and financial stability, thanks to the Fed's monetary policy and its role as a "lender of last resort." Some of these actions were aimed at stimulating economic activity by lowering interest rates; other actions were designed to provide liquidity in the financial markets so that companies have access to the necessary financing. In announcing its decisions, the Fed said that "COVID-19 has harmed communities and disrupted economic activity in many countries, including the United States." The US Congress passed a $ 1.9 trillion economic stimulus bill, designated the U.S. Rescue Plan Act (PL 117-2), which was signed by President Biden on March 11, 2021. On May 5, 2021, the U.S. Biden said he would support international discussions to lift intellectual property restrictions on the production of COVID-19 vaccines for emerging economies.[2]

Regarding the monetary and fiscal response to the economic downturn, Federal Reserve Chairman Powell said in a speech on October 6 that the monetary response included "the full range of instruments we have", including cuts in key interest rates, "unprecedented" purchases. assets, creating funds for emergency lending to households, businesses and state and local authorities and implementing targeted and temporary measures for banks to support their customers. These measures can be complemented by instruments of 1) Monetary Policy such as Forward Guidance and Quantitative Facility; 2) Liquidity actions such as Reserve Requirements, Derivatives, Discount Windows, Foreign Central

[2] On March 11, 2021, President Biden signed the $ 1.9 trillion U.S. Rescue Plan Act (P.L. 117-2) to stimulate the U.S. economy. The main features of the act include: • Extended unemployment benefits with a $ 300 weekly allowance until September 6, 2021. • $ 1,400. direct payments to individuals up to $ 75,000, $ 112,500 for single parents and $ 150,000 for couples. • Emergency paid leave, extended child tax credit up to $ 3,600 per child. • Over 50 billion grants and other payments to small businesses. • 350 billion dollars aid to state, local governments. • Financing of education: 130 billion. for schools; 40 billion for colleges and universities. • Nearly 50 billion for housing assistance • Over 160 billion in health-related programs, including COVID-19 vaccines, tests, contact tracking, and other • $ 50 billion. for transport services, including financing for airports, airlines and other railway services. • 10.4 billion dollars for agriculture, including debt relief for farmers. • 1.9 billion d. to improve cybersecurity. • Changes in other health care regulations;

Bank Swaps and Emergency Lending Facilities for the Non-Banking Financial System and 3) Fiscal Policy[3]

- Japan:

In response to the pandemic economic situation, the Bank of Japan injected $ 4.6 billion in liquidity into Japanese banks in March 2020 through short-term loans to buy corporate bonds and securities and twice as many exchange-traded funds to help Japanese businesses. The Japanese government has also promised to provide wage subsidies for parents forced to take leave due to school closures. In March, Japan also adopted an emergency fiscal package of about $ 1.1 trillion, roughly equal to 10% of Japan's annual gross domestic product (GDP). On April 27, 2020, the Bank of Japan announced that it would purchase unlimited amounts of government bonds and increase its purchases of corporate debt fourfold to keep interest rates low and boost Japan's economy. In May 2020, the Japanese cabinet proposed a second additional measure to provide $ 296 billion in spending and about $ 1.1 trillion in loans and guarantees financed by new bonds. This and previous set of expenditure measures were reported to be comparable to 40% of Japan's GDP and include grants to remuneration enterprises through the Japan Development Bank and small and medium-sized enterprise grants through the Regional Corporation for the Sustainability of Japan. Japan's economy, payments to help workers leave, and a reserve fund to provide capital injections to troubled companies through Japan Investment Corporation.

On monetary policy, the Bank of Japan (BOJ) has maintained its low interest rate policy of -0.1%, even as it increased its coronavirus credit facility from $ 700 billion to $ 1 trillion and said it would continue to buy commercial securities., corporate bonds and exchange traded funds amounting to ¥ 12 trillion per year. The COVID-19 loan facility has helped banks provide zero-interest loans to businesses. In a separate program, BOJ provided about ¥110 trillion for the purchase of commercial paper and corporate bonds and provided dollars through swap agreements with the US Federal Reserve. Japan said on August 17 that its economy contracted by 7.8% in the second quarter of 2020 compared to the previous quarter or at an annual rate of 27.8%. This decline in economic activity

[3] Marc Labonte, Specialist in Macroeconomic Policy, Government and Finance Division, CRS. CRS Insight IN11259, *Federal Reserve: Recent Actions in Response to COVID-19*, by Marc Labonte.

was accelerated by a decline in exports of 18.5% compared to the previous quarter (56.0% on an annual basis) and a decline in personal consumption by 8.6% (30.1% on an annual basis).

On July 19, 2021, the Bank of Japan issued a revised forecast, which is "very uncertain" that the impact of the pandemic will begin to decline in 2021 as a result of increased vaccinations. Japanese Prime Minister Suga announced on January 5, 2021, that Tokyo and three surrounding prefectures will launch a voluntary "soft" state of emergency on January 8, emphasizing long-distance work, limiting unnecessary travel and reducing sporting and cultural events. On April 23, 2021, Japan announced new two-week blockade protocols for Tokyo, Osaka and two other major cities due to an increase in viral infections. The blockades were intended to encourage workers to work from home, to close all establishments offering alcohol and supermarkets, but not schools. In April, May and June 2021, Japan again experienced a new wave with a total of 811,000 diagnosed cases. On July 8, Japanese officials announced that they would not be allowed to attend the Summer Olympics, which began at 23 July, after Japan declared a state of emergency again due to an increase in diagnosed cases of COVID-19.

On July 19, 2021, the Bank of Japan issued a revised forecast, which is "very uncertain" that the impact of the pandemic will begin to decline in 2021 as a result of increased vaccinations. Japanese Prime Minister Suga announced on January 5, 2021, that Tokyo and three surrounding prefectures will launch a voluntary "soft" state of emergency on January 8, emphasizing long-distance work, limiting unnecessary travel and reducing sporting and cultural events. On April 23, 2021, Japan announced new two-week blockade protocols for Tokyo,

Osaka and two other major cities due to an increase in viral infections. The blockades were intended to encourage workers to work from home, to close all establishments offering alcohol and supermarkets, but not schools. In April, May and June 2021, Japan again experienced a new wave with a total of 811,000 diagnosed cases. On July 8, Japanese officials announced that they would not be allowed to attend the Summer Olympics, which began at 23 July, after Japan declared a state of emergency again due to an increase in diagnosed cases of COVID-19.

- China

China was the first major country to resume economic growth since the outbreak of the COVID-19 pandemic. The government reported gross domestic product (GDP) growth of 3.2% in the second quarter and 4.9% GDP growth in the third quarter of 2020. However, China is still struggling with the economic consequences of the COVID-19 pandemic, including low domestic consumption, slow recovery in its leading export markets and reliance on government spending and exports to stimulate growth. China is also facing growing restrictions on its overseas trade, access to foreign technology and pressure on companies to diversify China-based supply chains. Against this background, the Chinese leadership is considering the country's economic direction and national industrial plans for the next 5 to 15 years.

To stimulate economic growth, China has provided $ 506 billion since February 2020 and has increased the government's budget deficit target to a record high of 3.6% of GDP, from 2.8% in 2019. China has cut value added tax value (VAT) and undertook a VAT exemption for certain goods and services. China's central bank has expanded monetary support by lowering interest rates, easing lending conditions and injecting liquidity into banks. Moving away from debt reduction efforts, the government announced the issuance of $ 142.9 billion in special treasury bonds for the first time since 2007; increase the quota for special bonds of the local government (source of infrastructure financing); and the rapid issuance of corporate bonds to cover the cost of a pandemic, but with potential broader applications. The IMF estimates that announced fiscal measures and financing plans amount to 4.1% of China's GDP by July 2020. The government says it seeks to control credit risk, but the need for additional fiscal and monetary support to boost growth may to undermine this goal.

- Europe

In the early stages of the pandemic, European countries did not adopt a synchronized fiscal policy, similar to that during the 2008-2009 global financial crisis. EU members basically used a combination of national fiscal policies and ECB bond buying to cope. with the economic impact of the pandemic. Individual countries have imposed quarantines and demanded the closure of business activities, travel and border restrictions, tax holidays for businesses, the extension of certain payments and guarantees on loans and subsidies to workers and businesses.[4] The European Commission has called for greater coordination among EU members in developing and implementing monetary and fiscal policies to address the economic consequences of the virus pandemic.

After lengthy debates, European leaders agreed on 21 July 2020 on a € 750 billion (about $ 859 billion) package for pandemic economic aid to European economies. On 11 December 2020, EU members finalized the agreement, which entered into force in February 2021.[5]

In assessing the crisis, the Commission argues that "the [risk] ... is that the crisis will lead to serious distortions within the single market and to profound economic, financial and social disparities between euro area Member States, which will ultimately could threaten the stability of Economic and Monetary Union. " According to this assessment, European countries will emerge from the recession at different rates and paths, reflecting differences in the timing of the introduction and elimination of social distancing measures, dependence on tourism and the scale and effectiveness of economic policies. The Commission also noted an increase in savings among EU households, which it said was largely unintentional rather than precautionary, and is expected to return to pre-crisis levels once consumers resume their usual spending patterns.

In previous actions, the European Commission has said it will ease sovereign debt rules to allow countries more flexibility in using fiscal policies. In addition, the European Central Bank (ECB) has stated its readiness to take "appropriate and targeted measures" if necessary. France, Italy, Spain and six other eurozone countries have argued for the creation of a "crown bond" - a joint common

---

[4] The WHO indicated in early January 2021 that 230 million Europeans were living under restrictions at the time and that 26 million Europeans became infected with COVID-19 in 2020. On 13 April 2021, the WHO estimated that 1 million Europeans have died from the disease, almost twice as many as in the United States. In an attempt to stop the spread of new strains of the virus, the United Kingdom, Ireland, Germany, Denmark and some northern Italian regions closed schools in January 2021 for several weeks.

[5] According to data published by Eurostat in August 2021, in the fourth quarter of 2020 and the first quarter of 2021, economic growth slowed by 0.4% and 0.1% in the EU and 0.6%, respectively. 3% in the euro area as a result of social constraints and business blockades during the period, which somewhat reduced expectations of a strong recovery in the EU in the first half of 2021. At 18.8%, the United Kingdom experienced the GDP growth in the second quarter of 2020 compared to the previous quarter among European countries, but the growth rate in the third quarter recovered by 16.0%, which is the third fastest rate after France (18.8%) and Spain (17.1%).

European debt instrument. Germany and the Netherlands, along with other eurozone members, opposed such attempts. However, as interest rates are already low, the Commission has indicated that it will expand its program of lending to EU banks, or buying up debt from EU companies, and possibly further lowering interest rates on deposits to negative levels in an attempt to support the euro exchange rate. ECB nominee Christine Lagarde has called on EU leaders to take more urgent action to avoid the spread of COVID-19. The Commission has provided a $ 30 billion investment fund to address the problems of COVID-19.

On March 31, 2021, French President Macron announced a four-week blockade of businesses across the country to limit the resumption of viral cases in French hospitals, and extended by one week the planned two-week school closure. The EU is also blocking shipments to the UK from the AstraZeneca vaccine, produced in Belgium and the Netherlands, until the EU's delivery commitments are met. At the same time, 16 European countries, including Germany, France, Italy and Spain, have suspended the use of AstraZeneca due to fears of possible negative side effects, despite assurances from EU drug regulators that the benefits outweigh the risks.

On 4 June 2021, the EU proposed its own three-point plan, which includes (1) maintaining export restrictions; (2) encouraging vaccine manufacturers to negotiate agreements with manufacturers in developing economies and increasing vaccine supplies to vulnerable countries; and (3) the use of existing WTO rules to grant licenses to manufacturers without the consent of the patent holder.

Given the macroeconomic and financial impact of COVID-19, decisive and coordinated economic policy measures should be taken to achieve the following objectives:

- To help save lives. To provide the necessary supplies, financial resources and investments for the control and treatment of the pandemic.
- Ensure the protection of workers in Europe (including the self-employed) against income loss and ensure that the most affected enterprises (especially SMEs) and sectors have the necessary support and financial liquidity.
- Reduce the impact on the whole economy, making full use of all available EU instruments and a flexible EU framework for action by Member States.

To offset the socio-economic impact of the COVID-19 epidemic, bold action is needed, taken in a timely and coordinated manner by all EU decision-making institutions. Crucial to this endeavor is the swift implementation of the measures identified by the EU. The announced measures relate to the current situation. We must be aware that this situation is changing on a daily basis. Further deterioration of the economic outlook cannot be ruled out.

4. Forecasts

4.1. General Forecasts

World GDP (excluding the euro area) is expected to increase by 6.2% this year, after slowing to 4.2% and 3.7% in 2022 and 2023, respectively. This reflects the interaction of factors, including the worsening pandemic in developed economies earlier this year and emerging market economies, as well as the macroeconomic impact of major US fiscal stimulus and improving prospects in other developed economies due to the rapid introduction of vaccines.

The projected global recovery from the pandemic crisis remains unchanged. In developed economies outside the euro area, the recovery is expected to continue unhindered and activity should reach the pre-pandemic trend next year, mainly due to the United States. In China, which was the first to be affected by the pandemic but recovered most quickly amid strong political support, real GDP returned to its pre-crisis trajectory as late as last year. In contrast, the recovery of other economies from emerging markets is expected to be slow. The recent increase in the number of those infected, as well as any delays in vaccination campaigns, could further increase these disparities.

The OECD estimates that economic recovery will take place over the next two years, but "recovery will be uneven between countries, potentially leading to lasting changes in the global economy." In addition, the pandemic is fragmenting the global economy due to growing trade and investment constraints , and the different policy approaches to tackling the crisis in different countries. According to the OECD analysis:

• The greatest impact of restrictions is on retail and wholesale trade, as well as on professional and real estate services, although there are significant differences between countries.

- Countries dependent on tourism are more severely affected, while countries with large agricultural and mining sectors have experienced less severe consequences.
- Economic effects are likely to vary from country to country, reflecting differences in the timing and extent of mitigation measures.

As a consequence of the slowdown in economic activity in the fourth quarter of 2020 and the projected slow growth and partial recovery in 2021, the OECD estimated that there will be long-term effects on the global economy, including:

- Production is projected to remain around 5% below pre-crisis expectations in many countries in 2022, increasing the range of significant fixed costs affecting disproportionately vulnerable populations.
- Smaller companies and entrepreneurs are more likely to go bankrupt.
- Many low-wage workers who have lost their jobs and are only covered by unemployment insurance may have difficulty finding a new job.
- People living in poverty and usually less covered by social security networks may suffer from deteriorating living standards.
- Children and young people of lower income and less skilled adult workers struggle to learn and work from home, with potential long-term damage.

According to the updated **IMF forecast** from October 2021, the world economy is recovering, but the recovery has been delayed due to new variants of the virus. The forecast also estimates a slower growth rate in developed economies than projected in April 2021 and a slower growth rate for emerging and developing economies. The IMF concluded that health risks continue to abound and hinder the full recovery of economic activity. In addition, the impact of the pandemic in critical units of global supply chains has "led to longer-than-expected supply disruptions", which have fueled inflation in many countries. The forecast concludes that economic recovery will be uneven across countries, depending on "access to medical interventions, the effectiveness of political support, exposure to spillovers in different countries and the structural characteristics of the crisis".

The IMF estimated that the global economic recovery may be weaker than expected as a result of continuing uncertainty about possible contamination, lack of confidence and permanent closure of businesses and changes in the behavior of businesses and households. The IMF concluded that the fiscal and monetary actions of developed economies are helping emerging and emerging market economies to avoid tightening monetary policy to stem capital outflows. Instead, the countries relied on their exchange rate movements while following developed economies in easing monetary policy, providing liquidity and using non-traditional monetary policy measures (such as buying government and corporate bonds).

In January 2021, the **World Bank** published its updated economic forecast, which indicated that in the absence of "substantial and effective reforms", the world economy will experience a decade of "disappointing growth". In particular, the bank assessed that all regions of the world remain vulnerable to renewed outbreaks of the virus, that there are logistical obstacles to the spread of effective vaccines and financial stress in addition to rising debt levels, and that the pandemic could have a greater negative impact. on income and growth.

An earlier forecast (June 8, 2020) shows that the economic recession in 2020 will be the deepest since World War II. He also estimated that the global economic recession would affect 90% of the world's economies, a percentage higher than that experienced during the Great Depression. Similar to OECD and IMF forecasts, the World Bank argues that the economic impact of the global recession will have the strongest impact on emerging and emerging economies that rely on world trade, tourism or remittances, as well as those that depend on from the export of raw materials.

The Bank also concluded that Global Value Chains (GVCs) were important channels through which pandemic macroeconomic indicators were transmitted across national borders. The economic consequences of the pandemic are spreading through trade links, which are exacerbated by quarantines, production closures and border closures. According to the World Bank, national measures have affected the world economy through four channels: declining employment due to factory closures and social distancing, trade shock due to rising commodity prices, tourist shock due to a sharp contraction in international tourism and a shock to services .

4.2. Eurosystem experts' macroeconomic forecasts for the euro area

The baseline forecast of June 2021 is based on the assumption of faster easing of restrictive measures and overcoming the health crisis by early 2022. The baseline assumption is that vaccination campaigns will continue in line with the EU's vaccine supply strategy. However, it is assumed that some restrictive measures will be needed by early 2022 for several reasons: demand constraints (eg vaccination readiness among the population), the emergence of new variants of COVID-19 outside the euro area and continuing uncertainty about the effectiveness of vaccines against them.

Significant monetary and fiscal policy measures, including the new generation EU package, will help support income and aggregate demand, prevent large-scale job losses and bankruptcies, and bridge the gap between the real economy and the financial sector. In addition to the monetary policy measures taken by the ECB by the end of the current forecasts, the baseline forecast includes discretionary fiscal stimulus related to the COVID-19 crisis and recovery, including measures financed by the EU's next generation ". Government guarantees on loans and capital injections should continue to help ease liquidity constraints. In addition, supervisory and macroprudential policies have freed up more bank capital to absorb losses and support credit flow to the real economy. Capital buffers have been released, guidelines have been issued to reduce pro-cyclical provisioning, and measures have been taken to maintain banks' loss-making capacity. It is assumed that monetary, fiscal and prudential policy measures in general will be able to prevent a serious vicious circle between the real economy and the financial sector during the forecast period.

Economic activity was expected to pick up strongly in the second half of 2021, as restrictive measures are expected to be eased. Real GDP is expected to reach its pre-crisis level in the first quarter of 2022 (a quarter earlier than expected in the March 2021 forecasts). In the last quarter of 2022, it should be 1.3% below the level predicted in the forecasts published before the start of the pandemic.

Private consumption is expected to resume in the second quarter, then rise sharply in the second half of 2021 with a gradual easing of restrictive measures and reach pre-crisis levels in the second quarter of 2022. The gradually weakening uncertainty and the recovery of disposable income also contribute, despite the reduction in net fiscal transfers, especially in 2022. Although private consumption is expected to be the main driver of the recovery, the baseline forecast does not latent demand, as the large amount of accumulated excess savings will remain largely unspent.

The household savings rate has fluctuated significantly since the beginning of the pandemic and is still rising, leading to an accumulation of surplus savings. The June 2021 forecasts assume that the savings rate will return to its pre-pandemic level by mid-2022 as the drivers of both forced and precautionary savings weaken and then remain This trend reflects the normalization of savings flows as a result of the successful exit from the health crisis and the easing of restrictive measures, which is expected to be completed by the beginning of 2022 and should also inspire confidence.

Correcting the accumulated surplus of savings requires balancing between several opposing forces. On the one hand, the increase in the saving rate during quarantine periods largely reflects forced savings, which are expected to decrease and be partially used for consumption after the restrictive measures have been eased (Dossche, 2020).

This can be aided by the fact that most of the additional savings appear to have been held primarily as bank deposits, which are highly liquid and can therefore be easily withdrawn for consumption. As uncertainty decreases, some precautionary savings may be spent. On the other hand, it seems unlikely that there will be a more significant release of surplus savings for consumption due to the concentration of savings in high-income households, which have a lower marginal propensity to spend income or wealth than low-income households (European Commission Technical Documents, 2021)·

Instead of spending the surplus on savings, households could also continue to hold them in the form of deposits or invest them in other assets - both financial and non-financial (eg real estate), or use them to repay debts. . Finally, as the current crisis is mainly due to a decline in the consumption of services, the potential for latent demand may be less pronounced, although this could be offset in part by a shift in favor of the consumption of durable goods. use.

Housing investment is expected to return to pre-pandemic levels in 2022. As for business investments, they are expected to remain sustainable and recover significantly in 2022, reaching pre-crisis levels by the end of the year. From now on, more stable improvement is expected with the recovery of global and domestic demand and the improvement of profit growth. This will be supported by favorable financing conditions and the positive impact of the "new generation EU" on business investment.

Taking all factors into account, the possibilities for relieving the accumulated surplus of savings for consumption after the mitigation of anti-epidemic measures appear to be generally limited. However, the speed and extent of the expected normalization of the savings rate are subject to considerable uncertainty. The mechanisms of interaction between pandemic and macroeconomic dynamics show a faster decline in the rate of savings in the short term. However, the model does not show a significant reduction in the surplus of savings - rather, it shows that the level of the savings rate will remain above the pre-crisis trend in 2022 and

2023 and will approach the baseline forecast only at the end of 2023 (Fisher, 2021).

Unemployment is expected to return to pre-crisis levels by the end of 2023. The contraction in employment growth in 2021 due to prolonged restrictive measures and a corresponding decline in activity has led to rising unemployment. It is assumed that a large proportion of workers covered by job retention schemes will return to their normal employment thanks to the strong recovery from the pandemic. Therefore, the unemployment rate is expected to be rather stable by the end of 2021, before gradually decreasing over the next two years and reaching 7.3% by the end of 2023.

Fiscal policy continues to mitigate the macroeconomic impact of the COVID-19 pandemic in 2021 and is at the heart of the recovery. As the restrictive measures remained in force in 2021, governments extended the emergency measures, gradually strengthened them and / or adopted new support measures. Most of the additional measures are temporary and are expected to be abolished in 2022. Some have been further extended along with other recovery measures, including EU-funded expenditure.

Most of the extraordinary support in 2021 represents additional costs in the form of subsidies and transfers to enterprises, including job retention schemes. Measures classified as "general government consumption" mainly reflect higher healthcare costs, including wages related to the vaccination campaign. In the revenue part, the measures relate to the reduction of direct and indirect taxes. Following an adjustment of the impact of EU New Generation grants on the revenue side of around 0.6% of GDP per year, the fiscal position is expected to be expansionary in 2021, tightening in 2022 and remain broadly neutral in 2023

The slight decline in the budget deficit in 2021 reflects a slightly better cyclical component and lower interest rates, which better offset additional stimulus measures not covered by the "new generation EU" grant. “In the revenue part. The significant improvement in the budget balance in 2022 is mainly due to the completion of most of the emergency stimulus measures related to the crisis and the much more favorable cyclical component. In 2023, with a generally neutral fiscal position and better cyclical conditions, the overall budget balance is projected to improve further. The decline in 2022-2023 is mainly due to the favorable differential between interest rates and growth, which more than compensates for continuing, albeit declining, primary deficits. Compared to the

March 2021 forecasts, the euro area budget deficit and debt have been revised upwards, especially for 2021 due to additional stimulus measures.

As there is still considerable uncertainty about the future development of the COVID-19 pandemic and its economic effects, two scenarios have been considered that are alternatives to the Eurosystem experts' baseline forecast of June 2021. They illustrate a range of possible impacts of the COVID-19 pandemic on the euro area economy.

In the mild scenario, the health crisis is expected to be overcome by the end of only temporary economic losses, while in the severe scenario a prolonged health crisis and permanent losses of potential GDP are allowed. Compared to the baseline scenario, the milder scenario envisages faster implementation, greater public acceptance and higher efficacy of vaccines, also against new variants of the virus. This will allow for faster easing of restrictive measures and their phasing out by the end of 2021.

In contrast, the severe scenario envisages a possible resumption of the pandemic in the coming months with the emergence of more contagious variants of the virus, which would also mean reducing vaccine efficacy and continuing some restrictive measures until mid-2023, which will have a negative impact. impact on activity.

Compared to the baseline scenario, the severe scenario is characterized by more severe damage to the economy, aggravated by increased insolvency and deteriorating creditworthiness of borrowers, which adversely affects the expected losses and capital costs of banks and therefore the provision of credit to the private sector. At the same time, even in the severe scenario, it is assumed that monetary, fiscal and prudential policies will limit the very severe multiplication of financial effects.

The banking sector must play a key role in tackling the effects of the proliferation of COVID-19, while maintaining credit flow to the economy. If the flow of bank loans is very limited, economic activity will slow down significantly as companies have difficulty paying their suppliers and employees. Banks need to have adequate liquidity to lend to their customers. The EU Commission takes note of the ECB's monetary policy decisions announced on 12 March 2020. The EU framework allows national governments to provide, where appropriate, in the form of state guarantees, support to banks if they themselves are experiencing difficulties in raising capital. Although there is no evidence that banks are currently experiencing liquidity difficulties, such a situation may arise for some banks if the crisis deepens significantly.

The non-banking financial sector will have to adjust to the new circumstances. Insurers can be expected to create new products related to both the risk of loss of life caused by the virus and the loss of income in the context of social distancing. The amount of the premium for some property insurance is likely to decrease because the insured will use their cars less often and will manage their movable and immovable property better. Due to the fall in the prices of shares traded on the domestic and international markets, the profitability of private pension funds will fall and may be negative for some time. On the other hand, new investments in stocks made during the recession have the potential for high returns. Thus, pension funds that invest in this asset class will be able to count on higher returns in the future. The same applies to personal investments in securities. In order to maintain the value of their savings and get a chance for real growth in personal wealth, households can take advantage of the ongoing economic slowdown and falling securities prices in international markets by investing in appropriate financial assets, relying on capital markets to recover from the crisis.

5. The pandemic situation in Bulgaria

Due to the spread of the infection and in order to protect public health, in particular to protect citizens from the direct physical threat of the virus, a state of emergency was declared in Bulgaria on March 13, 2020. Thus began the first phase of the crisis - strong restrictions on social and economic activities.

Currently, the Bulgarian economy is entering an economic crisis, the depth and duration of which may be very large. And although some slowdown in economic growth has been expected due to slowdown and problems in some of Europe's major economies, the current crisis is quite different - the result of the global pandemic caused by COVID-19.

Currently, the expectations of most consumers and entrepreneurs in Bulgaria for the future of their income are naturally pessimistic. In general, the banking system is facing the crisis with sufficient capital buffers and high liquidity. Bad credit, inherited from the previous crisis, has largely cleared up. But the problems of the real sector will be transferred to the banking system and will affect the work and performance of banks.

A decision of the banks, sanctioned by the BNB, to postpone loan installments until the end of the year is already underway, as a first reaction to the expected problems for the banking system. This will allow banks to operate temporarily more freely in terms of loan classification and provisioning, but at the same time will have a negative impact on their financial performance. After the moratorium, it can be expected that there will be a wave of bad loans that will test the stability of the banking system and this emphasizes the importance of the buffers available in it (Petranov, 2020).

Undoubtedly, the pandemic of COVID-19 changed the business and affected the national economic system in Bulgaria. As a result of health and restrictive measures in the country and globally, not only is international trade reduced, but there is also a significant change in global supply chains.

Moreover, the COVID-19 pandemic has not affected different countries and sectors equally. Although full restrictive measures in Bulgaria are implemented in only 3 months, the Bulgarian economy remains at the bottom of the EU economies with a decline of 6% in the last 2 years (2020 and 2021), and in some sectors this downward shift is more than 50%.

This requires an answer to 3 questions: Is the crisis in the economy caused by COVID-19 something unusual? How strong is the crisis compared to others like it? And what measures are needed to complement those already adopted by the government since the beginning of the pandemic?

A country's economy, and on a global scale, follows certain rules and never stands still. When new production technologies or new materials are developed: the economy grows, and when the "public contract" begins to not satisfy all individuals and companies, there is a decline in the economy. In this way, a normal economic cycle of growth and decline is formed. Considering the data on the Bulgarian economy, and in particular on industrial production, several significant "CRISES" can be identified, related to the subsequent change in "public relations" (Table 1)

Table 1. Comparison of COVID 19 with previous crises

1999 - 2008	• The growth of production is 18.3% • The growth rate of imports is 46.5% • The growth of exports is 36.8%. • Production is growing slowly with 0.14% growth rate on a monthly basis and 1.7% growth rate on an annual basis. • Imports in Bulgaria grew slightly faster (0.23% growth rate on a monthly basis and 2.79% growth rate on an annual basis) than exports of goods from Bulgaria (0.22% growth rate on a monthly basis and 2.67% growth rate on an annual basis)
2008 (GFC) -2020 (COVID-19)	• Growth in production is a total of 3.5% and the annual growth rate of production is 0.29%. • The growth rate of imports of goods decreased by 65% and reached 0.07% on a monthly basis and 0.84% on an annual basis • The growth rate of exports of goods decreased by 49% and outpaced imports, reaching 0.10% on an annual basis on a monthly basis and 1.21% on an annual basis
2020 (COVID-19) - 2021	• Production growth of 2.15% within the monthly growth rate of 0.16%. • Imports and exports increased significantly compared to the growth in the period 1999-2008, respectively: 6.13 times for imports and 3.73 times for exports

Main crisis points (GFC 2008-2009) and Covid-19 crisis (April 2020)	• October 2008: Production decreased by 8.5%, imports - by 8.5%, and exports - by 3.6% • April 2020: Production decreased by 6.0%, imports - by 6.7% and exports - by 3.3%

As can be seen from the data, the negative economic ones such as a decrease in production, an increase in unemployment, a decline in exports and others. are present, but with the necessary effort the pandemic situation can be overcome.

5.1. Recommendations

The measures implemented so far, both by Borissov's regular government and the caretaker government, can be considered necessary. However, the time of their implementation is not enough to assess the full effects of them.

As we have all witnessed, the current pandemic has affected thousands of people, and has affected almost all industrial sectors, causing historic losses to certain industries such as the transport sector, the oil market and tourism. The main reason why these sectors are most affected is that health and restrictive measures taken globally have affected sectors dependent on globalization and labor mobility. We should ask ourselves, what else needs to be done?

Changes in the country's Industrial and Economic Policy can be recommended in three main areas in order to be more flexible to future "economic shocks", regardless of the reasons that will cause them:

• Innovation: Investment in innovation infrastructure is needed, through which each individual has the opportunity to test, research and develop their innovative idea. The innovation infrastructure can cover various start-ups and business incubators. Business incubators should serve as a link between economic uncertainty and innovation, as the innovations they develop will be better adapted to the needs of individuals and there is a greater opportunity to develop new successful business models. In addition, economic growth will be accelerated by social growth through the construction of "public" business incubators. It is through them that they could include in the economy those individuals from marginalized groups who are currently excluded from economic life due to: violence, minority affiliation, disadvantaged people, permanent unemployment, etc.

- Entrepreneurship: Entrepreneurship is a tool that prevents job losses during economic crises. It is therefore necessary to enforce entrepreneurship policy and develop tools to support entrepreneurship. Some of the possible tools are: introduction of funds for fast entrepreneurship programs; launching bank guarantees for SME loans; release of budgetary funds to support innovative small and medium-sized companies.
- Establishment of value chains: Bulgarian industrial production is becoming increasingly dependent on the development of global supply chains. Thus, a successful industrial policy that prevents the negative effects of global crises must support not only global but also national supply chains. In this regard, industrial policy must support projects to diversify resources, including the development of appropriate domestic and international markets and the "double supply" of the same raw materials from suppliers in different countries. Such an approach should help to prevent negative shocks caused by existing (single or limited) value-added chains in the face of physical health and other constraints.

5.2. Forecasts for Bulgaria

Overall, the EU economy will grow by 5% in 2021 and by 4.3% in 2022, but will slow to 20% in 2023. Compared to the forecasts made in the spring, this is an increase of 1.3 percentage points, respectively. for this year and from 0.4 percentage points. for the next.

As for the euro area, the forecasts for this year and next are the same as for the whole of the European Union, but in 2023 the pace will be one idea slower - 2.4%.

However, this forecast depends largely on two factors: the development of the COVID-19 pandemic and the pace at which supply is adapting to the rapid recovery in demand after the reopening of the economy.

The European Commission has slightly raised its forecast for Bulgaria's gross domestic product (GDP) growth in 2021, but lowered it next year. According to its Autumn Economic Forecast, Bulgaria's economy will grow by 3.8% this year, while in the spring it was expected to grow by 2.7%. There will be a significant acceleration of the economy next year - by 4.1%, the report notes. In comparison, expectations in the previous forecast, however, were for growth of 4.9%, which still indicates a slowdown.

Inflation forecasts jump sharply. While in the previous report for this year an acceleration of 1.6% was expected, and for the next - 2.0%, now the forecasts have been revised to 2.4% and 2.9%, respectively. Brussels also presented forecasts for 2023 - economic growth will slow to 3.5% and inflation - to 1.8%.

The EC predicts that recent increases in energy and food prices are likely to shrink the purchasing power of low-income households. However, the increase in social benefits and pensions this year and next will compensate for the effect of higher prices on household budgets, according to Brussels. Exports of goods will grow along with external demand, but exports of services will grow more gradually. According to the Commission, higher energy and unprocessed food prices have caused inflation to accelerate in the second and third quarters of 2021. However, seasonal price increases in tourism services have been less pronounced, which has helped curb inflation in services such as whole.

Recovery of tax revenues will offset the impact on the deficit of still strong expenditure growth. The deficit is expected to narrow in 2022, as most emergency measures will be lifted and larger payments from the EU are planned to finance most of the projected growth in public spending.

The risks to Bulgaria's recovery are mostly related to the Covid-19 pandemic. According to the report, the introduction of a green certificate may not be enough to maintain the levels of new infections, and it may take longer to adapt to the new one. In addition, the impact of higher energy prices on core inflation and subsequently on private consumption may be stronger than expected.

The described economic consequences of the crisis require appropriate economic measures. The specific nature of the situation and the lack of Bulgarian and world experience make it difficult to find optimal solutions, but in all cases the public administration, business and economically active people must work together and find well-balanced solutions to limit the negative effects.

5.3. Advices for personal finance

The financial consequences of a global pandemic, such as COVID-19, are far-reaching. While we all take the necessary steps to put health and safety first, you may want to take steps to protect your finances.

As banks and other services reduce personal access and working hours, you may need to take a new approach to managing your finances during these uncertain times. Here are some steps you can take to begin the process of preparation for mediation (Wells Fargo,2021):

1) Plan and manage your finances actively: Personal financial planning is essential. Income, expenses, savings, investments and loans must be adjusted to the short-term and long-term needs, desires and life goals of the family. In a volatile global economic environment, it is important to seize opportunities as well as stay prepared for emergencies. Financial planning helps a person to remain responsible in both of these situations. It is also important to actively manage and review plans and implement changes in line with changing needs, desires and the overall economic scenario.

2) Review your budget and savings: Create an emergency fund before investing money: Such an emergency fund can help you stay afloat in times of financial crisis. Such a fund should be a minimum of 6 - 12 monthly family income. and be highly liquid. Most importantly, the fund should be considered sacred - available for use only in case of emergency.

Consider tightening your budget to ensure you have enough money to cover your basic expenses. If you have less income, prioritize your expenses and eliminate all unnecessary expenses. Creating a budget and sticking to it is a good strategy at all times, but especially when your finances have suffered an unplanned blow. If you receive a tax refund or other unforeseen profit, consider allocating a portion to increase your savings or create an emergency fund for future unexpected situations.

3) Life insurance and health insurance are important investments: Life is uncertain. The pandemic not only proved this to the world, but also showed how unpredictable life can be. Ensuring financial security for the family is therefore paramount. Health insurance is also mandatory, given the increase in lifestyle-related diseases and rising healthcare costs.

4) Avoid the debt trap: In an era of growing consumerism driven by a combination of factors such as better purchasing power, product innovation, stimulating marketing gimmicks and readily available personal credit options, one can find oneself in the debt trap. This debt trap not only damages financial planning, but can become devastating during an economic crisis.

5) Make payments on time: Although it can be difficult, try to make at least your minimum debt payments by the due date. Delays of 30 days or more can remain in your credit report for up to seven years, and 35 percent of your credit rating is based on payment history. Therefore, while higher credit card balances may also lower your credit rating, this impact may be easier to deal with over time than a missed payment. Many banks allow you to access your credit rating online;

5) Use credit wisely: If you need to carry balances or borrow more, make a list of your current credit sources, including current balances, credit limits, and annual interest rates (APRs). Note the end date of all zero-entry bids. Avoid maximizing each card. If necessary, split the costs between several cards.

6) Make the most of online banking: With online finance management or mobile banking, you can easily check account balances, pay bills, make transfers and meet many of your daily banking needs. Online tools can also help you monitor your spending habits and send and receive money. If you have difficulty, contact your creditors and credit card issuers. Financial institutions may have difficulty options that allow you to apply for short-term suspension of payments or possibly postpone or reduce your payments. Check the websites of your service providers. Many energy, telephone and internet companies can end outages during this time.

7) Diversification of investments: The basic principle of successful investment is to diversify investments in different asset classes - equity, debt, gold, real estate, etc. This helps not only to reduce the risk, but also to optimize the return. It is also important to keep in mind the duration of the investment and the objectives when choosing financial instruments (such as stocks).

8) Live a minimalist life: It's all about realizing that we don't need much to live a happy life. Excessive consumption - a bigger house, a better car, more clothes, the latest electronics, etc. just push our desires to the next level and always keep happiness out of reach. Living a simple life, focusing on needs, reducing desires and developing healthy eating habits not only ensures financial prosperity, but also contributes to mental and emotional well-being.

The coronavirus pandemic is changing the way we do many everyday things, including how we manage our finances. As the unprecedented Covid-19 pandemic swept the world like a storm, one of the most important lessons to be learned from this crisis was the need to properly plan and manage personal finances to build a secure future. To summarize, financial discipline and prudence are necessary for the next time disaster strikes.

Conclusion

The pandemic-related recession is characterized as being more global in nature than that experienced during the 2009-2010 global financial crisis as a result of its effects on developing economies. Through the various stages of the pandemic-related health and economic crises, governments responded with a number of policy initiatives that often attempted to balance competing policy objectives.

Compared to March 2021, the outlook for growth is stronger in 2022. This reflects the assumption that the pandemic will have a more limited economic impact given the progress of the vaccination campaign, significant additional fiscal policy measures - partly funded by the New Generation EU program - and an updated outlook for external demand, supported by recent US fiscal packages. Monetary, fiscal and macroprudential policy measures are expected to prevent a sharp increase in financial effects and reduce the economic damage from the crisis. As a result, real GDP is expected to be just 1.3% below the level projected in the pre-pandemic projections by the end of 2022.

In recent forecasts, it is projected geographic regions of the global economy would recover at different speeds, reflecting differences in the pace of vaccinations, the extent of policy support, and various structural conditions, such as the role of tourism in the economy.

Undoubtedly, the pandemic of COVID-19 changed the business and affected the national economic system in Bulgaria. As a result of health and restrictive measures in the country and globally, not only is international trade reduced, but there is also a significant change in global supply chains. The question is if the crisis in the economy caused by COVID-19 something unusual?

The negative economic consequences such as a decrease in production, an increase in unemployment, a decline in exports and others. are present, but the realized effects don`t seriously affect the development of the Bulgarian economy.

As the health crisis subsides and economic activity resumes, policymakers may consider evaluating the various policy approaches for lessons learned and for best practices to employ in addressing similar crises, should they arise. On the microeconomic perspective one of the most important lessons that came out of this crisis is the need to properly plan and manage one’s personal finances towards building a secure future.

References

1. Европейска комисия (2020) Координирани икономически мерки в отговор на пандемията от COVID-19, https://eur-lex.europa.eu/legal-content/BG/TXT/HTML/?uri=CELEX:52020DC0112&from=EN
2. Съвет на ЕС (2022) COVID-19: ответни действия на ЕС по отношение на икономическите последици, https://www.consilium.europa.eu/bg/policies/coronavirus/covid-19-economy/
3. Петранов, Ст., Златинов, Д. (2020) Икономически последствия от кризата с Ковид 19 и мерки за предотвратяването им, СУ „Св. Климент Охридски“
4. BIS Quarterly Review, March 2021, Bank for International Settlements, p. 10.
5. Brainard, Lael, Some Preliminary Financial Stability Lessons From the COVID -19 Shock, At the 2021 Annual Washington Conference, Institute of International Bankers March 1, 2021.
6. Cantu, Carlos, Paolo Cavalino, Fiorella De Fiore, and James Yetnam, A Global Database of Central Banks' Monetary Responses to COVID-19, BIS Working Papers No. 934, Bank for International Settlements, March 2021, p.5.
7. Congressional Research Service (2021) Global Economic Effects of COVID-19, https://crsreports.congress.gov, file:///C:/Users/PC/AppData/Local/Temp/FEBA-Analysis-COVID-19.pdf
8. Dossche, M., Zlatanos, S. (2020) COVID-19 and the increase in household savings: precautionary or forced?" ("COVID-19 and the growth of household savings - buffer or forced?") Economic Bulletin , ECB, Issue 6, 2020
9. Eurofound (2020 г.), Програмен документ за периода 2021—2024 г.: Към възстановяване и устойчивост, Дъблин
10. European Commission (2021) COMMUNICATION FROM THE COMMISSION TO THE COUNCIL One year since the outbreak of COVID-19: fiscal policy response
11. Federal Reserve Releases FOMC Statement, March 3, 2020, https://www.federalreserve.gov/newsevents/pressreleases/monetary20200303a.htm.

12. Fisher, J., Johnson, D. (2020) Estimating the marginal propensity to consume using the distributions of income, consumption, and wealth ("Calculating the marginal propensity to consume wealth"), Journal of Macroeconomics, Issue 65, 2020.
13. Global Financial Stability Report, International Monetary Fund, October 2020, p. 1.
14. IMF (2021) How will the world be different after COVID-19? https://www.imf.org/external/pubs/ft/fandd/2020/06/how-will-the-world-be-different-after-COVID-19.htm
15. Job Retention Schemes During the COVID-19 Lockdown and Beyond, Organization for Economic Cooperation and Development, October 12, 2020, p. 2.
16. Lessons in personal finance from the Covid-19 pandemic (2022) https://www.ageasfederal.com/blog/lessons-personal-finance-covid-19-pandemic
17. OECD Employment Outlook 2021, p. 15.
18. Smith, Colby, Camilla Hodgson, and Hudson Lockett, US Stocks Set Record High as Investors Look to New Administration, Financial Times, November 24, 2020. https://www.ft.com/content/433048a5-c489-4ddd-aebd-d56fb8f3edfc.
19. Special topic: Will consumers save the EU recovery? - Insights from the Commission's Consumer Survey (Special Topic: Will Consumers Save EU Recovery? - Findings from the Commission's Consumer Survey) in the European Business Cycle Indicators, European Commission Technical Documents, № 047, April 2021.
20. Telford, Taylor, and Hamza Shaban, "Dow Climbs More Than 800 Points as Vaccine News, Biden Victory Rev Up Markets," Washington Post, November 9, 2020.
21. https://www.washingtonpost.com/business/2020/11/09/stocks-markets-biden-trump-coronavirus/.
22. Wells Fargo (2022) Tips to help stay on top of your financial situation, https://www.wellsfargo.com/financial-education/basic-finances/financial-challenges/unexpected-expenses/tips-for-handling-your-finances-during-a-crisis/
23. World Economic Outlook, International Monetary Fund, October, 2021

Reporting in Islamic Banking

Sevgi Osman

[*1]Varna Free University (VFU), International Economics and Business, Economics, Varna, Bulgaria

***sevgi.osman@vfu.bg, 00359894797197**

Abstract

Islamic banking has become an undeniable reality that emerged in the 1970s and is now one of the important industries in the world as it plays an essential role in the financial stability of economies. Despite the degradation of the global financial system, the Islamic finance industry has seen remarkable growth. But Islamic banking in non-Muslim regions is still at a very early stage of development. Islamic finance is an ethical financial system based on Islamic law. It spread beyond the Muslim world, but with different theoretical and practical implications.

The main objective of the study is 1) to trace the progress of Islamic banking - past, present and future, and to clarify the main differences with conventional banking; 2) to see the different nuances of Islamic finance in individual countries - both from a legal and economic point of view and 3) to review the literature related to Islamic banking.

The main conclusion is that there is potential for high growth in all over the world as well. Given the risks that Islamic banks (IBs) face, they need legal, corporate and regulatory frameworks as much as other conventional banks. A sound legal framework is a key prerequisite for the safe development of Islamic banking. This report examines the various regulatory frameworks for Islamic banking in both the Muslim and non-Muslim worlds. The main differences with conventional banking are also presented. An important decision to be made by countries allowing Islamic banking is whether to maintain a unified set of banking laws and regulations for Islamic and conventional banking or separate ones.

Keywords: Islamic banking, finance, reporting, potential, performance, sustainability

Introduction

Islamic banking has become an undeniable reality that emerged in the 1970s and is now one of the important industries in the world as it plays an essential role in the financial stability of economies. Despite the degradation of the global financial system, the Islamic finance industry has seen remarkable growth. According to the World Database of Islamic Banking and Finance, Islamic banks are spread across 21 different countries such as Bahrain, UAE, USA, UK, Saudi Arabia, Pakistan and Indonesia.

Materials and methods

This report aims to trace the historical development of Islamic finance around the world as well as in Europe; to highlight the main principles of Islamic finance; to make a comparison between traditional finance and Islamic finance; to focus on the issue of reporting in Islamic banking and to summarize 60 researches in the field of Islamic finance for the period 2003-2018. The methodology used in the report is literature review and the analytical tool, the result of which is the table as an Annex at the end of the report.

Emergence of Islamic banks

Islamic banks represent a new wave of corporations whose social goals are as important as generating profit (Haniffa and Hudaib 2007, p. 98). They must be socially responsible regardless of financial results - positive or negative (Dusuki 2008a). The Islamic banking industry is progressing and becoming an increasingly significant segment within the global financial market. It is a competitive form of financial intermediation not only in Muslim countries, but offers a wide range of financial products and services in non-Muslim countries as well.

Among all Islamic financial institutions, banks appear the earliest (Sobol, 2015). Prerequisites for their appearance are the neo-revival movements among Muslim societies, on the one hand, and the growing wealth of the countries of the Middle East, on the other. One of the most influential movements was the "Muslim Brotherhood" in Al-Ismailija (Egypt) in 1928, founded by Hassan al-Banna. The Muslim Brotherhood criticizes the interest-based financial system in Egypt and other parts of the Muslim world and argues that Islam provides a comprehensive ideological framework for all aspects of life, which should include economic issues. The Muslim Brotherhood and other similar religious movements have followers both in the academic world and in the marketplace.

According to Kaplan (2019), the history of the Islamic banking system dates back to the 1940s. Before the partition of Pakistan and India, the Muslims who lived in that geography in 1946 came together and developed a different model of carrying out interest rate transactions. In this model, in addition to fulfilling the existing debt obligation, a Muslim who has granted a loan must pay the 'zakat' on the profit from the transaction to another bank (Mutlu, 2003: 298). Interest-free banking was first introduced in the modern sense of the word by Muhammad Uzeir, who lived in Pakistan in 1955. The interest-free banking system, which was established under the name "Savings Associations" in the 1960s, was further developed in the following years (Battal, 1999: 18). Since 1963 the Malaysian government established the Pilgrimage Management Fund (Tabung Haji) to assist Muslims wishing to perform their pilgrimage. (Alrifai, 2013: 101).

According to Di Mauro (2013), from a historical perspective, the idea of an Islamic financial system began to emerge in the second half of the 20th century, when decolonization and the creation of new countries with a majority Muslim population led to the foundation of Islamic banking. The Islamic financial system is seen as a segment of the overall Islamic economy that supports the Islamic social order and can be an alternative to capitalist liberalism and socialist planning. This offers believers the opportunity to combine their economic activity with their religious beliefs. Thus, historically, Islamic finance has developed over a long period with profound distinctive features.

The first Islamic bank was established in Egypt under the name "Mit Gamr" in 1963, and the first Sharia-based bank according to Sadoveanu (2011) was founded in 1963 in Egypt - "MitGhamr Savings Bank", renamed after of Nasser Social Bank. The first Islamic banks were "Dubai Islamique banque", "Kuwait Finance House" and "Bahrain Islamic Bank".

The factors for the emergence of Islamic banking are: 1) financial deregulations and innovations that allow the development of pure Islamic banking products and services; 2) the emergence of "visionaries" - people with deep knowledge of Islamic doctrine and banking; 3) the oil shocks of the first decade of the 1970s, which aided the accumulation of a large amount of petrodollars in Arab countries.

The rise in oil prices since the 1970s has led to the accumulation of significant amounts of foreign exchange reserves in oil-producing countries. The foreign trade surpluses of these countries flow to Western countries in the form of savings in petrodollars. There are also underdeveloped or developing Islamic countries that do not have rich oil reserves, but instead have idle natural resources and labor due to insufficient capital. Cooperation between Islamic countries with a capital surplus and countries with a capital deficit is economic factor for the creation of Islamic banks (Çobankaya, 2014: 11). The Islamic finance industry emerged on the global stage in the 1970s, when a huge influx of liquidity in the Gulf states was used to support the establishment of several institutions offering Islamic financial services – IIFS (Di Mauro, 2013). Since then, Islamic finance activity has grown significantly in both volume and scope.

According to Kaplan (2019), the reasons that led to the emergence of participatory banking can be religious, economic, social or political. According to the Islamic religion, interest is prohibited because it causes various damages, such as distorting the distribution of income, restricting development, causing excessive costs and risk in investment enterprises, and preventing the realization of projects with low profit but high social efficiency. Every social society consists of individuals with different capabilities, which also leads to the emergence of different classes in society. In order for these classes to continue their relations and for the economic differences between the classes to be reduced to a minimum, the interest-free banking system must be introduced. Income from savings is used for production, trade and industry and contributes to employment, thereby mitigating inequalities between classes and individuals in society (Kaya, 2013: 9-11).

The first interest-free bank established with the help of the state was Nasir Social Bank (NSB), which was also established in Egypt in 1971. The most important step in the history of Islamic banking was made in 1975 when the Islamic Development Bank was established in accordance with Islamic principles to support economic development and social development in Muslim countries (Sümer and Onan, 2015: 298).

Although the beginning of the history of Islamic finance can be traced back to the 1920s, the huge impetus for Islamic finance came from the Gulf countries as a result of the oil crisis and the huge increase in oil prices. Almost all Islamic banks established in the 1970s were partly or even entirely financed by oil revenues. Since then, Islamic finance has seen a growing importance. So far, banks have played a dominant role in the Islamic finance industry. The value of their assets amounts to about 80% of the assets of all Islamic financial institutions. Apart from banking services, other Islamic financial services that are developing dynamically are the issuance of Islamic bonds (sukuk), Islamic insurance (takaful) and Islamic funds.

The growing demand for interest-free banking products is accelerating the development of the Islamic banking system. Islamic banks are beginning to attract more and more customers, offering different financial products than commercial banks. Islamic banking is also becoming attractive in some non-Muslim countries (Salman and Nawaz, 2018: 155).

Islamic banking in European Union countries is still at a very early stage of development. There are only a small number of banks in the EU offering Islamic financial products and services. Most of them are located in the United Kingdom, which is considered the European Islamic financial center.

The first participation of European banks in interest-free financing took place already in the 20s of the 20th century. At the time, the Eastern Bank, the predecessor of Standard Chartered, was allowed to open a branch in Bahrain on the condition that it avoid all interest-based transactions. At the same time and under the same conditions, National Handelsbank of the Netherlands, a predecessor of ABN-Amro, was granted permission to establish a branch in Jeddah, the purpose of which was to provide money exchange services for pilgrims from Dutch Indonesia. The intervention of European banks in the Persian Gulf for the first time led to the demand for Islamic financing. And according to Wilson (2007), the beginning of IS in Europe is associated with the mentioned 2 events in the 1920s.

For the next fifty years, European banks involved in the Muslim world conducted their operations using interest, just like their local counterparts. It was only in the 1970s, when the first Islamic banks were established in the Middle East, that European banks again came into contact with interest-free banking. Newly established Islamic banks have problems managing their liquidity because they cannot use tools that are available to conventional institutions. As a response to this problem, a number of banks operating in London, notably Saudi International Bank and United Bank of Kuwait, are beginning to offer liquidity management services to Middle Eastern Islamic banks.

In the late 1970s, however, the perceptions of European bankers began to change, largely as a result of the emergence of Islamic banks in the Persian Gulf, with Dubai Islamic Bank being the first to be established in 1974, followed by Kuwait Finance House in 1977 and the Islamic Banks of Bahrain in 1978.

As for the first Islamic financial institutions in Europe, it should be noted that they appeared only at the end of the 1970s (Kurochkina ,2019). Gradually, with the change in national legislation, full-fledged Islamic banks or the so-called "Islamic windows" in conventional banks began to be created. Thus, in 1978, the Islamic

Banking System (later renamed Islamic Finance House Universal Holding) was established in Luxembourg, and in December 1982, the first Islamic insurance company Takafol was established (both for investors from the Persian Gulf countries).

In Switzerland, due to existing legal restrictions, the first full-fledged Islamic bank was founded only in 2006 (Faisal Private Bank). Another project of Islamic banking in Europe was the acquisition of the Hargrave Securities investment group in the United Kingdom in 1982 by the Saudi-based Al-Baraka, an organization that had a license to make bank deposits. According to Sobol (2015), this is a big step towards the implementation of Islamic banking services in European banks. However, the newly established Al Baraka International Bank serves the British Muslim community only to a limited extent.

In 1995, at a conference organized by the Islamic Foundation, the then governor of the Bank of England, Lord Edward George, gave a speech in which he drew attention to the dynamic development of Islamic banking in the Muslim world and its emergence on the international scene, as well as the need for attracting Islamic banks to the UK. It also points out a number of issues and difficulties associated with the development of Islamic banking in the UK. In practice in 2001, when a special commission was appointed, including representatives of the government, the Financial Services Authority (FSA), Muslim community banks, to determine the legal obstacles facing the further development of Islamic banking in the UK. 2004 brought a breakthrough in UK Islamic banking. In that year Islamic Bank of Britain (IBB) became the first fully Islamic retail bank to be licensed by the FSA. It is the first full-fledged Islamic bank not only in the UK but also in the whole of the European Union. In the following years, several fully Islamic banks were established in the UK. In 2014, six full-fledged Islamic banks already exist. In 2023 there are Abu Dhabi Islamic Bank (ADIB), Ahli United Bank, Bank of London and the Middle East, Al Rayan Bank, Gatehouse Bank, QIB UK

The foundation of interest-free banking or Islamic financial institutions is relatively recent compared to the history of the banking sector. Approximately 50 years have passed since the first Islamic financial institution appeared, to date there are many Islamic financial institutions operating according to Islamic rules and principles in many countries around the world and they maintain important functions in the financial system. (Schuster, 2013: 3). The Islamic financial system and the way it is perceived by all the major players has changed profoundly since the 1970s: there has been a diversification of products and participants and a strengthening of the cross-border dimension. Islamic finance is no longer seen as the opposite of the "secular" global financial system, but as an integral part of it. The industry began to target non-Muslim customers as Islamic financial companies began operating in Western countries in the 1990s. The existing Islamic financial system provides a variety of religiously acceptable financial services to both Muslim communities and non-Muslim clients seeking ethical investments and greater risk diversification. Today, the Islamic financial system is not limited to Islamic countries, but has gained popularity in Western countries, especially in Great Britain and the United States of America (Schuster, 2013: 3). In recent years, the Muslim population and Islamic banks, which remained stable during the Great Recession, have played an increasingly active role in the European Union's economy.

Basic principles of Islamic Financing

Conventional banking does not differentiate the goods and services provided from a religious point of view. At the core of the Islamic financial industry is the principle of interest-free banking, avoidance of transaction uncertainty, prohibition of speculation, and investment in halal-permitted goods and services (Hussain et al. 2015). The most important feature of Islamic banking is that it promotes a risk-sharing model - the risk is shared between the fund provider, the financial intermediary and the fund user, while in conventional banking the entire burden rests on the borrower's "shoulders". In addition, Islamic banking does not allow investing in haram or prohibited activities and industries such as gambling, alcohol and pork production (Ullah et al. 2014). Islamic banks confirm their socially responsible behavior in their economic activities by complying with Shariah principles of commerce (Cebeci 2012). This is a major 'differentiating point' of the social responsibility of Islamic banks that fundamentally distinguishes them from conventional banking.

The main differences between Islamic banking and conventional banking include not only the ways in which they operate, but also all the values that guide the entire operation and outlook of Islamic banking (Dusuki, 2008). These values prevail within the scope of Sharia (Islamic law) and are expressed not only in his dealings but also in his role in society. This requires internalizing the principles of Islamic financial transactions, both in form and substance. As Shariah-based companies, Islamic banks must fulfill social responsibilities that go beyond the conventional capitalist worldview of solely profit maximization (Dusuki, 2008). Islamic banks operate on the basis of Sharia principles and are far from conventional banks, which are highly motivated for profit through the so-called "concept of brotherhood", social obligations, and fairness are the main objectives of Islamic banks (Masruki et al., 2010).

Many scholars of Islamic banking (Ahmad, 2000; Iqbal and Molyneux, 2005; Lewis and Algoud, 2001; Warde, 2000) argue that Islamic banks perform mostly the same functions as conventional banks, but they do so in distinctly different ways. The most important features of Islamic banking and finance that make it different and unique from its conventional counterpart: first, Islamic banking strives for a fair, honest and balanced society as envisioned in Islamic economics. Second, Islamic banking is built on the principle of brotherhood and cooperation, which means that they are based on a system of capital, risk and equity sharing. Third, based on the ethical and moral framework of Shariah, Islamic banking is also characterized by ethical norms and social commitments (Dusuki, 2006). Fourth, Islamic banking is community-oriented, entrepreneur-friendly, emphasizing productivity and the physical expansion of economic production and services. Finally, Islamic banking operates within limits that ensure stability of the value of money and that reduce destabilizing speculation (Dusuki, 2011).

Islamic finance refers to "the application of Islamic law in the management of money" and encompasses intermediation activities and risk transformation similar to traditional finance. They are, however, unlike conventional financial, interest-free (ribā), real asset-based and capital-backed businesses that refrain from both taking risks (gambling) and exhibiting an excessive degree of uncertainty (gharar).

Broadly speaking, Islamic finance is based on divine law or Shariah as revealed in the Qur'an and Sunnah. These are respectively the Muslim holy text and real-life examples of the Prophet Muhammad. Islamic banking is a banking system in which profits, revenue or fees from any service are not spent or reinvested in interest-based activities or practices and is a system that avoids unethical and anti-social business transactions. While conventional banks earn a fixed income by charging compound interest rates, Islamic banks generate income by sharing risk, charging fees by providing services, leasing, trading and using other Shariah exchange contracts. Islamic banking and conventional banking differ in the following aspects:

1) Conventional banking is based on interest based principles and Islamic banking sector is based on interest free principles. The principle of profit and loss sharing (PLS) of the Islamic banking system creates an excellent relationship of financial trust and partnership between debtor and creditor. as well as an intermediary; 2) The conventional banking sector charges compound interest while the Islamic banking sector shares the losses; 3) Islamic banks act as partners with their depositors on the one hand and act as partners with an organization or entrepreneur on the other when an employee deposits funds for indirect investment compared to a commercial bank that is a borrower or lender of funds; 4) In conventional banking, money is a commodity that can be used to exchange and store value. Therefore, it can be sold at a higher price than its face value and can also be rented out. While in Islamic banking, money is not a commodity but can be used as a medium of exchange and storage of values. Therefore, it cannot be sold at a higher price than its face value; 5). There are rules that govern investment behavior in the Islamic banking sector.

- Avoiding interest based transactions such as (RIBA).
- The concept of Islamic tax like (ZAKAT).
- Prohibition of producing all those goods and services which are "HARAM" in Islam.

Islamic finance is an ethical financial system based on Islamic law. It spread beyond the Muslim world, but with different theoretical and practical implications. There is potential for high growth in Europe as well. There is a normative approach to the study of Islamic finance within a non-Islamic setting, namely the European Union (EU). The main focus is to argue for the normative autonomy of Islamic finance and Islamic rules applied to financial institutions within the EU legal order, analyzing the resulting regulatory challenges and opportunities for the European legislator.

The Great Recession and financial crisis led to a decline in the profits of financial institutions from 2007 to 2008. Many banks make high-risk loans to increase profits, which helps them be competitive in the market. Banks change loan rates according to market conditions. The interest rate has been vital for banks and other financial institutions to generate profits. In contrast, the relatively new financial practice-Islamic finance uses its different financing methods to generate profit. Charging interest on loans disrupts the circulation of wealth to those people who already have it, because the lender does not give loans to those people who cannot repay it, therefore, the gap between rich and poor is further widened, and therefore the interest rate forbidden in Islam.

Reporting issue in Islam Finance

A basic Muslim belief is that Allah will give an account of everything on the Day of Judgment and each person will be held accountable for whether their actions were in accordance with the Sharia or not. Therefore, reporting responsibility is the basic concept for Muslims, for the Islamic system and all relationships within any Islamic society (Aljirari, 1996). Emdadul (2010) affirms the concept of accountability in Islam in the following statement: "Accountability to Allah for all activities is vital to the Muslim faith. Sharia dictates how business should be conducted, organized and managed. According to Islam, the basic rule in business is honest and fair accounting and fair treatment of customers; such obligations impose the moral responsibility of the business community to Islam. Samuel and Stewart (2009) point out the consequences of the formation of sustainable accountability. They add that there is no sustainable accountability outside of Sharia - they are far from reality because they seek imposed accountability and ignore the responsibility that comes from the depths of faith such as morality and ethics. Lewis (2006) argues that "accountability to God and the community for all activities is paramount to the Muslim faith".

Al-Humaidhi (1999) states that the mainstream of accountability in Islam is seen at two levels. The first level is when each person is responsible for their actions. The second level includes the accountability for the persons and objects that are under his influence. Therefore, the accountability of intermediate units lies below the second level through accountability to all stakeholders. This accountability can be achieved and is provided through disclosure in annual reports and websites. In an Islamic context, the Ummah (nation) has the right to know how the corporations that are part of the Ummah affect its welfare (Maali et al., 2006). The responsibility to reveal the truth is a very important issue in the Islamic context, and this responsibility applies to both businesses and individuals. From an Islamic perspective, the primary objective of corporate reporting, which overrides other objectives, is to enable Islamic enterprises to demonstrate that they are Shariah compliant and serve society (Baydoun and Willett 2000). A corollary to this objective is that have a responsibility to disclose all information material to their stakeholders about their operations. Islamic banks have an obligation to disclose their Shariah compliance to stakeholders. Maali and others (2006) explain that "requiring Muslims to reveal the truth is intended to help the community understand the effect of a person or business on its well-being". Based on Islamic values, profit maximization should not be the sole objective of risk management and control. According to Hameed and Yahya (2003), every Islamic business institution is required not only to report its economic performance but also its Shariah compliance, social concern and environmental concern to its stakeholders. Stakeholders are expected to have broader objectives covering Shariah, social value; ethical behavior as well as financial which are a necessary part of their value proposition (Warde, 2013).

The perception of disclosure from the Islamic approach is based on two general requirements: the concept of social accountability, which contains Shariah and social disclosure, and the concept of full disclosure, which focuses on financial disclosure as well as Shariah and social issues (Baydoun and Willett, 2000; Haniffa, 2002; Haniffa and Hudaib, 2002). Haniffa and Hudaib (2002) argue that full disclosure of applicable and reliable information should assist external users in making both economic and religious decisions, in addition to assisting management in achieving their accountability to God, society and all other interested parties. Based on the debates, the IB has 3 reports - Sharia compliance, social and financial.

From an Islamic perspective, social issues are expected to be the main factor in the disclosure of companies' annual reports. As a result, every Shariah business entity is expected to be more transparent in its disclosure practice. Islamic banks must disclose full information to the ummah (Muslims) about how their activities are carried out based on the objectives of Shariah to improve public prosperity (Meutia; 2017). Most of the literature on Islamic banks confirms that they generally perform their CSR functions in the same way as conventional banks, although they have a different approach (Ahmad, 2000; Chapra, 2000; Warde, 2000; Henry and Wilson, 2004; Iqbal and Molyneux, 2005; Dusuki and Abdullah, 2007b; and Iqbal and Mirakhor, 2007). Islamic finance prohibits usury (interest rate), gharar (ambiguity), maisir (gambling) and some other pro ducts such as alcohol and pork (Rosly, 2010) and are based on the principles of participation in the real economy and social justice. Jaufeerally (2011) added two obligations of Islamic banking, namely, first, profit and loss sharing and second, financing that is supported by real assets. Unlike conventional banks, Islamic banks (IIBs) must adhere to Islamic law in their dealings. As a result, *there are differences in disclosure and reporting methods between Islamic and conventional banks.*

In an Islamic context, the main purpose of corporate reporting is to enable Islamic enterprises to demonstrate that they are Shariah compliant (Baydoun and Willett, 1997, p. 6). Other purposes of corporate reporting may include those known in the Western model, such as assisting economic entities in making economic decisions, but from an Islamic perspective these are secondary purposes. This view of the primary objective was adopted by the AAOIFI when it set out its Statement of Financial Accounting Objectives for Islamic Banks and Financial Institutions - Islamic firms must disclose all information necessary to advise the Umma (Islamic community) about their operations, even if the disclosure of such information would be against the company itself. In the Islamic context, the Ummah has the right to know how the individuals and organizations that are part of the Ummah affect its welfare. This obligation is emphasized in the Qur'an: "and do not conceal the truth with a lie, nor hide the truth that you know" About Islam God is omniscient - God says "I know what you reveal and what you conceal." Muslims are responsible for their actions and must consider this responsibility to the society in which they live because their actions affect society. Islamic businesses as well as individuals are required to undertake charitable activities and help the poor and needy. The requirement to pay Zakah is a clear example of such an obligation (the Qur'an lists eight uses for Zakah). The information provided by Islamic business enterprises, in addition to showing Shariah compliance, should therefore assist Muslims in fulfilling their religious obligations, especially the payment of zakat.

The conclusion of this discussion is that there are three broad objectives that can be used as a basis for identifying the social disclosures of Islamic business enterprises: 1. To demonstrate compliance with Islamic principles; 2. To show how business activity has affected the welfare of the Islamic community. 3. To help Muslims fulfill their religious duties.

Hasan and Siti-Nabiha (2010) argue that Islamic Banks accountability issues need further research. Recently, integrated reporting practices have attracted the attention of many scholars as a new evolutionary form of corporate reporting. The advantages and benefits of integrated reporting implementation highlighted by various studies. For example, integrated reporting improves information quality by linking financial and sustainability information (Baboukardos and Rimmel, 2016). Integrated reporting in the Islamic finance industry is not yet widespread. Critics note the need to introduce a new approach, with Gelmini (2017) arguing that Islam represents an extremely important area of study for integrated reporting. It qualitatively examines the integrated reporting of specific three

Islamic banks to identify the reasons why these banks issue integrated reporting. To study the adoption of an integrated reporting framework in Islamic financial institutions, Ramli et al. (2018) explores the principles of integrated reporting that are aligned with Islamic non-profit organizations that trace their origins to waqf, zakat and sadaqa (charity). To overcome the shortcoming of conventional reporting models in reporting waqf revelations Mansor et al. (2017) proposed a new integrated accounting system for "waqfs" through integrated accounting based on Islamic accounting principles. Masruki et al. (2020) also proposed an integrated waqf reporting model that covers four different disclosure areas, first, waqf performance; second, waqf financial and non-financial information; third waqf administration; and finally waqf socio-economic effect.

Results

Table 1. Summary of researches for Islamic finance

Year	Author(s)	Research	Object	Findings
2002	Haniffa and Hudaib	"A theoretical framework for the development of the Islamic perspective of accounting."		They argue that from an Islamic perspective, full disclosure along with social responsibility disclosure is important in the context of Islamic banking and highlight certain dimensions of social disclosure.
2003	Harahap	"The disclosure of Islamic values—annual report. The analysis of Bank Muamalat Indonesia's annual report"	The Islamic Bank of Indonesia	Reveals Certain Islamic Values of Islamic Bank Indonesia Through Interpretive Content Analysis of Annual Reports 1992–2000.
2006	Maali	„Social reporting by Islamic banks."	29 full-fledged Islamic banks in 16 countries.	This study is related to the social disclosure of Islamic banks. The disclosure index examined 30 items across 6 dimensions. The sample of the study was 29 fully-fledged Islamic banks in 16 countries. Content analysis was performed on annual reports for 2000–2002

2007	Dusuki and Abdullah	„Maqasid al Shari'ah, Maslahah, and corporate social responsibility“		They define the maslahah pyramid as a framework for implementing CSR. This framework is based on general ethical guidelines derived from an understanding of the objectives of the Shariah and the public interest in the light of Islamic axioms
2007	Dusuki and Abdullah	„Why do Malaysian customers patronise Islamic banks?“	750 customers of two leading full-fledged Islamic banks in Malaysia	The factors that customers consider important when choosing an Islamic bank are defined.
2007	Farook	„On corporate social responsibility of Islamic financial institutions“		It classifies CSR for Islamic banks into two forms - mandatory and recommended according to the degree of importance
2007	Haniffa and Hudaib	„Exploring the ethical identity of Islamic Banks via communication in annual reports.“	2002–2004 Annual Reports of 7 Islamic Banks in the Gulf Region	They develop an ethical identity index to assess the social disclosure of Islamic banks. The index examines 78 items across the eight dimensions.
2008	Dusuki	„What does islam say about corporate social responsibility?“		A continuum of levels of CSR has been defined - irresponsible, minimalist, apathetic, tactical and the highest level, called taqwa-centric.

2008	Dusuki	„Understanding the objectives of Islamic banking: a survey of stakeholders' perspectives."	1,500 stakeholders such as customers, employees, community members, managers, regulatory officers and Islamic banking Shariah advisors from two full-fledged Islamic banks in Malaysia	Explores stakeholders' perspective on the philosophy and objectives of Islamic banks in Malaysia's dual banking environment.
2009	Hassan and Latiff	„Corporate social responsibility of Islamic financial institutions and busi- nesses."		Considers CSR in the context of philanthropy. The central focus is on how to increase charity (other than Zakat and Qard al Hassan)
2010	Aribi and Gao	„Corporate social responsibility disclosure: a comparison between Islamic and conventional financial institutions."	Annual reports of 21 IFIs and 21 CFIs for 2004..	The study aims to compare CSR disclosure between Islamic Financial Institutions (IFIs) and Commercial Financial Institutions (CFIs) operating in the Gulf region.
2010	Hassan and Harahap	„Exploring corporate social responsibility disclosure: the case of Islamic banks."	The Annual Reports (for 2006) of seven Islamic banks in seven countries	A CSR disclosure index was developed, which consists of 78 items in eight dimensions.
2010	Hassan et al.	„Ethical gaps and market value in the Islamic banks of Bangladesh"	6 Islamic Banks in Bangladesh	The impact of ethical identity on the market value or performance of Islamic banks in Bangladesh is investigated.
2010	Rahman et al.	„Corporate social reporting: a preliminary study of bank Islam Malaysia Berhad (BIMB)."	Reports for 1992–2005. of an Islamic bank in Malaysia.	Analysis of CSR disclosure

2010	Williams and Zinkin (2010)	„Islam and CSR: a study of the compatibility between the Tenets of Islam and the UN global compact.“		Checking the compliance of the principles of Islam with the ten principles of the United Nations Global Struggle for Socially Responsible Business
2011	Aribi and Gao	“Narrative disclosure of corporate social responsibility in Islamic financial insti-tutions.”	The annual reports for 2004 of 21 Islamic financial institutions from the Gulf region	The influence of Islam on CSR is explored
2011	Farook et al.	“Determinants of corporate social responsibility disclo-sure: the case of Islamic banks.”	47 banks from 13 countries	Through content analysis method, the determinants of CSR disclosure of Islamic banks are explained.
2012	Cebeci	“Integrating the social maslaha into Islamic finance.”		The paradigm of sustainability and long-term social development in the true spirit of Islamic finance is argued
2012	Christine Mallinb, Hisham Faraga	„Corporate social responsibility and financial performance in Islamic banks“	90 Islamic banks from 13 countries/	The paper finds a positive relationship between CSR and financial performance in Islamic banks, and a highly significant relationship between the size of the Sharia Supervisory Board (SSB) and CSR disclosure.
2012	Zahid and Hassan	„Corporate social responsibility to employees: considering common law vis-a-vis Islamic law principles.“		They argue that the employer's obligations are similar to Islamic legal principles. While common law looks at issues from a temporal

				perspective, Islam takes it as a holistic view
2013	Almunawar and Low	„Islamic Ethics and CSR.“		CSR in Islamic banks is based on certain axioms of Islamic ethical philosophy such as tawhid (unity), adl (justice), ikhtiar (free will), fard (responsibility) and ihsan (benevolence).
2013	Kamla and Rammal	„Social reporting by Islamic banks: does social justice matter?“	19 Islamic banks in 11 countries	Emphasize disclosure and social reporting of Islamic banks in terms of social justice and poverty eradication. They address 5 topics and 11 disclosure analysis points.
2013	Khan	„Developing a conceptual framework to appraise the corporate social responsibility per- formance of Islamic banking and finance institutions.“	10 Islamic banks in seven countries	It assesses the CSR performance of Islamic banks through content analysis and based on interpretive and discursive analysis. It conceptualizes the framework of CSR from the Islamic principles of Shariah, community welfare, brotherhood, socio-economic development and Western literature on CSR.
2013	Rahman and Bukair	„The influence of the Shariah supervision board on corporate social respon-	Отчетите за 2008г. на 53 ислямски банки от региона на Персийския залив	This study explains the influence of Shariah supervisory board, bank size and performance on CSR

		sibility disclosure by Islamic banks of Gulf co-operation council countries.“		disclosure of Islamic banks in the Gulf region.
2013	Rashid et al.	„Customer-centric corporate social responsibility: a framework for Islamic banks on ethical efficiency“	The reports for 2008 of 53 Islamic banks from the Gulf region	They divide the ethical identity index (Haniffa and Hudaib 2007) into two layers, viz. religious commitment and commitment to stakeholders. The study sample also contains multiple were considered for content analysis of CSR disclosure
2013	Sairally	„Evaluating the corporate social performance of Islamic financial institutions: an empirical study.“	46 Islamic financial institutions (36 Islamic banks in 20 countries)	It assesses and describes the CSR performance of Islamic banks. The research framework begins by identifying the principles of CSR, examines the management of CSR, and finally evaluates the effectiveness of CSR.
2014	Darus et al.	“Social responsibility reporting of Islamic banks: evidence from Indonesia.	Annual reports for 2007–2011 years of 3 Islamic banks in Indonesia	Investigating the CSR disclosure of Islamic banks in Indonesia. .
2014	Darus et al.	“Corporate social responsibility towards the community: evidence from Islamic financial institutions in Malaysia.”	The 2012 Annual Reports of 37 Islamic Financial Institutions, including 17 Islamic Banks of Malaysia	They explore society-oriented CSR disclosure.

2014	Hamdan	“Corporate social responsibility of Islamic banks in Brunei Darussalam.”	Two Islamic banks in Brunei	It investigates the CSR perspectives of two Islamic banks in Brunei. The study takes data for this purpose from secondary sources viz. bank website, magazines, magazine articles, news, etc. and also from some informal conversational interviews with several employees of Islamic banks
2014	Khurshid et al.	„Developing an Islamic corporate social responsibility model (ICSR)“		Carroll's (1979) theory of CSR is reviewed from an Islamic perspective according to the doctrine of Shariah al-Muamalat.
2014	Koku and Savas	„On corporate social responsibility and Islamic marketing.“		They explore the concept of CSR and its relationships with Islamic marketing. They define Islamic marketing with its components and consider them under the lens of CSR.
2014	Mallin et al.	“Corporate social responsibility and financial performance in Islamic banks.”	2010-2011 Annual Reports of 90 Islamic Banks in 13 Countries	The relationship between CSR and financial performance in the context of Islamic banks is empirically investigated.
2014	Ullah et al.	“Socially responsible investment: insights from Shari’a departments in Islamic financial institutions.”	Two Islamic banks from UAE and Pakistan	Investigate socially responsible investing (SRI) of Islamic banks.

2014	Zaidi and Low	„The koranic discourse on corporate social responsibility.“		They refer to the facts that the concept of CSR according to the views of the Qur'an has a different paradigm that promotes socio-economic development, social justice and an interest-free economic system
2014	Zaki et al.	“The association of Islamic bank ethical identity and financial performance: evidence from Asia”	The 2006–2010 Annual Reports of Seven Islamic Banks in Asia	They examine the effects of ethical identity on financial performance following the approach of Haniffa and Hudaib (2007)
2015	Alamer et al.	“A new business process and outcome oriented corporate social responsibility index for Islamic banking”		They propose a process- and business-oriented CSR index, while arguing for the need for standardization and a comprehensive disclosure index.
2015	Aribi and Arun	„Corporate social responsibility and Islamic Financial Institutions (IFIs): manage-ment perceptions from IFIs in Bahrain.“	The 2006, 2008 and 2010 Annual Reports of 7 Islamic Financial Institutions in Bahrain	This study investigates CSR disclosure by ch. of managers' understanding of the nature and practice of CSR.
2015	Belal et al.	“Ethical reporting in Islami Bank Bangladesh Limited (1983–2010)”	Islamic Bank in Bangladesh for a period of 28 years (1983–2010)	Ethical practices and disclosures over a 28-year period (1983–2010) are examined. The survey index contains 149 items for 16 groups.
2015	Jusoh et al.	“An Islamic perspective on corporate social responsibility		They argue for accountability through the theocentric exposition

		of Islamic banks "		of divine appointment and human responsibility
2015	Nor and Hashim	„SR and sustainability of Islamic banking: the bankers view. "		They investigated the perception of CSR practices through 11 interviews with key employees of Islamic banks in Malaysia. They aim to explore bankers' understanding of Islamic banking, its objectives, CSR and sustainability, and also gauge opinion on CSR activities, reporting and benefits as well as challenges to Islamic banking
2016	Azis and Mohamad	„Islamic social business to alleviate poverty and social inequality"		They present the case for CSR by emphasizing that Islamic banks can introduce innovative products for social and small enterprises while using different financing instruments such as Islamic microfinance and qard al-hasan
2016	Bakar and Yusof	„Challenges in CSR engagements: the case of bank Islam"	Islamic Bank in Malaysia	They investigate the challenges of CSR engagement for a particular Islamic bank in Malaysia.
2016	Bakar and Yusof	„Managing CSR initiatives from the Islamic perspective: the case of Bank Islam Malaysia Berhad (BIMB) "	29 interviewees belonging to the design, implementation,	They describe the framework and processes of managing CSR initiatives through a particular Islamic bank in Malaysia

			monitoring and recipient groups of CSR initiatives.	
2016	Di Bella and Al-Fayoumi	„Perception of stakeholders on corporate social responsibility of Islamic Banks in Jordan“	210 respondents belonging to various stakeholder groups such as customers, managers, employees, Shariah advisors, regulators and community members	This study aims to assess the perception of different stakeholder groups regarding the CSR of Islamic banks operating in Jordan.
2016	El-Halaby and Hussainey	„Determinants of compliance with AAOIFI standards by Islamic banks“	The 2013 annual reports of 43 Islamic banks from the MENA region	They examine the compliance and level of disclosure of Islamic banks with respect to AAOIFI standards. The CSR index contains 95 items in 12 areas.
2016	Helfaya et al.	„Qur'anic ethics for environmental responsibility: implications for business practice“		They argue that Islam emphasizes responsible behavior towards the environment and its elements and present a discursive analysis of Qur'anic verses in the area of environmental responsibility
2016	Khan	„CSR standards and Islamic banking practice: a case of Meezan Bank of Pakistan.“	Pakistan Islamic Bank 2012, 2013 and 2014 Annual Reports, e-newsletters, media reports, websites and other sources	It examines the CSR engagement of Pakistan Islamic Bank in relation to certain stakeholders

2016	Maulan et al.	„Measuring halal brand association (HalBA) for Islamic banks“	121 customers of Islamic banks	They examine the factors of 'brand' association in the context of Islamic banking. The factor analysis concluded that there are three dimensions of Halal in the context of Islamic banking, viz. god consciousness, Sharia compliance and CSR
2016	Menne	„Evidence of CSR practices of Islamic Financial Institutions in Indonesia“	The Annual Reports (2010–2014) of 9 Islamic Banks in Indonesia	It examines the empirical relationship between CSR and financial performance. using Zakat and Qard al Hassan funding as indicators of CSR and profit as an indicator of financial performance.
2016	Mostafa and ElSahn	„Exploring the mechanism of consumer responses to CSR activities of Islamic Banks“	203 customers of Islamic banks operating in Bahrain	They examine the relationship of Islamic bank customers' perception of CSR and its impact on consumer and bank identification, as well as examining the mediating role of Islamic ethics.
2016	Nobanee and Ellili	„“Corporate sustainability disclosure in annual reports: evidence fromUAE banks: Islamic versus conventional.	16 banks, including conventional and Islamic, operating in the UAE	They empirically examine the relationship between corporate sustainability disclosure and financial performance. Sustainability disclosure was measured by the energy and environmental reporting indicator,

				and financial performance by the short-term deposit growth indicator.
2016	Platonova et al.	„The impact of corporate social responsibility disclosure on financial performance: evidence from the GCC Islamic banking sector“	The 2000–2014 Annual Reports of 24 Gulf Islamic Banks	They investigate the impact of CSR disclosure on the financial performance of Islamic banks. The survey design includes an index to measure CSR disclosure, return on assets as an indicator of financial performance.
2016	Rahman et al.	„Determinants of ethical identity disclosure in Islamic banks: an analysis of practices in Bahrain and Malaysia“	2007–2011 Annual Reports of 21 Islamic Banks	They investigate CSR disclosure in Islamic banks from Malaysia and Bahrain. using the Haniffa and Hudaib (2007) index to measure ethical identity.
2016	Turker			She revised Carroll's (1979) model according to the Islamic paradigm
2017	Ahmed and El-Belihy	„An investigation of the disclosure of corporate social responsibility in UK Islamic Banks“	The Annual Reports (2007–2009) of Islamic Banks in the United Kingdom	They investigate CSR disclosure by Islamic banks in the UK and conclude that four Islamic banks in the sample adopt Haniffa and Hudaib's (2007) index.
2017	Amran et al.	“Social responsibility disclosure in Islamic banks: a comparative study of Indonesia and Malaysia”	3 domestic Islamic banks from Indonesia and 3 from Malaysia for the period 2007-2011.	They present a comparative analysis of CSR disclosure made by Islamic banks in Malaysia and Indonesia based on six areas and 78 items

2017	Migdad	"CSR practices of Palestinian Islamic banks: contribution to socio-economic development."	3 Islamic banks from UK	The CSR practices of the Palestine Islamic Bank are examined through the 2015 annual reports and 11 interviews with six practitioners at the decision-making level and five members of the banks' Shariah board.
2017	Rawashdeh et al.	„Philanthropy, markets, and Islamic financial institutions: a new paradigm"		They build an argument based on the assumption that the market and philanthropy are not mutually exclusive but complementary, based on a participatory approach. They emphasize the need to spread charitable CSR activities by offering Islamic financial instruments to enterprises.
2018	Franzoni and Allali	"Principles of Islamic finance and principles of corporate social responsibility: what convergence?"		They provide a comparative analysis of traditional and Islamic CSR and conclude that the only difference of traditional CSR is the obligation of Islamic banks to take responsibility mostly for religious reasons. They also argue that if religious obligations are excluded from the CSR of Islamic banks, the concept converges with the

				expositions of Carroll's (1979) model.
2018	Jaiyeoba et al.	“Are Malaysian Islamic banks' corporate social responsi-bilities effective? A stakeholders' view”	193 stakeholders including employees, customers and community members of Islamic banks from Malaysia	They investigate the CSR performance of Islamic banks operating in Malaysia through a stakeholder opinion survey.
2018	Muhammad Bilal Zafar, Ahmad Azam Sulaiman	„Corporate social responsibility and Islamic banks: a systematic literature review“	A Literature Review on CSR in Islamic Banks.	It is concluded that there are various studies which are descriptive in nature, investigating CSR in Islamic banking in different regions and contexts, but they are less compared to the studies to reveal CSR in Islamic banking.
2018	Murphy and Smolarski	“Religion and CSR: an Islamic political model of corporate governance.”		A normative model of critical Islamic perceptions in the field of governance is proposed
2018	Shabbir et al.	“Corporate social responsibility and customer loyalty in Islamic banks of Pakistan: a mediating role of brand image.”	350 customers of Islamic banks	They examine the relationship between CSR and customer loyalty based on stakeholder theory, taking customer loyalty as a performance indicator.

Discussion

In summary, it can be argued that research is contradictory – according some authors Islamic and conventional banking are not drastically different. Others are of the opinion that the two systems function on the basis of fundamentally different principles and ethics. The answer to this question also depends a lot on the specific country and the legal regulation in which the banks operate.

Conclusion

Islamic finance has become a key dimension of the relationship between Arab banks and their European counterparts. While Arab banks imported most of their conventional financial products from Europe in the past, European banks are now importing Sharia-compliant products from the Arab world, and not just for their overseas Arab clients, but also for Europe's growing Muslim population. Thanks to the emergence of Islamic banking, the transfer of knowledge in finance has become a two-way process - European banks have as much to learn from the Arab world as the latter have from Europe. The growing proliferation of Sharia-compliant finance is transforming Euro-Arab financial relations into a partnership in the twenty-first century.

References

1. Antoniazzi, S., 2022. Islamic Banks and the European Banking Union: An Overview of Critical Issues and Perspectives. European Journal of Islamic Finance, 9(1), pp.37-55.
2. Committee on Payments and Market Infrastructure – World Bank Group (2015), Payment aspects of financial inclusion. Consultative report, 9f., Available at: http://www.worldbank.org
3. Di Mauro, F., Caristi, P., Couderc, S., Di Maria, A., Ho, L., Kaur Grewal, B.,
4. ... and Zaheer, S. (2013). Islamic finance in Europe. ECB Occasional Paper, (146).
5. Hajjar, M. ed., 2019. Islamic finance in Europe: a cross analysis of 10 European countries. Springer.
6. Hamad, S., Lai, F.W. and Jan, A.A., 2020. Using integrated reporting to disclose the value-based intermediation information: evidence from Islamic banking industry. International Journal of Advanced Science and Technology, 29(10s), pp.1085-1098.
7. Hidayat, S. E., Nadeem, M. M., AlMadaifa, A. J., and Ali, Z. (2018). Impacts of Basel III on Islamic finance. Journal of Islamic Financial Studies, 4(02), 123-133.
8. Houssem eddine BEDOUI (2016) Overview Of Islamic Finance Regulatory Framework And Development; Available at: https://www.researchgate.net/publication/326832316_Overview_Of_Islamic_Finance_Regulatory_Framework_And_Development
9. IMF POLICY PAPER (2018) THE CORE PRINCIPLES FOR ISLAMIC FINANCE REGULATIONS AND ASSESSMENT METHODOLOGY
10. Jusoh, W.N.H.W. and Ibrahim, U., 2017. Corporate social responsibility of Islamic banks in Malaysia: arising issues. Islamic Economic Studies, 25(Special Issue), pp.155-172.
11. Juso h, W.N.H.W. and Ibrahim, U., 2019. Corporate Social Responsibility of Islamic Bank's Practices: An Exploratory Study. IJIBE (International Journal of Islamic Business Ethics), 1(2), pp.95-109.
12. KAPLAN, H. E. (2019). Islamic Financial Institutions in The World and Turkey. JOEEP: Journal of Emerging Economies and Policy, 5(1), 90-100.
13. Kazim, R., Mughal, Kh., Khan, N. (2022) Profitability of Islamic banks verses conventional banks in Pakistan.

14. Kurochkina, I. and Us, U., 2019. The development and special aspects of Islamic finance in Europe at the present stage. In SHS Web of Conferences (Vol. 67, p. 06033). EDP Sciences.
15. Maali, B., Casson, P. and Napier, C., 2006. Social reporting by Islamic banks. Abacus, 42(2), pp.266-289.
16. Mallin, C., Farag, H., and Ow-Yong, K. (2014). Corporate social responsibility and financial performance in Islamic banks. Journal of Economic Behavior and Organization, 103, S21-S38.
17. Sadoveanu, D., 2011. Islamic banking in European union countries: challenges and opportunities. CES Working Papers, 3(4), pp.592-598.
18. Sherif, E.H., Khaled, H., Mohamed, M. and Hussien, M., 2018. The determinants of financial, social and Sharia disclosure accountability for Islamic banks. Risk Governance and Control: Financial Markets and Institutions, 8(3), pp.21-42.
19. Sobol, I. (2015). Islamic banking in the European Union countries. European Integration Studies, 9(1), 184-197.
20. Sobol, I., 2015. Islamic banking in the European Union
21. Sociology International Journal, Volume 6 Issue 2 – 2022, https://medcraveonline.com/SIJ/SIJ-06-00263.pdf
22. Syarif, F. (2019). Regulatory framework for Islamic financial institutions: lesson learnt between Malaysia and Indonesia. Journal of halal product and research (JPHR), 2(2), 79-85.
23. Wilson, R., 2007. Islamic finance in Europe.
24. Zafar, M. B., and Sulaiman, A. A. (2019). Corporate social responsibility and Islamic banks: a systematic literature review. Management Review Quarterly, 69(2), 159-206.
25. Zakiaha, S., Takdir, D. Samdin (2018) Effects of Intelectual Capital on Disclosure of Corporate Social Responsibility in Islamic Banks, Available at:
https://www.academia.edu/36906951/Effects_of_Intelectual_Capital_on_Disclosure_of_Corporate_Social_Responsibility_in_Islamic_Banks

Sukuk Bonds – Innovative Investment Market for European Banks

Sevgi Osman[1]

[1] Department of Economics, Varna Free University, Varna, Bulgaria, sevgi.osman@vfu.bg

Abstract

The growth of Islamic banking can certainly be traced back to the spread of investment funds and Islamic bonds. Sukuk has been developing as one of the most important Islamic financial instrument in the capital markets which are acceptable according to Islamic laws. The Islamic bond market has gained significant consideration even among conventional investors because these instruments are linked to material assets and, therefore, with a high degree of security. Sukuk could be attractive to both Muslim and non-Muslim investors as an alternative to conventional bonds for those looking for diversification options.

The article introduces to a very innovative and different market with its strengths, weaknesses, opportunities and threats, compares it with the conventional bonds market, glances at sukuk related literature, looks at sukuk market`s trends and tries to give answer for the question – could this innovative market be a good alternative to traditional conventional bonds?

The conclusion is that there is a positive outlook on the prospects for the sukuk market. What is more there's a significant overlap between Islamic finance and sustainability which hint the growing demand for green and sustainability sukuk from investors in Western markets such as the US and Europe.

Key words: Islamic bonds, innovation, regulation, sukuk, Europe

1. Introduction

Islamic finance and banking showed a great performance and are still expanding rapidly in recent years and just in 2019 it increased by 11.4%, due to COVID (Islamic Finance Outlook, 2021). Total value of Islamic financial assets is US$2.88 trillion in 2020 and expected to be US$3.69 trillion in the end of 2024 (Hasan, Islamic Finance Senior Proposition Manager, Refinitiv). Because of its promising future Islamic financial instruments are not only performed in Muslim countries but also being used in many non-Muslim countries (Yusoff and Shamsuddin, 2003-Alharbi, 2016).

There are Islamic banks in France, Germany, Italy, Ireland, Luxembourg, United Kingdom and Turkey. Additional to Islamic banks there are some conventional banks in Europe offering 'Islamic Window' for the customers who are interested in Islamic financial products, such as Bank of Ireland, Barclays, Citigroup, Deutsche Bank and HSBC Amanah. On the one hand there is still low interest to Islamic finance in Europe, on the other hand there is a potential for the future in terms Islamic finance in Europe because of several reasons. First of all, there is a significant amount of Muslims in Europe and their proportion in the population tends to increase.[6] Second is the growing interest to Islamic financial products in some countries by non-Muslims like in Malaysia.

Although there are conceptual similarities in terms of financial products between conventional and Islamic finance, they are entirely different financial systems. Despite Islamic finance's small size in the conventional finance world, its promising growth makes Islamic finance a hot topic both in academia and business world. Today customers can access sophisticated Islamic financial products not only in Muslim countries but also in Europe.

[6] There are 1.9 billion Muslim in the world and it 25% of the world population. Only 20% of Muslims live in Middle East and the largest community in Asia with 62%. 25.8 million Muslim live in Europe and it is the 4.9% of the population. According to Pew Research Center Muslim population in Europe will be increased to 7.4% by 2050 even Europe accepts no Muslim refugee. Same research center estimates the Muslim population in USA as 8.1 million which is 2.1% of population by 2050, that is twice more than today.

2. Literature Review and Hypotheses Development

Compared to the literature on conventional bonds, the existing research on sukuk is relatively thin, largely consisting of qualitative rather than quantitative work in the form of market reports, articles in popular magazine, blogs, and conference papers. Very few research papers on sukuk are published in top scientific academic journals with impact factors. The underdeveloped literature on sukuk, especially in the scholarly empirical research, can be attributed mainly to a lack of available historical, consistent, and reliable data as well as the limited number of Islamic journals and funding for Islamic finance research.

The bulk of the literature focuses on operational matters of sukuk issuance and structure in practice, which revolve around their need to be Shari'ah-compliant. Limited literature has undertaken study on capital markets and corporate financial aspects of sukuk, followed by their theoretical nature, and very few studies examine the implications of sukuk for the real economy.

According Zulkhibiri (2015) the sukuk researches could be classified into three groups. In the first group of research, the literature revolves around the underlying theoretical and legal nature of sukuk from the perspective of Shari'ah. Debate is still ongoing among Islamic scholars on the theoretical and legal aspects of sukuk. The second group of literature focuses on the operational aspects of sukuk with respect to issuance, risk, and structure. This includes legal and regulatory considerations, performance, and innovation in sukuk. The third group research focuses on the development aspects of economic sectors by using sukuk as instruments for capital market development and as an alternative financing tool for economic development.

The paper of (Cakir, 2007) shows evidence that Sukuk are different types of instruments than conventional bonds, as evidenced by their different price behavior. If an investor is ready to allocate certain amount of funds in the bonds of a certain issuer, diversification by including Sukuk in the investment portfolio could significantly reduce the portfolio's VaR compared to a strategy of investing only in conventional bonds of that issuer. The results were broadly the same in both methods that were used in this analysis, namely the delta-normal approach and the Monte-Carlo simulation.

The results of the study indicate that the VaR of a portfolio consisting of sukuk and bonds is not similar to a portfolio which represents only bonds. Although there is some reduction in VaR which can be gained by adding another instrument, this reduction is not because of adding an instrument in the portfolio; rather it is an outcome of the different behaviour of sukuk prices in the secondary market compared with conventional bonds.

In relation to this, Godlewski et al. (2013) found that the investors responded differently to the issuance of sukuk and bonds. Hence, sukuk can be considered a different type of instrument compared with bonds because of their different price behaviour. Finally, the VaR concept is a very useful tool for financial institutions with regards to their risk management, and international fixed-income investors are advised to incorporate sukuk in the investment portfolio along with bonds which may help to gain diversification benefits as shown from this study. In this context, this study uncovered the attractive opportunities in terms of diversification benefits with credit quality and Shariah-compliant financial sector exposure for investors who want to invest in fixed-income securities (Bhuiyan, 2020).

Mimouni (2019) examines the impact of Sukuk market development on banks' profitability using a dataset of 71 Islamic banks (IBs) and 146 conventional banks (CBs) spanning 13 countries over the 2003–2014 period. The results suggest that Sukuk development reduces IBs' profitability but has no impact on CBs' performance. In addition, the evidence shows that these adverse effects on IBs' profitability are substantially lower after the 2008 global financial crisis. Accordingly, their findings suggest that IBs were able to overcome Sukuk competition after the crisis.

The study of Alim (2021) investigate the comparative impact of conventional and Islamic bonds over returns. It provides useful insights to investors to diversify investment by lowering the risk to the optimum level. This study examines the impact of the conventional and Islamic portfolios on returns through simple OLS regression, suggesting that Sukuk returns are positive and significant. Simultaneously, conventional bonds show a negative trend, but in the long run, the returns are significant. It indicates that the market is volatile due to macroeconomic factors that can reduce risks through portfolio diversification. Thus, this research suggests that investment can be secured by taking a rational portfolio decision that confirms robustness.

Birgaip (2021) investigate the contribution of Sukuk in diversification of bond portfolios by comparing Turkish bond funds that invest exclusively in conventional bonds (pure conventional bond funds), in Sukuk (pure Islamic bond funds), and in both (mixed bond funds) among each other for the period of 2014–2019. The results suggest that bond funds, of which the portfolios are composed of a combination of Sukuk and conventional bonds (i.e. mixed bond funds), have a relatively "lower risk-higher return" profile. Moreover, including Sukuk to conventional bond portfolios theoretically offers significant diversification opportunities for investors, particularly when the economy worsens.

The empirical results of Ledhem (2022) show that the sukuk markets are complementary to the Islamic Banks (IBs) and maintain their financial stability, which results in decreasing risk-taking by these banks. Moreover, to the best of our knowledge, of all the existing studies on the link between IBs and sukuk market development, this paper is the first that finds a complementarity effect of sukuk market development on IBs. Developed sukuk markets are becoming more widely recognized as an important component of stable financial systems. Accordingly, this study demonstrates that sukuk market development is complementary to IBs and promotes stability and reduces riskiness at IBs.

Using a sample of 68 sukuk securitizations issued by 68 companies operating in seven countries between 2004 and 2020, study of Mseddi (2023) concludes that sukuk securitization has a positive impact on the systematic risk of the issuing companies. These findings align with previous empirical results (Franke & Krahnen, 2006; Hansel ¨ & Krahnen, 2007; Iglesias-Casal et al., 2016, 2020; Lockwood et al., 1996; Uhde & Michalak, 2010). The findings are interesting for investors concerned about modifying their portfolio management strategy as they help them adjust their financial structure to enhance the performance of funding sources. It is important to study whether the impact of securitization on changes in systematic risk varies based on the type of sukuk.

Regardless such a limited number of studies on Islamic funds in Europe, this cursory look at their performance gives us a signal that they could be a good diversivication tool for portfolio management of conventional financial institutions. An effective diversification strategy will provide possible scope for European markets to retain financial stability and boost system efficiency, which is essential for policymakers, portfolio managers and investors.

2.1. Islamic finance in Europe – legal aspects

In Europe, there has been a significant growth of interest in Islamic finance and banking, Islamic bond products and other credit collection instruments. Very significant was the position of the Financial Service Authority which, in 2004, issued an authorisation to operate to the Islamic Bank of Britain and to the first European Islamic Investment Bank. Other European countries have experimented with Islamic financial products, albeit in a limited way. In this context, it is interesting to look further at the possible relations between the conventional bank model that operates in the EU market and the Islamic bank that follows religious criteria (e.g., the prohibitions of riba and gharar), but with issue regarding risk control and data transparency, regulation and prudential supervision, especially in relation to the current European system, capital requirements and the Basel III Agreement

Not only Muslim investors are involved, as they formally conform to Islamic principles, but also European ones, given the financial crisis caused mainly by the circulation of instruments that have unsafe mechanisms, based as they are on interest and debt. Indeed, Islamic securities are currently traded in the largest secondary markets mainly because of their security qualities.

The growth of Islamic banking can certainly be traced back to the spread of investment funds and Islamic bonds; the establishment of the Islamic Bank of Britain, which is an expression of this evolution also by means of innovative management methods in order to acquire credibility in the markets, notwithstanding its very particular and distinct framework compared to conventional banks. Regarding taxes, the legislation in the UK facilitated the practical implementation of traditional models of acquisition avoiding interest, which are compatible with Islamic law. New rules have been implemented to levy the stamp duty only once in cases of Islamic mortgages and at first HSBC Amanah first offered such Islamic mortgages, with other banks following suit. However, it is necessary to highlight the problematic issues of compatibility with the conventional market, regulation in the classical sense and the necessary transparency of requirements, when Islamic banks operate in European countries. It is necessary to consider the supervision exercised by the ECB and national central banks, according to the approach of European banking supervision (Reg. (UE) 15 October 2013, n. 1024 and Reg. (UE) 16 April 2014, n. 468 and related disciplines) and many rules (Basel III, EBA) that impose obligations of capital requirements and procedures of necessary transparency (e.g., the "stress test" for banks) about aspects of accounting and internal decisions that can only be based on the adoption of technological innovations for communications.

Islamic finance schemes present interesting aspects from the perspective of a sustainable and socially oriented finance, but the critical issue is the certainty of the rules and their effective knowability through widely available technological tools. It is, therefore, necessary to have a high level of transparency in internal controls by the Shariah Boards, which plays a role analogous to the ethics committees, but according to Islamic ethical-legal rules from which derives a certain unpredictability in the application of rules of conduct by way of interpretation. Moreover, a certain uniformity of rules would be necessary, given the obvious differentiation according to the countries of origin, an objective in theory constantly affirmed by the Gulf Cooperation Council (GCC), but difficult to implement even for the discipline of competition.

More sophisticated Islamic financial instruments can help the Muslim communities living in non-Muslim countries. Islamic Finance can be a fresh way to attract money to European countries and at the same time it can help the Muslim population to integrate the country by involving them into the financial system. European Union acts as a single market by establishing movement of goods, services, capital and people freely. Unfortunately Germany has little interest to Islamic Finance when it is compared other leading countries in the world. "We all know the UK will be the Islamic finance hub in Europe." (Adham Charanoglu, DAR). Beside UK government's pro-Islamic finance regulations helping them to achieve to be an Islamic finance center in Europe in the future, the other European countries' governments showed little interest and they actually lead to UK in a position with respect to Islamic banking and finance that has not been achieved in nowhere else in Europe (Wilson, 2007). However, post Brexit it seems there is an uncertainty for the Islamic financial services and they are going to make a choice whether staying and operating in UK which will be more costly or moving to countries such as France or Germany to provide services.

These aspects are of considerable interest to European legal systems as an opportunity and alternative source of financing. In Europe, there is a significant presence of "Islamic counters" that have opened in conventional banks for depositors wishing to implement religious principles, but **regulatory innovations** must be introduced for supervision and regulation, in the sense that the EU member states where these banks are located should adopt their legislation considering all the potential risks in relation to this new financial activity.

From the European perspective, the pandemic has confirmed the importance of a solid system of rules capable of directing banks towards virtuous and prudent behaviour and strengthening the ability of the system to cope with the crisis. Moreover, the United Nations published a study in 2016 highlighting the possible contribution of Islamic finance to promoting the sustainable development goals of the 2030 Agenda to finance infrastructure. However, sustainable finance requires rules and techniques to manage risk and technology to enable knowledge of standards and accounting rules for the maximum transparency in transactions, and control of compliance with Islamic law as well as compatibility with the conventional system: objectives that are very complex to achieve. In particular, the ECB cultivates international relations for cooperation with countries outside the EU with Article 8 of Reg. (EU), 15 October 2013, no. 1024, on banking supervision "to establish contacts and enter into administrative arrangements with supervisory authorities, international organisations and administrations of third countries, subject to appropriate coordination with the EBA (Antoniazzi, 2022).

The context of reform of the international rules and global difficulties have undoubtedly aggravated the relevant complexity of the multiple tasks carried out by the Islamic Finance Stability Board (IFSB) as regulator and supervisor of the Islamic banks and as an authority that adopts the choices of necessary alignment to the conventional system for obvious interests in international markets.

2.2. What is Sukuk?

Sukuk has been spreading all over the world in recent years. It is also attracting both Muslim and non Muslim people. From this aspect, we can say that Sukuk has been developing as one of the most important Islamic financial instrument in the capital markets which are acceptable according to Islamic laws.

There are lots of different types financial activities but at the end who decides that those activities are Islamic or not. There is no unique set of rules that can be used to check a financial activity whether it it Islamic or not. However, there are two important organization which are recognized by many countries, investment banks, banks, institutions, etc. They are Accounting and Auditing Organization for Islamic Financial Institutions (AAOIFI) and Islamic Financial Services Board (IFSB).

Sukuk is translated mostly into English as Islamic bond. It represents ownership of an asset or its usufruct and it is an investment certificate consisting of ownership claim in a pool of assets. AAOIFI defines Sukuk as being: “Certificates of equal value representing after closing subscription, receipt of the value of the certificates and putting it to use as planned, common title to shares and rights in tangible assets, usufructs and services, or equity of a given project or equity of a special investment activity”.

The Islamic bond market has gained significant consideration even among conventional investors as well in the last decade precisely because these instruments are linked to material assets and, therefore, with a high degree of security. The global sukuk market has proven itself as an effective measure of some of the fastest-growing economies in the world, while also providing steady cash flow. Unlike traditional fixed income investments, sukuk offer a stake in the underlying assets and pay investors a percentage of profit at predefined regular intervals.

Underlying sukuk are assets or transactions permissible under Sharia principles. The most common sukuk are the following (Kusuma, 2014) :

- Sukuk al-Ijara: based on leasing (sale and leaseback) transactions
- Sukuk al-Murabaha: based on sale-and-purchase contracts with predetermined cost and profit
- Sukuk al-Mudharaba: based on a partnership or profit-sharing agreement between capital providers (investors) and an entrepreneur
- Sukuk al-Musyaraka: based on a joint venture with an obligor
- Sukuk al-Salam: based on a forward contract, usually commodity
- Sukuk al-Istisna: based on a contract for a future delivery of manufactured or constructed asset(s)
- Sukuk al-Wakala: based on a contract with an agency that makes investment decisions on behalf of the investors

Sukuk Markets evolution

Europe’s first Sukuk was issued in 2004 by Germany. The issuer was actually not the German federal government, the issuer was the state of Saxony-Anhalt (this Sukuk issuance was called as Saxony-Anhalt Sukuk). The face value of Islamic bond (another name for Sukuk) was 100 million Euro. The state of Saxony-Anhalt was part of the East German before reunification of Germany and this state can be considered as underdeveloped state in Germany (there are 16 states in Germany and Saxony-Anhalt is the 13th richest state in Germany). Raised debt in Islamic rule was never done before in Europe, therefore what the state Saxony-Anhalt did was certainly a success for Germany in terms of Islamic finance. Although the high debt of the state of Saxony-Anhalt was a big motivation to find a new way to fund debts, it was nevertheless a promising step for the future of Islamic finance in Germany. The state wanted also a new place for not only for funds from Islamic world but also all investors and entrepreneurs. Actually the demand for Saxony-Anhalt Sukuk was strong at that time, more than 50% was bought by investors in Bahrain and UAE and the rest was bought by European investors-the majority was from France and Germany.

There were three Sukuk worth $336 million in 2000 and by the end of 2006, just after six years it reached to 77 Sukuk with over $27 billion funds under management.

Sukuk has grown more than 20% during the period of 2008 and 2013. Sukuk is the fastest growing Islamic financial product and it has second largest total asset value in Islamic finance after Islamic banking. After 2010s non-Muslim countries like UK, Hong Kong and Luxembourg started to issue Sukuk and in the near future some Asian and African countries will be added to the list. Sukuk has a wide range of usability like for a new source for renewable energy, ethical investments, infrastructure projects, financing for small&medium enterprises and so on.

Sukuk issuance started in UK in 2007 and UK government became the first Western government in Europe as sovereign Sukuk issuer. This Sukuk issuance was in 2014 and it received a strong a demand. Total value of first UK government's Sukuk issuance was 2.87 billion Euro (almost 29 times more than Germany's first Sukuk issuance). Muslim population in UK is less than both in France and Germany. However, UK is the leading country in Europe in terms of Islamic finance. More than 65 Sukuk with more than value of US $50 billion were issued in London Stock Exchange to 2021. UK is the bigger sovereign Sukuk issuer among the western countries. Regularity developments which started in the mid-90s and were get into practice at the beginning of 2000s played a crucial role in the success of UK in terms of Islamic finance. UK is also very strong in Islamic financial education (Sekreter, 2021).

Total global Sukuk issuance in 2018 was about US $120 billion and total international Sukuk issuance in Germany from 2004 to 2018 was around US $200 million on the other hand in UK in the same time interval it was more than US $1.7 billion.

Sukuk could be attractive to both Muslim and non-Muslim investors as an alternative to conventional bonds for those looking for diversification options. As evidenced during the start of the global pandemic in early 2020, the sukuk market witnessed a more muted downturn relative to traditional bond markets and experienced a quick recovery afterward. This resilience during volatile times is often tied to the high-quality nature of issuers and strong credit fundamentals of the underlying sukuk structure. Despite a small decrease in market size for 2020, the U.S. dollar denominated sukuk market has experienced a compound annualized growth rate of nearly 20% since 2013, as measured by the Dow Jones Sukuk Total Return Index (ex-Reinvestment) and the S&P Global High Yield Sukuk Index. As capital needs evolve and investor awareness broadens, the global sukuk market is well positioned to build on its current momentum (S&P Dow Jones Indices). Offering unique advantages for investors and issuers alike, Sukuk presents exciting possibilities for diversification, ethical investing, and economic development.

3. Material and methods

3.1. Theoretical Framework

This study is based mainly on SWOT analysis which is is an analysis method used to evaluate the 'strengths', 'weaknesses', 'opportunities' and 'threats' involved in an organization, a plan, a project, a person or a business activity. It can be applied at different analytical levels -individual level, organizational level, national level, international level-. It can be used by educational institutes, non-profit organizations, markets, industries, countries, governments, projects, etc. Combined with a short look at literature review it has made an attempt to show off some advantages of Sukuk bonds in comparison with conventional ones.

3.1.1. Strengths

A Sharia-Compliant Investment Vehicle

Sukuk provides a gateway to financial markets for Islamic investors seeking instruments that align with their religious beliefs. This inclusivity not only broadens the investor base but also increases capital flow into markets, potentially reducing the cost of capital for issuers. The Sharia compliance of Sukuk ensures they meet certain ethical standards, attracting not only Islamic investors but also those interested in ethical or socially responsible investing (SRI). This alignment with ethical investment principles can enhance the global appeal of Sukuk as an investment vehicle.

Diversification of Investment Portfolios

Sukuk structures are underpinned by a diverse range of assets, including real estate, infrastructure projects, and various business ventures. This allows investors to diversify their portfolios across different asset classes, sectors, and geographies, potentially reducing risk. Unlike conventional financial instruments, Sukuk's performance is often linked to returns from real assets or business profitability rather than fluctuating interest rates. This lower correlation with traditional assets makes Sukuk a valuable tool for portfolio diversification, helping to smooth out returns over time.

Support for Economic Development

Sukuk is particularly well-suited for funding large-scale infrastructure and development projects that align with Islamic principles. This is especially important for emerging markets and Islamic countries, where such funding supports economic development and improves public welfare. Since Sukuk must be backed by tangible assets or projects, they often finance ventures in the real economy, such as renewable energy projects, sustainable agriculture, and community-benefiting infrastructure. This focus on real economic activity promotes sustainable development goals (SDGs) and responsible investment practices.

Stimulating Financial Innovation

The growth of the Sukuk market drives financial innovation, particularly in developing Islamic financial instruments that meet the diverse needs of modern economies while adhering to Sharia principles. This innovation can lead to more efficient financial markets and stimulate economic growth by unlocking new forms of investment.

Broadening Impact

The unique characteristics of Sukuk, including their ethical foundations, asset-backed structures, and potential for diversification, help making financial markets more inclusive and foster an environment conducive to sustainable economic development. As the Sukuk market evolves, it could play a crucial role in channeling investments into sectors and regions vital for global economic stability and growth, particularly in areas underserved by conventional financial systems. As awareness and understanding of Islamic finance grow, Sukuk could increasingly be seen as a viable and attractive option for a broader range of investors, further integrating Islamic finance into the global financial system.

3.1.2 Weaknesses

While the Sukuk market is growing, it faces several challenges that can impact its development and the ease with which investors and issuers engage with it. Understanding these challenges is crucial for participants in the Islamic finance market and regulators (Yesuf, 2016).

Complexity and Cost of Structuring Sukuk

Ensuring that Sukuk structures comply with Sharia law adds layers of complexity to their issuance. This process involves securing approval from Sharia scholars, who assess the structure's adherence to Islamic principles. The involvement of these scholars and the need to design instruments that reflect the real economic activity and asset ownership required by Sharia can make the structuring process more time-consuming and costly than conventional bonds. The necessity for Sukuk to be backed by tangible assets means issuers must identify and manage these assets, adding another layer of complexity. This requirement can limit the flexibility in the types of financial products offered and increase the logistical and legal challenges involved in structuring and managing Sukuk.

Varied Interpretations of Sharia Principles

Islamic finance is guided by principles interpreted by scholars, leading to differences in the application of these principles across jurisdictions. This variability can affect the uniformity of Sukuk structures, making it challenging for investors to compare different Sukuk or for issuers to standardize offerings across markets. The lack of standardized global regulations for Islamic finance compounds the issue, as each country may have its own set of rules governing Sukuk issuance and trading. This fragmentation can deter international investors and issuers, limiting the market's growth and the cross-border flow of Islamic finance.

Liquidity in the Secondary Market

Compared to the well-established global market for conventional bonds, the Sukuk market is relatively young and still developing. This has historically resulted in lower liquidity in the secondary market, with fewer buyers and sellers. This liquidity issue can lead to higher transaction costs and price volatility, making it less attractive for some investors. The diversity of Sukuk structures, coupled with the relatively small number of issuances in some markets, can make it difficult to establish benchmarks for pricing and risk assessment. This lack of benchmarking can further exacerbate liquidity challenges, as investors may find it harder to assess the value and risk of Sukuk investments.

3.1.3. Opportunities

Current market trends

In 2019 total value of global Sukuk is almost $146 billion (IIFM Sukuk Database). According to IIFM Sukuk Database, Germany had three Sukuk issues between 2001 and 2019 with the value of $206 million which is less than Luxembourg. Luxembourg had also three Sukuk issues in the same time period however their total value is $280 million. On the other hand UK has 10 Sukuk issues and their value is more than $1.7 billion.

Sukuk has a special place in Islamic financial products since it is a promising product in non-Muslim countries. In 2019 it has increased by more than 18% and reached the value almost USD 146 billion globally (IIFM). Sukuk has continued to attract attention in 2020 despite the Corona Pandemic. Sukuk has performed the same year well in not only in Muslim countries like Egypt but also in non-Muslim countries like Taiwan and gained new issuers. However for many years Malaysia, Indonesia and Saudi Arabia are major Sukuk issuers and they are dominating Sukuk market. Moreover Turkey, Bahrain and Pakistan tend to increase their Sukuk issuance in the following years.

The overall Islamic capital market (ICM) segment, consisting of sukuk, Islamic funds, and Islamic equities registered a slower, single-digit, growth rate for the first time in five years. ICM's value of USD 966.3 billion accounted for a share of 29.8% of global IFSI assets as of the end of 2022. In 2022, the growth of the sukuk sub-segment was moderate due to unfavourable global economic conditions and reduced sovereign issuances. Sovereign funding needs in the GCC region were low, and there was a narrow domestic investor base, lack of market depth, and secondary market activities in other jurisdictions. However, there was a slight positive impact from sustainability-linked sukuk issuances for development projects and new sovereign issuances in response to the global economic recovery. The Islamic equities indices were affected by global market volatility and negative returns, while Islamic funds contracted due to liquidity strain and susceptibility to runs during stressed conditions.

Large corrections were observed in the capital markets in 2022, affecting both equity and fixed-income markets. Islamic equity markets were impacted similarly to global equity markets, with significant market volatility and negative returns across most indices and sectors. However, Islamic equity indices performed better in the longer term, as they are inherently less prone to more severe impact due to the constituents of Islamic indices being generally less leveraged. Activity in primary Islamic capital markets, particularly sukuk issuances saw continued but moderate growth, in contrast to bond markets which saw a decline. Islamic funds have also remained largely resilient, however, the pace of growth has slowed down (IFSB report, 2023).

Regional break-up of the Domestic Sukuk Market for 2011 year shows that from Europe only Germany have 1 sukuk issuance for 123 USA$ millions which is 0,1% of total value. The analogical table for 2022 year shows that number of issuances for Europe (including Turkey) is 32. Regional break-up of the **Domestic** Sukuk Market (2001-2022) shows 4,91% for Europe. Regional Break-up of **International** Sukuk issuance (Jan 2001 – Dec 2022) shows that number of issues for Europe and others is 66 (2001-2022) – Turkey (42), UK (12), USA (4), Germany (3), Luxemburg (3), France (1), Kazakhistan (1).

According to statistics from 2001-2022 (A Comprehensive Study of the Global Sukuk Market August 2023, 12th Edition) it could be seen that Total Global Short Term Sukuk Issuances for all currencies for the period 2001-2022 is approximately 1022 (7,2%) as Total Global Short Term Sukuk Issuances – All Currencies for 2022 is 22 (0,62%).

Based on the investor type, Banks had the highest allocation (68%) including 91% Islamic Banks, followed by Supranational/ Sovereign Wealth Fund (SWF)/ Ministry of Finance (MoF)/ Central Banks, and Pension Funds/ Asset Managers with 27% and 4%, respectively. Islamic investors were still dominating primary market in 2022, accounted around 85% from total allocation across the tenors, compared to 15% allocated to conventional investors (International Islamic Financial Market report 2023).

For the past 20 years, the global sukuk market has been dominated by issuers and investors from the GCC region, as well as Malaysia, Indonesia, and Turkey. Looking ahead, the investment landscape is poised for significant evolution driven by product innovation, sustainability targets, and new market entrants. It could be expected that sukuk will continue to attract the attention of some of the world's largest and most significant institutional investors in the U.S., Europe, and Asia, as many may view sukuk as an effective way to invest in some of the fastest-growing regions of the world.

Many institutional investors are shifting towards responsible investing by incorporating ESG components within their investment strategies, which is helping to drive demand for ESG financial products. However, there remains a shortage in the global supply of ESG investments, and green and sustainability sukuk have the potential to fill some of this gap, particularly for investors seeking Shariah compliance as well. As the global sukuk market evolves, sukuk indices, like those offered by S&P DJI, will play an integral role in the investment decision-making process, providing tools to better measure, benchmark, and replicate various sectors of the market (S&P Dow Jones Indices).

It must be mentioned also that there are various similarities between the principles of Islamic finance (e.g., in the case of sukuk) and the principles of public-private partnership for infrastructures, regarding risk sharing, the lender as partner, the exclusion of speculative intentions and certainty in the definition of contractual performance. The comparison could be the topic for interesting studies in the future.

3.3.2. Recent case studies for Sukuk issuance from European banks

Dubai Islamic Bank PJSC ("DIB"), rated A3 by Moody's and A by Fitch, is the second largest Islamic bank in the world and the largest Islamic bank in the United Arab Emirates, measured by total asset size. In November 2022, DIB successfully priced its inaugural Sustainable Sukuk – a landmark USD 750 million 5-year senior issue with a profit rate of 5.493% per annum representing a spread of

155bps over 5-Year US Treasuries.[7] This deal once again demonstrated an established and strong investor following from Europe, Asia and the Middle East. The Sukuk was priced after completing a comprehensive marketing exercise where DIB updated investors on its positive financial performance as well as its Sustainable Finance Framework.

On 9 February 2022, Riyad Bank executed a USD 750mn Sustainable AT1 RegS Sukuk issuance. This was a landmark deal in several ways, however most importantly, it was the first-ever sustainable AT1 Sukuk issuance globally, first-ever sustainable AT1 from an EM issuer and first-ever sustainable bank capital issuance from the GCC region. It is listing on International Securities Market of the London Stock Exchange and the Sustainable Bond Market of the London Stock Exchange. Joint Global Coordinators are HSBC Bank plc, Riyad Capital and Standard Chartered Bank (B&D). Riyad Bank is committed to supporting the Kingdom's energy transition agenda and the environmental targets of Vision 2030 and its dedicated Green and Renewable Banking offering contributes to accelerating the energy transition and driving a new wave of investment in line with the Kingdom's goal to achieve Net Zero by 2060.

3.1.4. Threats

Sukuk vs Conventional bonds

Conventional bonds that yield interest, or riba, are prohibited under Shariah law. Islamic bonds (sukuk) have economic characteristics similar to those of a conventional bond, but are structured so as to be compliant with Shariah law enabling them to be sold to Islamic investors. Sukuk, sometimes referred to as Islamic bonds, are better described as Islamic investment certificates.

This distinction is as crucial as it is important. The distinction is important as a bond is a contractual obligation whereby the issuer is obliged to pay bond holders, on certain specified dates, interest and principal. In comparison, under a sukuk

[7] The Sukuk was issued in line with DIB's Sustainable Finance Framework which was created to facilitate financing of green and social initiatives and projects. This sukuk is listing on Euronext Dublin and Nasdaq Dubai. Sole Sustainability Structurer is Standard Chartered Bank. Joint Lead Managers and Joint Bookrunners Bank ABC, Dubai Islamic Bank, Emirates NBD Capital, First Abu Dhabi Bank, HSBC, KFH Capital, Sharjah Islamic Bank, Standard Chartered Bank and The Islamic Corporation for the Development of the Private Sector.

structure, the sukuk holders each hold an undivided beneficial ownership in the underlying assets. Consequently, sukuk holders are entitled to share in the revenue generated by the sukuk assets as well as being entitled to share in the proceeds of the realisation of the sukuk assets. This case describes the differences between conventional bonds and sukuk.

What is a conventional bond?

A bond is a "security" showing that a borrower owes a specified sum. This claim protects the holder in circumstances in which the issuer is unable to pay the amount due. The investor who buys bonds lends the issuer money in return for interest payments. When the bonds mature, the investor will receive the principal amount of the bonds back. Legal documentation for a bond is required to specify the terms for both interest and principal payments. Interest can be paid monthly, semi-annually or annually. Most bonds pay interest semi- annually in North America. "Eurobonds", which trade in Europe, pay interest annually. Mortgage-Backed Securities (MBS) and Asset-Backed Securities (ABS) pay interest monthly, reflectingthe payment terms of the underlying mortgages and loans. The currency of payments is important. Some bonds have the coupon paid in one currency and the principal in another. Bonds which pay part of their principal before maturity are said to "amortize" their principal. This is the case with many mortgage bonds. The Bond market comprises a primary market and a secondary market. The primary bond market is where the bonds are initially issued, while the secondary market is where the bonds are resold to other investors. Islamic bonds also have primary and secondary markets. The main difference, however, is the way the bonds are issued and traded afterwards.[8] (AIMS education, IBF 513)

Even with controversies surrounding the issuance of Sukuk, Sukuk have witnessed strong surge in the issuance in Malaysia and Gulf Co-operation Council countries, there is strong evidence on Europe, Japan and Korea patronizing Sukuk in their respective countries. The continual growth of Sukuk has raised question

[8] In the process of Islamic bond issuance *bay' al- Thah* is sometimes used to securitize the instrument in the primary market, while in the secondary market, bay' al-Dain is used in order to legalize reselling of the bonds. This process is mostly used in the Malaysian market, while most of the Middle-Eastern countries do not accept this concept and apply alternative techniques

whether Sukuk can play the role of an alternative source of financing which might replace the conventional bond. Although a common starting point for explaining sukuk is to use bonds as a comparison point, it is important to understand that there are certain fundamental differences.

Sukuk adhere to an Islamic view of finance, avoiding *Riba* (generating money from money, i.e. interest or usury), bonds are securities that are *Riba* due to the fact that they have a fixed interest.

There are five important differences between sukuk and traditional bonds:

1. Sukuk indicate ownership of an asset. Bonds indicate a debt obligation.
2. The assets that back sukuk are compliant with Shariah. Assets backing bonds may include products or services that are against Islam.
3. Sukuk are priced according to the value of the assets backing them. Bond pricing is based on credit rating.
4. Sukuk can increase in value when the assets increase in value. Profits from bonds correspond to fixed interest, making them *Riba*.
5. When you sell sukuk, you are selling ownership in the assets backing them. The sale of bonds is the sale of debt.

Sukuk are backed by tangible assets, rather than by debt. Sukuk ownership indicates ownership of an asset that has value. Although, a bond may also indicate this, the real definition of a bond simply indicates a debt obligation. At its root, the relationship between the issuer of a bond and the consumer is very different from the relationship between the issuer of sukuk and the purchaser of sukuk. In the case of a bond, the consumer is acting as the loaner and the bond issuer as a loan recipient. In this case, the loan has a fixed interest, therefore being *Riba.* In sukuk, the purchaser is purchasing an asset that has value rather than participating in an implicit loan agreement.

Another important difference between bonds and sukuk is that the assets involved in sukuk certificates comply with all laws of Islam. In the case of bonds, the bond certificate may be backed by assets that are not compliant with Shariah, which may be bundled together with other types of assets without the consumer's knowledge. The consumer of sukuk is assured that the value of the certificate corresponds to assets that are in the public good and not related to activities or products that are against Islam.

Although some may argue that the differences between sukuk and bonds are merely technicalities, these differences matter to Muslims. In fact, the practice of profiting from money alone, at the expense of productivity and real people has been one of the drivers for many of the economic problems that have plagued the world in the last decade. Interest and artificial inflation of prices based on debt rather than on real value is the main reason why bubbles form, burst, and then lead to recessions and depressions. Sukuk, unlike bonds, are priced according to the real market value of the assets that are backing the sukuk certificate. Bond pricing is based on the credit rating of the issuer. This is necessary in the case of bonds because when you sell a bond on the secondary market, you are actually selling the debt in the underlying loan relationship. The sale of a sukuk on the secondary market is simply the sale of ownership in the asset.

The main advantage of sukuk over traditional bonds is that their value increases in relationship to the assets backing the sukuk certificate. If the asset raises in value, then the value of the ownership of that asset, backed by the sukuk, increases. Bonds do not have this characteristic. It is not possible to raise the main debt in a bond and increase in revenue from a bond is the direct result of the fixed interest rather than in any kind of tangible increase in value or productivity.

This is not to say that bonds and sukuk are not similar in certain ways. Both can be turned into cash by selling them on the secondary market. Based on the strength of their backing, both bonds and sukuk can be ranked by ranking institutions. There is also similar variance in bond and sukuk designs and issuers, allowing consumers to have a variety of options when looking into these financial instruments.

Table 1. Sukuk versus Conventional Bonds

	Sukuk	Conventional Bonds
1	Income is generated from assets	Income is derived from debt instrument
2	Return is expected	Return is interest and pre-determined
3	Negotiability is restricted to specific types of Sukuk	Negotiable financial paper
4	Sukuk issue is a seller of assets	Bond issuer is a borrower
5	Sukuk holder is an owner of assets	Bond holder is a lender
6	Seller-buyer relationship	Lender-borrower relationship
7	Business risk-return relationship	Issuer guarantees the payment of face

		value and periodic interest
8	Major risk lays with underlying assets	Major risk is with issuer-credit risk
9	Return is expected from underlying assets	Interest payment is an obligation
10	Return of investor`s capital cannot be guaranteed	Issuer is obligated to return investor`s capital (face value)

Source: Afshar, T. A. (2013)

It has been mentioned that according to the Accounting and Auditing Organization for Islamic Financial Institutions, sukuk can be described as "certificates of equal value representing undivided shares in ownership of tangible assets, usufruct, and services, assets of particular projects or special investment activity". Conventional bonds differ significantly from sukuk in such a way that the return to bondholders or investors signify the right to claim indebtedness for borrowed money, whereas the return to sukuk holders signifies the right to avail payments from a trade transaction and claim ownership of business venture or a specific asset (Kuwait Finance House Research Ltd., 2015). Moreover**, sukuk is an innovative financial instrument** having a flexible structure based on Islamic financial contracts, unlike a bond which is based on the ancient structure of a loan imposed with interest. Sukuk is not an interest based financial instrument but one that promotes real economic activities and generates a return based on sharing or leasing acceptable assets (RAM Rating Services Berhad, 2008). Furthermore, sukuk differs considerably from conventional bonds in terms of risks related to investment. Sukuk is influenced by the Shariah compliance risk, which is associated with the structure that originates from the usage of Islamic finance contracts. Apart from this, sukuk faces similar risks associated with bonds such as credit risk, business risk, foreign exchange risk, liquidity risk, commodity risk and market risk which are considered an interest rate risk and equity price risk (Tariq, 2004). Both financial instruments are successful in generating capital for corporations and governments. However, these two instruments differ in nature, given that sukuk instruments are based on equity, whereas conventional bonds are debt-based instruments.

4. Recommendations for future development of Sukuk market

A number of steps can be taken to benefit European markets from the Islamic stock market:

a) Developing standardized guidelines for Sukuk issuance and trading, possibly through international Islamic financial institutions, could harmonize practices across jurisdictions and reduce complexity.
b) Increasing awareness and u
c) nderstanding of Sukuk and Islamic finance among investors and financial professionals could expand the market, potentially leading to improved liquidity.
d) Leveraging financial technology (FinTech) to facilitate Sukuk issuance, trading, and management could reduce costs and complexity. Blockchain technology, for example, could offer a transparent and efficient platform for managing the ownership and trading of Sukuk.
e) First, the two instruments are not quite identical. Although there are various fundamental differences between the sukuk and conventional bonds, both instruments tried to solve the same common financial problem of raising capital for needed entities. They offer quite different solutions to the same financial problem. Therefore, their differences are not originated from financial interests but it is from the religious backgrounds.
f) Second, sukuk instruments are a good mechanism to attract those investors who are away from participating in conventional system due to their religion. The Sukuk issues are available to all financial institutions and investors regardless of their religious background and believe. Which method of financing should be considered, is a matter of choice and whether the bond issuer and/or bondholder would like to benefit from the growing market share of the religiously conscientious financial market.
g) Third, the two financial instruments are exposed to some specific risks. Certain risks will affect only either conventional bonds or sukuk instruments. Some events which can bring a risk to conventional bonds will have a gain to sukuk instruments. One reason for this is their dissimilarities in nature. Therefore,
    - If there is an active management approach supported by deep research, it can help investors to avoid undue risk.
    - One of the most important risks for Sukuk is Shari'ah

compliance risk. Therefore, institutions and governments should have proper Shari'ah advisory board before issuing any forms of Sukuk.

- To overcome the liquidity problem, conventional financial institutions have various instruments to manage their liquidity. However, there are only very few options available to Islamic financial institutions. Therefore, development of appropriate secondary market is crucial for Sukuk instruments.

h) Fourth, based on the analysis Global Sukuk has shown relatively strong performance with lesser volatility compared to conventional bonds. Sukuk were effective in achieving high returns as compared to conventional bonds. They offer better risk adjusted returns than other conventional bonds.

i) Fifth, Sukuk also provides diversification benefits gained from their diversity by region and currency, attractive correlation with major asset classes, and their diversity sukuk structure. Therefore, an active portfolio management can change exposures to individual countries or currency that are performing poorly, overweight countries or particular market sectors that are performing well, and may help investors expand their income opportunities by allowing them to take advantage of the diversification attributes sukuk instruments have to offer.

j) Sixth, the use of Sukuk instruments along with conventional bonds will create a business opportunity for bond issuers. Therefore, creating suitable regulatory environment for sukuk instruments will make easy the issuance and trading of sukuk. Creating proper Islamic financial regulatory bodies (like IIFS) in every country will be difficult, but it is possible to establish a dedicated department within existing government structures that will do at least the basic tasks of Islamic financial regulatory bodies. It will be also important to create cooperation among different regulatory bodies to form institutional frame work for sukuk within the existing system.

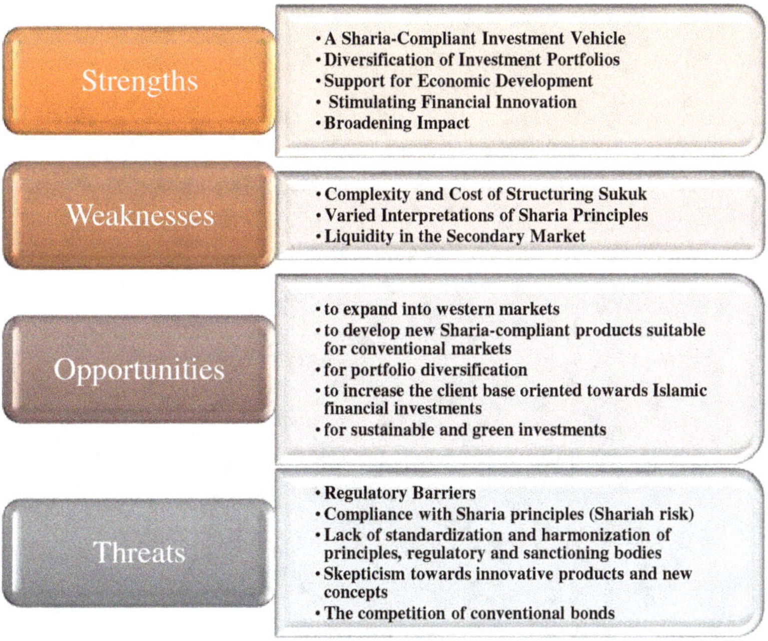

Fig. 1. Schematic representation of the variables of the study

Source: Authors' Compilation, 2024

5. Conclusion

Several factors could spur future growth in the sukuk market. These include the resolution of regulatory standards related to existing sukuk structures, the establishment of clearer guidelines on rights and remedies in default scenarios, greater harmonization of legal documents and the development of a standardized interpretation of Shariah law across diverse regions.

Although Islamic finance is growing rapidly, it remains still as a mystery especially in western world and it continues to be a poorly analyzed and paid attention by western communities. Since there is no Christian or Jewish finance or banking, almost all European countries are skeptical to Islamic finance and image of Islam in Europe is also feeding this skepticism although there is a high number of Muslims in European countries (Wilson, 2007).

Looking ahead, hovewer, remains the hope about the continued expansion and maturation of the global sukuk market, particularly as investor interest broadens beyond the core GCC and Asian countries. On the other hand, there is growing demand for green and sustainability sukuk from investors in Western markets such as the US and Europe, where ESG priorities are becoming increasingly widespread. Combined with regular demand from Shariah-compliant investors, this will broaden the investor base for green and sustainability sukuk.

The presented advantages of these relatively less risky and stable bonds compared to conventional ones and their diversifying effect, give us reason to conclude that they would be a good alternative/addition in the portfolios of European companies. The availability of Islamic benchmark indices from leading providers such as FT Russell, S&P, Dow Jones and JP Morgan is also a positive technical catalyst as these indices not only provide valuable information but also bolster the marketability and liquidity of sukuk instruments.

Additionally, the growing trend among issuers to leverage the sukuk market for significant financing needs in infrastructure and development projects across both developed and emerging markets should further propel market growth. In conclusion, there is a positive outlook on the prospects for the sukuk market.

References

1. AIMS education, IBF 513: Islamic Commercial & Investment Banking how do Islamic Bonds (Sukuk) differ from conventional bonds? https://aims.education/
2. Afshar, T. A. (2013). Compare and contrast sukuk (Islamic bonds) with conventional bonds, are they compatible? Journal of Global Business Management, 9(1), 44.
3. Antoniazzi, S. (2022). Islamic banks and the European Banking Union: an overview of critical issues and perspectives. European Journal of Islamic Finance, 9(1), 37-55.
4. Kusuma, K. A., & Silva, A. C. (2014). Sukuk markets: a proposed approach for development. World Bank Policy Research Working Paper, (7133).
5. The Resilience and Relevance of Global Sukuk, S&P Dow Jones Indices
6. Yesuf, A. J. (2016). A comparative analysis of Sukuk and conventional bonds. In Chaos, Complexity and Leadership 2014 (pp. 417-438). Springer International Publishing.
7. Sekreter, A., Einstein Visiting Fellow (2021) Islamic Finance: Its Theory, Products and a Brief View of Islamic Finance in Europe, https://www.dpublication.com/abstract-of-4th-icbmf/f7-117/
8. Islamic financial services industry stability report 2023
9. Sukuk reports, International Islamic Financial Market, https://www.iifm.net/sukuk-reports
10. The Resilience and Relevance of Global Sukuk, S&P Dow Jones Indices
11. https://www.sukuk.com/education/important-differences-sukuk-traditional-bonds-2207/#/?playlistId=0&videoId=0
12. Zulkhibri, M. (2015). A synthesis of theoretical and empirical research on sukuk. Borsa Istanbul Review, 15(4), 237-248.
13. Cakir, S., & Raei, F. (2007). Sukuk vs. Eurobonds: Is there a difference in Value-at-Risk?
14. Bhuiyan, R. A., Puspa, M., Saiti, B., & Ghani, G. M. (2020). Comparative analysis between global sukuk and bond indices: value-at-risk approach. Journal of Islamic Accounting and Business Research, 11(6), 1245-1256.
15. Mimouni, K., Smaoui, H., & Temimi, A. (2019). The impact of Sukuk on the performance of conventional and Islamic banks. Pacific-Basin Finance Journal, 54, 42-54.
16. Alim, W., & Ali, A. (2021). The Impact of Islamic Portfolio on Risk and

Return.
17. Pirgaip, B., Arslan-Ayaydin, Ö., & Karan, M. B. (2021). Do Sukuk provide diversification benefits to conventional bond investors? Evidence from Turkey. Global Finance Journal, 50, 100533.
18. Ledhem, M. A. (2022). The financial stability of Islamic banks and sukuk market development: Is the effect complementary or competitive? Borsa Istanbul Review, 22, S79-S91.
19. Mseddi, S. (2023). International issuance of Sukuk and companies' systematic risk: An empirical study. Borsa Istanbul Review, 23(3), 550-579.
20. Yesuf, A. J. (2016). A comparative analysis of Sukuk and conventional bonds. In Chaos, Complexity and Leadership 2014 (pp. 417-438). Springer International Publishing.
21. Green and sustainability Sukuk Report 2022: financing a sustainable future

Ecological sustainability indicators of banks

Sevgi Mertkan

Varna Free University "Chernorizets Hrabar", Department of Economics

sevgi.osman@vfu.bg, https://orcid.org/0000-0002-5108-5476

Abstract

The increased interest in measuring sustainable development stems from studies that highlight the difficulties in measuring non-financial information and offer guidelines for developing common evaluation frameworks. The reporting of environmental information is currently often underestimated and lags behind the information on financial, economic and social indicators due to the indirect impact of the banking sector on climate change. After the detailed analysis of the literature review, it is found that banks have an interest in measuring environmental sustainability to meet the expectations of stakeholders rather than financial gain. The paper focuses on the importance of mandatory regulations for environmental sustainability in the European context, and more specifically on those that have been introduced in recent years and for which there are many questions. The specific indicators proposed by the various working groups and initiatives for measuring environmental sustainability, their pros and cons and the corresponding future recommendations were also examined.

Keywords: sustainability, ecological indicators, EU banks, regulations

Introduction

The sustainable finance market is growing, supporting real economic change. Despite the challenging macroeconomic environment due to the COVID pandemic, European ESG bond and loan issuance has increased 58.8%, just in 2020, amounting to €398 billion.[9] While a lot has been achieved, the scale of what will be needed to meet the objectives of the Paris Agreement and the Sustainable Development Goals cannot be understated. According to a recent report by the Global Financial Markets Association and Boston Consulting Group, investment needs will amount to $100-$150 trillion over the next three decades, to fund the transition to a low-carbon economy. This translates to at least $3–$5 trillion of investment per year – an increase of five to eight times from current levels. The United Nations has estimated that for the complementary ambition of reaching the Sustainable Development Goals, the annual funding gap is $2.5 trillion per year. It is evident that the challenge is staggering – and the financial sector will be crucial in meeting it.[10]

Banks are subject to a plethora of sustainability requirements. Some of these are mandatory, imposed by regulatory authorities, whereas others are voluntary. The main problem in the implementation of voluntary codes is their focus primarily on the business side of sustainability. Or in other words, they can be accepted by any financial institution without completely changes the business and towards sustainable development.

Financial institutions are both impacted by and capable of contributing to climate risks in a number of ways. This is why many global regulators are prioritising appropriate climate risk disclosures as part of ensuring the broader transition of the financial services industry to more sustainable, and positively impactful, business models. To do this it is essential that financial institutions develop a framework that both identifies the required disclosure standards and their materiality triggers, alongside a comprehensive understanding of precisely which activities of the institution influence their entity level disclosures.

---

[9] https://www.afme.eu/Publications/Data-Research/Details/AFME-European-ESG-Finance-Quarterly-Data-Report-Q4-2020

[10] https://www.un.org/press/en/2019/dsgsm1340.doc.htm

1. Government environmental measures and initiatives

Climate change and environmental protection are among the most significant challenges of our time to achieve sustainable development. The global importance of sustainability is reflected in changing consumer expectations, as well as in national and international regulations (Appendix A).

The ESG disclosure requirements applicable to banks are contained in a number of different regulatory reform initiatives, which address multiple aspects of the transition to sustainable finance. Banks accordingly need to map the obligations that they (and their divisions – e.g. lending, corporate finance, wholesale markets, asset management and private banking) are subject to across the ESG framework in order to:

- Manage the risk of conflicting or inconsistent information being disclosed
- Ensure consistency and/or alignment of disclosures
- Identify the overlaps in the reporting pillars where common reporting metrics can be leveraged.

The identification of common or overlapping disclosures allows for the mapping of disclosure requirements by disclosure category or "pillar" (for example, governance, risk, monitoring, etc.), in order to facilitate a central framework based on common terminology where possible. Accordingly, the aim is to identify the overlaps and alignments between the different ESG regulatory reform initiatives from which it has been identified the following common reporting pillars:

- Governance
- Business Strategy
- Risk Management
- KPIs

A central component to unlocking change at the scale needed is for the regulatory framework to enable the procurement and disclosure of high-quality, comparable ESG data. The European Commission's Non-Binding Guidelines on Non-Financial Reporting (June 2017) contain 6 key principles for good non-financial reporting, namely that disclosed information should be:

1. Material;
2. Fair, balanced and understandable;
3. Comprehensive but concise;
4. Strategic and forward-looking;
5. Stakeholder oriented; and
6. Consistent and coherent.

The global financial sector has the potential to support the transition to a sustainable economy by linking financing needs to global sources of funding. Scaling up sustainable finance worldwide is a challenging task, for which coherent definitions of sustainability across jurisdictions and a higher degree of standartisation and transparency on data are necessary. Europe is one of the most advanced jurisdictions in this area, with both regulators and financial institutions demonstrating an unparalleled level of ambition on sustainability and showcasing credible commitments and consistent rules to reach the global goals. The EU needs to keep the level of its ambition, without losing sight of the global developments should it wish to become a beacon for international action, paving the way for other jurisdictions to follow suite.

European Union (EU) legislation requires large companies to disclose information on social and environmental challenges. Since 1973, the EU has adopted six Environmental Action Programs (EAPs). In 2001, the EU launched its Sustainable Development Strategy, which complements the Lisbon Strategy for Promoting Growth and Jobs with an Environmental Dimension. In line with these strands, the Europe 2020 strategy[11] aims to deliver "smart, inclusive and sustainable growth". The "Resource Efficient Flagship Initiative in Europe"[12] identifies the path to sustainable growth and supports the transition to a resource-efficient, low-carbon economy. The EU's ambition to maintain its leadership in environmental protection is reflected in its long-term vision for 2050. Europe to

[11] In 2013, the Council and the Parliament of Europe adopted the Seventh Environment Action Program for 2020, entitled "Living well within our planet". Based on the Program, it also emphasizes the need for better implementation of EU legislation in the field of environment, state-of-the-art science, investment and the integration of environmental aspects into other policies. The Europe 2020 strategy is the EU's agenda for growth and jobs for the current decade. It emphasizes smart, sustainable and inclusive growth as a way to address structural weaknesses in the European economy, increase its competitiveness and productivity, and maintain a sustainable social market economy (Europe 2020 strategy).

[12] Europe's resource efficiency strategy is part of the Europe 2020 strategy - the EU's growth strategy for a smart, inclusive and sustainable economy. It supports the transition to sustainable growth through resource efficiency and a low-carbon economy.

be the first climate-neutral continent. The Community is introducing new key climate and energy measures to stimulate the "contribution" of clean energy to zero net greenhouse gas emissions in Europe by 2050 (Gercheva, 2020).

1.1. Link between environmental reporting and financial performance of banks

ESG factors became the hallmark of sustainable finance, and their integration in the DNA of banks and financial institution encompasses strategy to investment and credit decisions to risk management all the way to external reporting. Between 2015 and 2020, only about 40% of studies focused on the banking sector, and most of them showed conflicting results. They support the current thinking that adopting a strategic focus on ESG issues can lead to financial outperformance (Kotsantonis, 2019).

Previous researches (up to 2019) globally in the field of sustainability reporting in the banking sector has been grouped into (Osman, 2020): 1) researches analyzing the development of disclosure of information about sustainability and its environmental aspect (**Appendix D**); 2) studies analyzing the impact (negative and positive) of sustainability information on banks' financial performance (**Appendixes E,F**); 3) studies analyzing the impact of sustainability reporting (CSR) initiatives/ frameworks on banks (**Appendix G**)

From the first group of studies to 2019 it has been clear that no special attention is paid to the environmental aspect of sustainability. It is considered alongside the social factor or as part of sustainability. Therefore, banks should further develop in the area of sustainability reporting by focusing on its environmental aspect as well. From the second group of previous studies it can be argued that there is a relationship between sustainability and financial indicators of banks, although indirect at first glance. The most frequently used financial indicators in the scientific literature are ROA and ROE, which can also be used in other studies, especially for European countries. Recently focusing on the importance of financial performance, Dhar (2021) aims to show how environmental accounting reporting practices influence financial performance. The research of Felita (2021) shows that sustainability reporting positively influence the banking company performance. The study for 220 Sub-Saharan African banks for the period 2007-2018 finds that sustainable banking initiatives improve the financial performance of these banks. Positive impacts of environmental reporting on banks' FP were identified in Vietnam banks by Chi (2022). The study for African banks (2022) concludes that increased sustainability reporting enhances bank performance in the long term. Among others, the study of Attah-Botchwey (2022) recommends that policymakers must develop a sustainability framework specific to the banking industry's needs.

However, the empirical results of Fijałkowska (2018) reveal that in case of banks in the Central and Eastern Europe (CEE) region being socially responsible is not reflected in the bottom line. The results of De Silva (2019) conclude that there's no significant difference in sustainability disclosures between listed banks and financial institutes and the number of disclosures has no significant influence on institutes' financial performance.

In EU, despite the presence of a common market, the analysis reveals that the orientation toward the SDGs is different between the Member States (Cosma,2020). The "scope" of contribution to SDGs from the European banks is narrow. It is higher in emerging countries such as Estonia, Croatia, and Poland with significant differences in comparing banks operating in the same country.

Study of Buallay (2021) which investigates the relationship between the level of sustainability reporting and banks and financial services sectors' operational, financial and market performance using data from 4458 observations in 60 different countries for 10 years (2008– 2017) pinpoint a negative relationship between ESG on one hand and operational performance (ROA), financial performance (ROE) and market performance (TQ) on the other hand. The results of Bătae (2021) show a positive relationship between emission reductions and financial performance but market investors do not value a bank's involvement in social responsibility initiatives and do not endorse the adoption of best governance practices that could reduce the riskiness of a bank's portfolio. Companies are using ESG disclosure to demonstrate that their corporate activities do not damage the environment and society, and the board of directors are engaging in an open dialogue with stakeholders (Tariq, 2021).

According to the study of Dogan (2021) whether the banks' sustainability score is high or low does not cause any change in their financial performance. Results of Koundouri (2022) showed that such a connection seems to exist at least for some specific parameters, while for others, such a claim cannot be supported.

In summary, it can be concluded that the reporting of environmental information by banks has a positive impact on financial performance in developing countries, while in the EU such a correlation is not found in most (almost all) of the studies reviewed.

In that case, the question is why do banks strive to adhere to certain requirements and report according to certain frameworks, regulations, etc. Next, the report examines the purspose of adoption and compliance of known sustainable development initiatives, frameworks and regulations and how stakeholders are responding to them.

1.2. Link between environmental reporting and stakeholder theory

Banks and financial institutions endeavored to reinvent their business, realign capital flows toward sustainable investments and integrate sustainability in risk management to restore trust, transparency and longevity. This leverages the growing attention of stakeholders to the new socially responsible practices and the application of proper governance. The attention on ESG issues in the bank decisionmaking processes (particularly for lending decisions) is driven by heightened pressure from shareholders and different stakeholders (Kotsantonis, 2019)

This is in accordance with the studies of stakeholder theory. Freeman described two definitions of Stakeholders: generally as a "group of people or individual, who have an im-pact, or is impacted by the organizations objectives' achievements", and specifically, as the "group of people or individual, who play an essential role in the survival and success ofthe company". Zeitlberger believed that the pressure of environmental concerns is leading to the environmental responsibility taken by businesses around the world. Thus, after 15 years of massive investment into US economy, the European banking system is shifting towards domestic markets primarily due to social responsibility aspects.

Following the stakeholder theory, some authors such as Post, Preston, and Sachs argue that companies should apply those social, environmental, and corporate governance aspects that are necessary, regardless of the costs incurred or the income they produce.

Many of the decisions of these interested parties could be based on the environmental aspects of the services offered. Therefore, there is an increasing pressure that forces banks to change their management systems to meet these growing demands. Meanwhile, although it is true that the banking industry cannot generate serious problems of environmental pollution, it is also true that great savings can be achieved in the billing of electricity, water, fuel, and the use of paper, among others, if corrective measures for environmental improvement are adopted (Jeucken, 2010). In this sense, it is necessary to highlight the works of Jo et al.(2015), Finger et al. (2018), and Laguir et al.(2018), who strictly analyzed the creation of value through the environmental activities carried out by banks. Specifically, Jo et al. examined whether corporate environmental responsibility plays a role in improving operational performance in the financial services sector of 29 countries. Their results show that the reduction of environmental costs requires at least one to two years before improving financial performance, being the fastest process in developed markets and slowest in the developing markets. Finger et al., who also distinguished between banks from developed and emerging countries, analyzed the effect of the adoption of the Equator Principles on banks' financial performance. Their results show that in developed (emerging) countries, the adoption of the Equator Principles is associated with an increase (decrease) in financing activity and the participation of interest income. They also indicate that these results show that the adoption of the Equator Principles is a strategic decision for banks in emerging countries and a form of greenwashing in developed countries. Meanwhile, Laguir et al. focused on the French banking sector, and document that the environmental and financial performance of banks is mutually reinforcing, suggesting that there is a complex bidirectional relationship between both magnitudes. The results of Quirós (2019) reveal that there is great pressure from financial stakeholders to adapt banks' management systems and incorporate environmental aspects.

Therefore, banks are more likely to adopt sustainable and environmental reporting requirements to meet stakeholder expectations and be ethical than financial benefits. But there is definitely a need for transparent disclosure of environmental sustainability, given the scale of environmental issues and the banking sector's potential for change.

1.3. Voluntary or mandatory environmental reporting?

Again from studies up to 2019 (Appendix G) it is clear that there are conflicting opinions about initiatives and voluntary codes of conduct in the field of sustainable development reporting, including and environmental sustainability as the trend is towards standardization of reported information. (Osman, 2020) The main problem with them is in their implementation itself, since they are voluntary. But even they help to integrate sustainability into the core business of banks and create certain pressures on those who do not accept such codes of conduct (Weber, 2015).

Facing sustainability issues and criticism by non-governmental organizations (NGOs), the financial sector has adopted various voluntary codes of conduct to manage sustainability risks, such as environmental and social risks in lending, project finance and investment. Thes codes of conduct do not enable an adequate climate change performance to be observed for three general reasons. First, codes of conduct are voluntary, and it is unknown what changes in processes, financial risks and socio-ecological impacts they are associated with.

Furthermore, differences in reporting quality are mainly caused by the size of members. It seems that environmental reporting is a function of the size of the reporting entity and depends on financial resources. Reporting about complex interactions needs expertise that is usually only available at bigger financial institutions.

Other voluntary codes of conduct[13] have guidelines about how financial institutions should address social and environmental issues, including climate change, but they do not have guidelines about how to report on them. Moreover, even if the codes of conduct do include guidance on disclosing compliance, empirical studies find that only positive aspects are reported.

For instance, Weber (2018) found that the disclosure behaviour of banks is relatively similar and follows an isomorphism trend. Without any external pressure and regulations, members of codes of conduct agree on certain practices that work for all members. This means that there is no incentive to become the most transparent reporting institution, but there is, rather, the trend to mimic the relatively low reporting standards. These weaknesses of the voluntary codes of conduct led to the argument that they are more for reputational purposes as opposed to substantive climate change management integration.

[13] such as the Impact Investing and Reporting Standards (IRIS), the GABV, the United Nations Environment Programme Finance Initiative (UNEPFI) and the United Nations Principles for Responsible Investment (UNPRI)

Empirically, banks and the financial sector have received limited attention in the environmental accounting literature. The financial sector has not been regulated with regards to its environmental impacts, and, therefore, research has been focused on determining what is reported in voluntary disclosures. According to Esposito et al. (2019), extant literature lacks studies that focus on the role of regulatory changes in determining actors' attitude and actions toward sustainable finance (Bengo, 2020). This concern is shared by other scholars such as for example Nicholls (2010) and Brest and Born (2013).

The poor quality in disclosure is also influenced by institutional and methodological accounting aspects. Institutionally, it appears that the voluntary nature of reporting incentivizes the use of voluntary reporting largely as a reputational tool.

Climate-related reporting in the financial industry is still in its infancy, not very transparent and fragmentary. The indirect relation between banking and climate change is one of the reasons why banks struggle with climate-related reporting. Missing standards and institutional pressure from regulators or by sectoral peers could be reasons for the current state of climate-related reporting

There is a need for stronger participation of financial regulators with regard to climate-related financial risks and risk reporting. It is evident that the financial sector's connection to climate change is twofold and includes both risks and opportunities. Finally, the role of financial regulators and central banks should be addressed (Folger, 2018).

Cerrone (2022) describes the change of banking regulation toward governance and environmental sustainability challenges. It shows that it has not been fully understood how these new types of environmental risks affect differently banking activity. As risks are global and systemic, it is necessary regulatory coordination.

Regulators are now aware that there are linkages between natural disasters and financial market instability. For this reason the European regulatory framework for sustainable finance has greatly developed. European leadership in sustainable finance has given rise to several regulations. In particular, banks will consider the CRR Pillar 3 and EU taxonomy disclosures, also because EBA is also aligning its position to this view.

The structural shift toward the green transition and the climate crisis is exposing banks to physical and transition risks, which they need to be ready to manage.

Banks will need to strengthen their risk management frameworks and reassess their business strategies. A recent ECB assessment shows that banks have made some progress in adapting their practices to manage these risks, but none are close to meeting the supervisory expectations (ECB, 2021).[14] For this reason, supervisors have already planned a number of specific measures for next years and beyond, including a thematic review of banks' environmental risk management practices and a stress test on climate-related risks. Many of the proposed regulatory changes actually stem from research conducted by the European Banking Authority and the ECB and are focused on issues identified in the use of internal models by European banks. Regulators and supervisors are running in giving guidelines and new frameworks to induce banks to pay more and more attention to these risks.

The whole supervisory process is reshaping by introducing the measurement of ESG risks and climate-related risks but the greatest problem is due to the huge relevance of these risks and the overlapping of rules, regulations, and guidelines that are still at an early stage but are renewing the banking activity whose main role to bring the economy to put in practice a real new green deal (Cerrone, 2022). Wift action by governments to steer the transition towards a greener economy could fruitfully interact with financial stability-focused prudential regulation to ensure that the financial sector contributes effectively to the economic transformation. Through a combination of carbon taxes and subsidies as well as guarantees, public authorities should seek to meet emissions reductions targets and, also, to facilitate an orderly transition to a more sustainable economy. At the same time, this policy mix would help to reduce the overall exposure of the financial system to both physical and transition risks. Combined with a well-designed climate-related microprudential framework, this could help the banking system to manage these risks and, thus, to contribute effectively to the economic transformation (Coelho, 2022).

Report of Financial Stability Board (2022), based on a review of current practices, provides recommendations to assist supervisory and regulatory authorities in developing their responses to monitor, manage and mitigate risks arising from climate change and to promote consistent approaches across sectors and jurisdictions. The recommendations encourage authorities to accelerate in the

---

[14] ECB. The State of Climate and Environmental Risk Management in the Banking Sector. 2021. Available from: https://www.bankingsupervision.europa.eu/ecb/pub/pdf [Accessed: 2021-12-10]

identification of their data needs for supervisory and regulatory objectives, identify relevant types of data and metrics that they may require from financial institutions and provides key policy considerations to assist authorities in their future work, where appropriate, towards expanding regular standardised regulatory reporting requirements.

Therefore, it has become important for banks to start to incorporate climate change into their risk management frameworks and strategic planning, by assessing their current loan portfolios and banking operations for any physical and transition impacts. Therefore, banks should start to improve the accuracy of information available on climate risks and developing internal systems to manage and monitor climate risk. In recent years, there is also an expectation from banks to adapt a responsible and sustainable banking model to make societies resilient to environmental shocks. This introduces another layer of challenge and complexity to banks' strategies and risk management (Feridun,2020).

As climate-related financial risks continue to receive increasing attention, regulatory authorities are be expected to set regulations with respect to banks' public disclosure, capital planning, and governance processes.

Next, in this article is showed the progress of regulations and supervisory approaches with respect to the management of financial risks from climate change. Although the development of regulations is still in progress across the world, this does not mean that banks can be complacent. For instance, the EBA explicitly expects banks to act on climate-related risks as soon as possible, rather than waiting for the related rules to be finalized. This paper reviews, from a technical point of view, the challenges that authorities would face in seeking to adjust the prudential framework to cope with climate-related financial risks, and discusses different policy options.

2. Proposed kpis from european regulators the cons of proposed KPIS

2.1. Understanding the recent relevant frameworks in EU

The regulatory framework for sustainable finance has developed at a rapid pace over the past few years in the EU. A mandatory disclosures regime for financial and non-financial companies was already developed back in 2018 and constituted the second block in the EU action plan on financing sustainable growth. In 2021 the European Commission's revised Strategy for Financing the Transition to a Sustainable Economy proposed a series of ambitious actions to strengthen sustainability disclosures standards in the EU, for example by improving science-based target-setting, as well as disclosure and monitoring of the financial sector's commitments.

Corporate transparency on sustainability issues is a prerequisite to enable financial market actors to properly assess the long-term value creation of companies and their management of sustainability risks. Environmenatal reporting is ineffective when longer-term risks are not fully transparent or are not reported in a uniform, comparable way and thus cannot be taken into account or used for comparability purposes. Corporate transparency on sustainability will not only inform market participants, but also help to steer companies in a more sustainable and long-term direction.

The sustainability initiatives considered by AFME (Association for Financial Markets in Europe)[15] include: The Non-Financial Reporting Directive (**"NFRD"**); the guidelines of the Task Force on Climate-related Financial Disclosures (**"TCFD"**); the Taxonomy Regulation (**"Taxonomy"**); the Sustainable Finance Disclosure Regulation (**"SFDR"**); the Low Carbon Benchmark Regulation (**"LCBMR"**); the ECB Guidelines on climate-related environmental risks and the European Commission guidelines on non-financial reporting and climate risk; and the changes proposed to Pillar 3 disclosures under the Capital Requirements

[15] AFME (2021) ESG Disclosure Landscape for Banks and Capital Markets in Europe, https://www.afme.eu/Portals/0/DispatchFeaturedImages/FINAL_%20AFME%20White%20Paper_%20ESG%20Disclosure-2.pdf

Directive ("**CRD**"), Capital Requirements Regulation ("**CRR**"), Investment Firms Directive ("**IFD**") and Investment Firms Regulation ("**IFR**").

It is nonetheless important to flag certain other initiatives relevant to the European ESG disclosures landscape.These are the:

- IFRS Foundation's Consultation on Sustainability Reporting that is believed to establish a foundation for the development of comparable and consistent global sustainability reporting standards;
- Global Reporting Initiative (GRI) Sustainability Reporting Standards which set out best practice for reporting publicly on a range of economic, environmental and social impacts (including positive and negative contributions to sustainable development); and
- Sustainability Accounting Standards Board (SASB) Standards which are industry-specific standards that set out a minimal set of sustainability topics and associated accounting metrics.

This article will focus on the ***NFRD, SFDR, Taxonomy Regulation and changes proposed to Pillar 3*** which are mandatory and challenging to them.

2.2. Non-financial Reporting Directive

To foster transparency and long-termism, the EU Commission has adopted the NFRD (2014/95/EU). It requires large public interest entities with over 500 employees (including banks and insurance companies) to disclose non-financial information. Further, they should include in public reports material issues and policies implemented in relation to:

- environmental protection
- social responsibility and treatment of employees
- respect for human rights
- anti-corruption and bribery
- diversity on company boards (in terms of age, gender, and educational and professional background).

Within this framework, in June 2019, the EU Commission published Non-Binding Guidelines on Reporting Climate-Related Information in order to foster accurate climate reporting. These guidelines integrate the recommendations of the

Financial Stability Board's Taskforce on Climate-related Financial Disclosures (TCFD) and take account of the EU Taxonomy on sustainable activities.The most commonly referenced framework in the case of climate disclosures is the TCFD framework. In recognition of this, regulators in the EU have referenced the TCFD framework throughout the development of legislation and supporting guidance on climate related disclosures. A number of financial institutions throughout the EU already make TCFD-aligned disclosures since they have global applicability and recognition and are a useful starting point when considering which standards a global financial group should adhere to. While not currently binding, the guidelines contain reporting requirements for companies under the scope of NFRD and include a separate annex for banks and insurance companies, whereby they are recommended to report (Supplement on reporting climate-related information, 2019)[16]

The EU Commission is also assessing responses to the public consultation on the need to revise NFRD provisions. It is expected that the scope of the Directive will be enlarged in respect to the reporting entities as well as its content, in particular on aspects related to climate change. Respondents called for consistency between the EU legislation, and more specifically, for an alignment of the NFRD with EU Taxonomy regulation requirements. It is also expected that common European Non-Financial Reporting Standards will be developed, as per the recent mandate given to the European Financial Reporting Advisory Group (EFRAG) to start preparatory technical work, though the final decision on the need for such standards is still pending.

---

[16] For example:

- Volume of financial assets funding sustainable economic activities that contribute substantially to climate Mitigation and/or Adaptation, according to the EU Taxonomy (in absolute figures and compared with total exposures, i.e. green asset ratios).
- Volume of collaterals related to assets or activities in climate change mitigating sectors. This information provides relevant information on, for example, retail mortgage portfolios.
- Total amount of fixed income portfolios invested in Green Bonds.

COMMUNICATION FROM THE COMMISSION (2019) Guidelines on non-financial reporting: Supplement on reporting climate-related information, https://ec.europa.eu/finance/docs/policy/190618climaterelatedinformationreportingguidelines_en.pdf

2.3. Sustainable Finance Disclosure Regulation (SFDR)

The new policy of the EU Sustainable Finance Disclosure Regulation (SFDR) 2019/2088 came into force on March 10th, 2021. The SFDR stresses social and environmental compliance disclosure and reporting obligations for financial services participants such as asset managers and investment funds, which are now required to define their strategic positioning with respect to sustainability.

Sustainability is becoming the main character of the financial industry in Europe, especially after the SFDR. Such regulation defines a new institutional context in which sustainability issues can become a game changer for the functioning of the financial sector. However, despite the various types of obligations and top-down indications for disclosing and reporting sustainability practices provided by this new policy, financial actors still lack a comprehensive framework on how to track and measure their social and environmental contributions within the perimeter of this novel institutional context. In particular, one of the main limitations is that it hardly reconnects to the practices of social impact measurement that are currently available for financial actors to assess their environmental, social and governance contributions (from now on ESG).

The SFDR was introduced by the European Commission alongside the Taxonomy Regulation and the Low Carbon Benchmarks Regulation as part of a package of legislative measures arising from the European Commission's Action Plan on Sustainable Finance. Is SFDR different to the taxonomy regulation?

Yes – but they interrelate. The Taxonomy Regulation is the EU Commission's principal mechanism to address "greenwashing" as it sets out criteria for determining if an activity is environmentally sustainable, including whether the activity contributes to, or does not significantly harm, one or more specified environmental objectives. The Taxonomy Regulation requires further disclosures which need to be made in addition to those set out in the SFDR. The taxonomy regulation is effective from 01 January 2022.[17]

The European Commission adopted on 6 April 2022 a technical standards to be used by financial market participants when disclosing sustainability-related information under the Sustainable Finance Disclosures Regulation (SFDR). Today's Delegated Regulation specifies the exact content, methodology and

---

[17] KPMG (2022) SFDR- Snapshot, https://assets.kpmg/content/dam/kpmg/ie/pdf/2021/03/ie-sustainable-finance-disclosure-reg-sfdr.pdf

presentation of the information to be disclosed, thereby improving its quality and comparability. Under these rules, financial market participants will provide detailed information about how they tackle and reduce any possible negative impacts that their investments may have on the environment and society in general. Moreover, these new requirements will help to assess the sustainability performances of financial products. Compliance with sustainability-related disclosures will contribute to strengthening investor protection and reduce greenwashing. This will ultimately support the financial system's transition towards a more sustainable economy. The requirements will now be subject to scrutiny by the European Parliament and the Council. They are scheduled to apply from 1 January 2023 (KPMG,2022).[18]

2.4. Corporate Sustainability Reporting Directive

On 21 April 2021 the European Commission adopted a proposal for a Corporate Sustainability Reporting Directive (CSRD) to amend the existing reporting requirements of the Non-Financial Reporting Directive (NFRD). The NFRD had proven insufficiently reliable and comparable, and investors were still finding it difficult to access data. Companies were also unsure which information to disclose and how to disclose it. The Commission, the European Parliament, and the Member States in the EU Council, are currently negotiating a final legislative text on the basis of the proposal.

While banks will be affected by several layers of regulation applicable to all corporates, some financial sector-specific guidelines and standards are also being developed at both international and EU level.

In addition to the specific elements included in sustainable finance regulations, European banks will be required to disclose as part of the Pillar 3 disclosure requirements of Capital Requirements Regulation 2 (CRR II). In October 2021 the European Commission published a proposal to amend the **CRR**, under which the requirement to disclose information on ESG risks would be applied to all institutions, (i.e. beyond large, listed banks to which the existing requirement applies from 2022). However, the proposal also suggests that the future standards be tailored in terms of periodicity and detail to the size and complexity of the

[18]https://ec.europa.eu/info/businesseconomyeuro/bankingandfinance/sustainablefinance/sustainability-related-disclosure-financial-services-sector_en

institutions, thus respecting the proportionality principle. The Basel Committee is currently exploring using Pillar 3 of the Basel framework to promote a common disclosure baseline for climate-related financial risks across internationally active banks. This work will consider the availability and reliability of sufficiently granular data for banks and their counterparties, and of defined risk metrics. The Pillar 3 work is part of the Committee's holistic approach to addressing the range of climate-related financial risks to the banking system, spanning regulatory, supervisory and disclosure-related elements. This Pillar 3 work will be performed in cooperation with the ISSB.[19]

Large financial institutions with publicly listed issuances will be required to disclose information on ESG risks, including physical and transition risks. The European Banking Authority (EBA) is drafting implementing technical standards (ITS), specifying uniform disclosure formats and associated instructions for Pillar 3 disclosure of prudential information on ESG risks. The ITS will initially focus on climate change related risks, aligned with the EU Taxonomy regulation, including both quantitative and qualitative information and metrics, as well as qualitative information on other environmental, social and governance risks. These uniform disclosure formats aim to collect sufficiently comprehensive and comparable information to allow users to assess institutions' risk profiles.

The ITS include: 1) tables for qualitative disclosures on ESG risks, 2) templates for quantitative disclosures on climate change transitional risk, 3) a template for quantitative disclosures on climate change physical risk, 4) templates for quantitative information and key performance indicators (KPIs) on climate change mitigating measures, including the green asset ratio (GAR). The ITS are applicable to large institutions with traded securities and provide for disclosure of an ambitious range of metrics, for instance in relation to financed emissions, alignment metrics and physical risk. Institutions must disclose this information from June 2022. The first disclosure will take place on an annual basis, and thereafter disclosures will take place twice-yearly. This means that the first disclosure will take place in 2023 for a disclosure reference date of end-December 2022.

The EBA's work on Pillar 3 ESG disclosures will leverage other disclosure initiatives, such as the EU Taxonomy and the Commission's non-binding

[19] ECB (2022) **Supervisory assessment of institutions' climate-related and environmental risks disclosures**, ECB report on banks' progress towards transparent disclosure of their climate-related and environmental risk profiles

guidelines on climate change reporting and TCFD recommendations. In the development of ITS, the EBA will follow a sequential approach. The ITS will initially focus on climate change related risks, aligned with the EU Taxonomy regulation, including both quantitative and qualitative information and metrics, as well as qualitative information on other environmental, social and governance risks (Raux,2021). In future, the ITS will require institutions to disclose relevant alignment metrics by sector and estimate the distance between their financing and the 2030 milestones defined by the IEA scenario.[20]

2.5. The EU Taxonomy Regulation

The EU Taxonomy Regulation is an ambitious effort by the European Union to classify what is "environmentally sustainable" and, among other things, require in-scope entities to report on the extent to which their activities and/or financial products qualify as "environmentally sustainable." The Taxonomy Regulation seeks to standardize the growing universe of sustainable finance products and environmental-related disclosures, aiming to promote investments in environmentally sustainable activities and reduce "greenwashing." There was no mandatory obligation for banks to report the Taxonomy alignment of their exposures to non-NFRD companies, although EBA is proposing mandatory KPIs on such exposures in their final draft ITS on Pillar 3 ESG disclosures, that are still subject of adoption process of the European Commission (UNEP FI, EBF, 2022). Tackling the "greenwashing" risk, the EU Taxonomy provides a clear, science-based classification of economic activities

On February 26, 2021, the three European Supervisory Authorities (the European Securities and Markets Authority (ESMA), the European Insurance and Occupational Pensions Authority (EIOPA) and the European Banking Authority (EBA), collectively the "ESAs") responded to the Commission's call for advice on implementing Article 8, and published sector-specific proposals for KPIs to be published by financial and non-financial undertaking (Sullivan & Cromwell LLP, 2021). Through the provisions of Article 8 of the EU Taxonomy Regulation—complemented by the Article 8 Disclosures Delegated Act—banks are expected to report the extent to which their balance sheets support economic activities that contribute substantially to achieving the EU net-zero target in 2050. Moreover,

[20] EBA/ITS/2022/01, final report implementing technical standards on prudential disclosures on ESG risks in accordance with Article 449a CRR.

the bulk of the data that banks need to meet these reporting obligations will be provided through the EU Taxonomy disclosures of their clients, as specified under the on Article 8 Disclosures Delegated Act.

In summary, the Non-Financial Reporting Directive (NFRD) requires large EU "public interest" corporates to publish data on the impact their activities have on ESG factors. The Taxonomy Regulation introduces a sustainability classification system through which these corporates must classify investments based on NFRD data (and other datasets). The SFDR (as supplemented by the Taxonomy) requires banks and investment firms to disclose:

- The environmental sustainability of an investment and the provenance of any ESG claims made;
- The risks investments present to ESG factors;
- The risks ESG factors present to investments.

Banks feed the analysis into the SFDR disclosures by way of Articles 5 and 6 of the Taxonomy Regulation, which is the principal mechanism through which the regulation makes its presence felt in the world: In many respects, the Taxonomy can be regarded as a very elaborate set of marketing rules. Articles 5 of the Taxonomy Regulation interfaces with Article 9 of the SFDR and adds taxonomy-specific pre-contractual and periodic reporting disclosures. Articles 6 of the Taxonomy Regulation does the same for Article 8 of the SFDR. Meanwhile, Article 7 of the Taxonomy Regulation applies the following boilerplate pre-contractual and periodic reporting disclosure to all otherwise in-scope financial products that are not "sustainable investments" and that do not promote their ESG characteristics (in accordance with Articles 8 and 9 of the SFDR, respectively): "The investments underlying this financial product do not take into account the EU criteria for environmentally sustainable economic activities."

The Taxonomy Regulation also introduces new disclosures for corporates subject to the NFRD. Specifically, Article 8 requires entities subject to the NFRD to disclose in their non-financial statements "information on how and to what extent their activities are associated with environmentally sustainable economic activities under Articles 3 and 9 of the Taxonomy Regulation" [21]

This lack of synchronisation and synergy between different EU legislative initiatives associated with sustainability disclosures creates a significant challenge

[21] https://insight.factset.com/eu-taxonomy-regulation

for companies and banks in both identifying and understanding the co-dependencies (or conflicts) between the differing disclosure expectations that will impact them institution wide.

"The synergy between different pieces of legislation (in particular the Non-Financial Reporting Directive (NFRD), the Taxonomy Regulation, and the Sustainable Finance Disclosure Regulation (SFDR) can contribute significantly to enhancing sustainability in the economy. However, neither the timings nor the concepts of these different pieces of legislation are fully synchronized or aligned with one another."(ESMA, 2020) [22]

[22] ESMA 22-106-2858 14 September 2020

3. Proposed KPIS from european regulators

As climate-related data will increasingly serve as important informational inputs into supervisory reporting and risk assessments of financial institutions exposures to climate-related risks, financial institutions need strong governance, processes and controls around risk data aggregation and reporting (internally and externally) of climate-related data. As stated in the report of the Task Force on Climate-Related Financial Disclosures (TCFD, 2020), each organization must clearly disclose how to measure climate risks and opportunities. Access to the indicators and objectives used by the banks allows investors and other stakeholders to better assess the organization's risk-adjusted return, ability to meet financial obligations, overall exposure to climate risks, and progress in management or adapting to these risks. Therefore, they should consider the use of climate indicators in their disclosures, such as GHG emissions from 1, 2 and 3, as well as other key performance indicators (**Annex C**). In general, the most appropriate choice of indicator is a function of the purpose of the analysis (Thomä and Dupré, 2018). The advantages and disadvantages of the different groups are presented in **Annex B.** This article also summarizes the proposed KPIs by the main European regulatory authorities (**Table 1).**

In its Guide on climate-related and environmental risks, **ECB Banking Supervision** published a set of expectations related to disclosures. The expectations cover not only the content of the disclosures, but also the policies, processes, methodologies, definitions and criteria associated with them. In terms of content, institutions are expected to disclose climate-related risks that are material, with due regard to the Commission's Supplement on reporting climate-related information. They are expected to disclose their GHG emissions for the whole group, including downstream emissions, as well as the KPIs and key risk indicators they use for strategy-setting and risk management.[23]

Data is the lifeblood of financial markets. Without a clear regulatory framework to ensure financial institutions and investors have access to comparable ESG data

---

[23] ECB (2022) **Supervisory assessment of institutions' climate-related and environmental risks disclosures**, ECB report on banks' progress towards transparent disclosure of their climate-related and environmental risk profiles

from borrowers and issuers, allocating capital to supporting real economy transition plans will remain challenging. For example, in it recent report EFRAG.

As climate-related data will increasingly serve as important informational inputs into supervisory reporting and risk assessments of financial institutions exposures to climate-related risks, financial institutions need strong governance, processes and controls around risk data aggregation and reporting (internally and externally) of climate-related data. As stated in the report of the Task Force on Climate-Related Financial Disclosures (TCFD, 2020), each organization must clearly disclose how to measure climate risks and opportunities. Access to the indicators and objectives used by the banks allows investors and other stakeholders to better assess the organization's risk-adjusted return, ability to meet financial obligations, overall exposure to climate risks, and progress in management or adapting to these risks. Therefore, they should consider the use of climate indicators in their disclosures, such as GHG emissions from 1, 2 and 3, as well as other key performance indicators (**Annex C**). In general, the most appropriate choice of indicator is a function of the purpose of the analysis (Thomä and Dupré, 2018). The advantages and disadvantages of the different groups are presented in **Annex B.** This article also summarizes the proposed KPIs by the main European regulatory authorities (**Table 1).**

In its Guide on climate-related and environmental risks, **ECB Banking Supervision** published a set of expectations related to disclosures. The expectations cover not only the content of the disclosures, but also the policies, processes, methodologies, definitions and criteria associated with them. In terms of content, institutions are expected to disclose climate-related risks that are material, with due regard to the Commission's Supplement on reporting climate-related information. They are expected to disclose their GHG emissions for the whole group, including downstream emissions, as well as the KPIs and key risk indicators they use for strategy-setting and risk management.[24] Data is the lifeblood of financial markets. Without a clear regulatory framework to ensure financial institutions and investors have access to comparable ESG data from borrowers and issuers, allocating capital to supporting real economy transition plans will remain challenging. For example, in its recent report[25] EFRAG

[24] ECB (2022) **Supervisory assessment of institutions' climate-related and environmental risks disclosures**, ECB report on banks' progress towards transparent disclosure of their climate-related and environmental risk profiles

[25]https://www.efrag.org/Assets/Download?assetUrl=%2Fsites%2Fwebpublishing%2FSiteAssets%2FEFRAG%2520PTFNFRS_A5_FINAL.pdf

inventorised circa 70 ESG KPIs that banks should be reporting on across three core legislative measures (NFRD, SFDR and Taxonomy).[26]

[26] AFME (2021) ESG Disclosure Landscape for Banks and Capital Markets in Europe, https://www.afme.eu/Portals/0/DispatchFeaturedImages/FINAL_%20AFME%20White%20Paper_%20ESG%20Disclosure-2.pdf

Table 1. Proposed KPIs by EU regulators

Regulation	Category	Proposed KPIs
TCFD	GHG emissions (Absolute Scope 1, Scope 2,and Scope 3; emissions intensity)	• Absolute Scope 1, Scope 2, and Scope 3 GHG emissions • Financed emissions by asset class • Weighted average carbon intensity • GHG emissions per MWh of electricity produced • Gross global Scope 1 GHG emissions covered under emissions-limiting regulations
	Transition risks (Amount and extent of assets or business activities vulnerable to transition risks)	• Volume of real estate collaterals highly exposed to transition risk • Concentration of credit exposure to carbon-related assets • Percent of revenue from coal mining • Percent of revenue passenger kilometers not covered by Carbon Offsetting and Reduction Scheme for International Aviation (CORSIA)
	Physical risks (Amount and extent of assets or business activities vulnerable to physical risks)	• Number and value of mortgage loans in 100-year flood zones • Wastewater treatment capacity located in 100-year flood zones

		• Revenue associated with water withdrawn and consumed in regions of high or extremely high baseline water stress • Proportion of property, infrastructure, or other alternative asset portfolios in an area subject to flooding, heat stress, or water stress • Proportion of real assets exposed to 1:100 or 1:200 climate-related hazards
	Climate-Related Opportunities (Proportion of revenue, assets, or other business activities aligned with climate-related opportunities)	• Net premiums written related to energy efficiency and low-carbon technology • Number of (1) zero-emissions vehicles (ZEV), (2) hybrid vehicles, and (3) plug-in hybrid vehicles sold • Revenues from products or services that support the transition to a low-carbon economy • Proportion of homes delivered certified to a thirdparty, multi-attribute green building standard
	Capital Deployment (Amount of capital expenditure, financing, or investment deployed toward climate-related risks and opportunities)	• Percentage of annual revenue invested in R&D of low-carbon products/services

		• Investment in climate adaptation measures
	Internal Carbon Prices (Price on each ton of GHG emissions used internally by an organization	• Internal carbon price • Shadow carbon price, by geography
NFDR	GHG emission	Direct GHG emissions; Indirect GHG emissions from the generation of acquired and consumed electricity, steam, heat, or cooling; All other indirect GHG emissions that occur in the value chain of the reporting company; GHG absolute emissions target
	Energy	Total energy consumption and/or production from renewable and non-renewable sources; Energy efficiency target; Renewable energy consumption and/or production target
	Physical risk	Assets committed in regions likely to become more exposed to acute or chronic physical climate risks; Percent turnover in the reporting year from products or services associated with activities that meet the criteria for substantially contributing to mitigation of or adaptation to climate change as set out in the Regulation on the establishment of a framework to facilitate sustainable investment; Percent capital expenditure (CapEx) and/or operational

		expenditures (OpEx) in the reporting year for assets or processes associated with activities that meet the criteria for substantially contributing to mitigation of or adaptation to climate change as set out in the Regulation on the establishment of a framework to facilitate sustainable investment.
	Green Finance	Climate-related Green Bond Ratio: Total amount of green bonds outstanding (at year-end) divided by (a 5-year rolling average of) total amount of bonds outstanding Climate-related Green Debt Ratio: Total amount of all green debt instruments outstanding (at year-end) divided by (a 5-year rolling average of) total amount of all debt outstanding.
	Bank specific KPIs	
	GHG emissions	In disclosing indicators related to GHG emissions, banks and insurance companies should focus on their Scope 3 GHG emissions, despite the well-known challenges. Scope 1 and Scope 2 GHG emissions (direct emissions and indirect emissions from the generation of purchased energy) are likely to be small when

		compared to other indirect emissions (Scope 3). Amount or percentage of carbon-related assets in each portfolio in MEUR or as a percentage of the current portfolio value; Weighted average carbon intensity of each portfolio, where data are available or can be reasonably estimated Volume of exposures by sector of counterparty
	Lending and investment activities	Credit risk exposures and volumes of collateral by geography/country of location of the activity or collateral, with an indication of those countries/geographies highly exposed to physical risk.; Volume of collaterals related to assets or activities in climate change mitigating sectors; Volume of financial assets funding sustainable economic activities contributing substantially to climate

		mitigation and/or adaptation (absolute figures and compared to total exposures). Total amount of the fixed income portfolios invested in green bond certified according to a potential EU Green Bond Standard if and when such a standard is approved, or according to any other broadly recognised green bond framework (at year-end) divided by (a 5-year rolling average of) total amount of holdings in fixed income portfolios.
	Insurance underwriting activities	Breakdown of underwriting exposure by lines of business to economic sectors (life / non-life / reinsurance); Percentage of products incorporating climate-related risks into the underwriting process for individual contracts (life / non-life / reinsurance); Number and value of climate-related underwriting products offered (Non-life / reinsurance); Maximum Expected Loss from natural catastrophes caused by climate change (life / nonlife / reinsurance); Total losses attributable to insurance payouts from (1) expected natural catastrophes and (2) non-expected natural catastrophes, by

		type of event and geographic segment (net and gross of reinsurance);
	Asset-management activities	Breakdown of assets under management by business sector across asset classes (equity / bonds / infrastructure / real estate / structured products / MBS / derivatives)
SFDR		**List of PAI indicators:** 1. GHG emissions (Scope 1, 2, 3 and total) 2. Carbon footprint 3. GHG intensity of investee companies 4. Exposure to companies active in the fossil fuel sector 5. Share of non-renewable energy consumption and production 6. Energy consumption intensity per high impact climate sector 7. Activities negatively affecting biodiversity sensitive areas 8. Emissions to water 9. Hazardous waste ratio 10. Violations of UN Global Compact principles and Organisation for Economic Cooperation and

		Development (OECD) Guidelines for Multinational Enterprises 11. Lack of processes and compliance mechanisms to monitor compliance with UN Global Compact principles and OECD Guidelines for Multinational Enterprises 12. Unadjusted gender pay gap 13. Board gender diversity 14. Exposure to controversial weapons (antipersonnel mines, cluster munitions, chemical weapons and biological weapons) 15. GHG Intensity 16. Investee countries subject to social violations 17. Deforestation 18. Supplier Codes of Conduct **PAIs applicable for real estate investments** 1. Exposure to fossil fuels through real estate assets 2. Exposure to energy-inefficient real estate assets 3. GHG emission generated by real estate assets

		4. Energy consumption intensity Waste Production (Share of real estate assets not equipped with facilities for waste sorting and not covered by a waste recovery or recycling contract)
Taxonomy Regulation with proposal of EBA		Taxonomy-eligible and Taxonomy non-eligible economic activities in their: • total turnover, • capital expenditures, and • operational expenditures. Green Asset Ratio: the proportion of assets linked to Taxonomy-compliant economic activities as a share of total eligible assets. Additional off-balance sheet KPIs: • Green ratio for financial guarantees (of corporates subject to NFRD disclosure obligations) • Green ratio for assets under management (AuM) • Green ratio for fees and commissions
EBA	Lending activities and equity holdings	***EBA advice to the Commission*** 1. Green asset ratio (GAR) 1.1. Green asset ratio for lending activities and equity holdings with non-financial

		corporates (NFC) subject to NFRD disclosure obligations • Green asset ratio: methodology for loans and advances – Non-financial corporates subject to NFRD disclosure obligations • Green asset ratio for debt securities – Non-financial corporates subject to NFRD disclosure obligations • Green asset ratio for equity holdings – Non-financial corporates subject to NFRD disclosure obligations • GAR on total financing to NFC subject to NFRD disclosure obligations (lending plus equity holdings) 1.2. Green asset ratio for lending activities, equity holdings of financial corporates 1.3. Green asset ratio for retail exposures • Residential real estate lending • Retail - Credits for consumption • Retail – other considerations 1.4. GAR for exposures to NFC not subject to NFRD disclosure obligations (including small- and medium-sized enterprises – SMEs)

		1.5. GAR for loans and advances financing public housing 1.6. Other on-balance-sheet exposures – Repossessed real estate collateral 1.7. TOTAL GAR
	Off-balance-sheet exposures	2. Green ratio for financial guarantees of corporates subject to NFRD disclosure obligations (FinGuar KPI) 3. Green ratio for assets under management (AuM KPI)
	Services other than lending – Fees and commissions (F&C KPI)	4. F&C KPI - Proportion of the institution's fee and commission income from corporates subject to NFRD disclosure obligations, derived from products or services other than lending associated with taxonomy-aligned economic activities that contribute to the environmental objective of climate change mitigation, climate change adaptation or other environmental objectives, compared to total fees and commissions from corporates subject to NFRD disclosure obligations from products or services other than lending.
	Other disclosures: trading portfolio	• Total trading during the disclosure period in taxonomy-aligned instruments, including absolute

		• purchases plus absolute sales of taxonomy-aligned securities. • Total trading during the disclosure period of eligible securities, including total absolute purchases plus total absolute sales of eligible securities. • Trading KPI: Ratio of absolute purchases plus absolute sales of taxonomy-aligned securities compared to total absolute purchases plus total absolute sales of eligible securities.

The **ECB**'s Guide on climate-related and environmental risks sets out expectations as regards disclosure of Scope 3 financed emissions. Scopes 1, 2 and 3 are categories that can be used by organisations as a conceptual tool to formalise their GHG emission accounting while avoiding double counting. The Greenhouse Gas Protocol is a common reference in that regard. Scope 3 covers all indirect GHG emissions that occur in the value chain of the reporting company, including both upstream and downstream emissions. In the case of a credit institution, this includes the emissions of counterparties linked to lending portfolios, or in other terms "financed emissions", and which are expected to represent the large majority of emissions. Although the ECB does not prescribe the use of a specific measurement and/or attribution methodology, institutions are encouraged to adopt a granular approach to measuring carbon emissions, while remaining consistent with the GHG Protocol, as set out in the European Commission's Supplement on reporting climate-related information. Furthermore, the EBA ITS on Pillar 3 disclosures on ESG risks will also require large banks with traded securities to disclose Scope 3 financed emissions for selected portfolios.

The transition to a low-carbon and more sustainable economy requires a structural transformation of economic activities, and in particular the production, transportation and consumption of energy. Financial institutions (FI) have endeavoured to assess and disclose the alignment of their financing activities in these key transition sectors against science-based pathways. As pointed out by the NGFS[27], such context-based metrics are critical to gaining a better understanding of how exposures will evolve over time and comparing these against trendlines. While the ECB encourages banks to disclose results from pilot exercises that have been conducted, it points out that institutions are required to comprehensively disclose their risk profile. [28] Because financial institution disclosure is linked to their products and services, financial institutions are users of information disclosed by third parties (clients, investee companies, etc.). Therefore, it is key to find coherence between a reporting of direct impacts of FIs' clients and investees companies and a reporting of indirect impacts of FIs.

The European Supervisory Authorities (ESAs) have developed draft Regulatory Technical Standards (RTS) with regard to the content, methodologies and

[27]Progress report on bridging data gaps", Network for Greening the Financial System, May 2021.

[28] ECB (2022) **Supervisory assessment of institutions' climate-related and environmental risks disclosures,** ECB report on banks' progress towards transparent disclosure of their climate-related and environmental risk profiles

presentation of sustainability-related disclosures under empowerments Articles 2a, 4(6) and (7), 8(3), 9(5), 10(2) and 11(4) of "**SFDR**". The 32 core indicators put forward by the ESAs will add up to the indicators laid down in the Taxonomy Regulation (sustainable proportion of turnover, capital expenditure and operating expenditure) and to the KPIs that will come out of the review of the NFRD.[29]

Large companies required to provide a non-financial statement under the Non-Financial Reporting Directive (**NFRD**), covering financial (including banks) and non-financial corporations (Article 8 of the EU Taxonomy Regulation).

- ▪ The proportion of turnover aligned with the EU Taxonomy
- ▪ Capital Expenditures (CapEx) and Operational Expenditures (OpEx) aligned with the EU Taxonomy
- ▪ Other KPIs for financial institutions, including specific KPIs for credit institutions(banks)—defined in the Article 8 Disclosures Delegated Act published on 6 July 2021.

In its recent report, EFRAG highlighted that KPI mentioned in different guidelines, framework and standards are numerous and are not granular enough to provide key information to FIs:

- Climate-related KPIs are the most mature ones in terms of definitions, scopes and methodologies. However, when it comes to social, governance or other environmental topics, KPIs are few, with sometimes unclear definitions and methodologies.
- But even on climate-related issues, the definitions and calculation methodologies are not yet mature: many climate indicators coexist, with different calculation methodologies. In addition, the lack of transparency, frequent changes in methodologies and their complexity are a challenging issue for FIs.
- ESG KPIs used by the three main EU regulations shows that there is no convergence

In conclusion, data methodologies are not standardised and not transparent, information is not frequently audited, hence not comparable: nevertheless, high quality, comparable and verifiable disclosure is a prerequisite to enable FIs to

[29]https://www.eba.europa.eu/sites/default/documents/files/document_library/Publications/Draft%20Technical%20Standards/2021/962778/JC%202021%2003%20%20Joint%20ESAs%20Final%20Report%20on%20RTS%20under%20SFDR.pdf

correctly assess the risks and opportunities in their investment decision-making process and to respond correctly to current and upcoming EU regulations.[30]

The three key performance indicators for non-financial undertakings laid down in Article 8(2) of the **Taxonomy Regulation** (turnover, capital expenditure and operating expenditure) were considered by the European Banking Authority (EBA) irrelevant for assessing the environmental sustainability of financial activities (including lending, investment and insurance) and, therefore, not appropriate to demonstrate to what extent the economic activities of financial undertakings are taxonomy-aligned (EBA in its March 2021 response to the European Commission's call for advice from September 2020).

EBA instead suggested using the green asset ratio (GAR), which measures the share of a credit institution's taxonomy-aligned balance sheet exposures versus its total eligible exposures.

The comprehensive list of KPIs for banks has been specified also in Annex V of the Article 8 Disclosures Delegated Act.[31] For banks, the benefits of having their clients' Article 8 disclosures are two-fold: 1) it helps them understand their client's degree of EU Taxonomy alignment; and 2) it helps them fulfil their obligations under Article 8.

Given that Article 8 of the Taxonomy Regulation does not specify any KPIs to be used by financial undertakings (that is credit institutions, asset managers, investment firms and insurance and reinsurance undertakings). The key performance indicators for financial undertakings are specified by delegated act - Commission Delegated Regulation (EU) 2021/2178 of 6 July 2021 supplementing Regulation (EU) 2020/852 of the European Parliament and of the Council by specifying the content and presentation of information to be disclosed by undertakings subject to Articles 19a or 29a of Directive 2013/34/EU

[30]https://www.efrag.org/Assets/Download?assetUrl=%2Fsites%2Fwebpublishing%2FSiteAssets%2FEFRAG%2520PTF-NFRS_A5_FINAL.pdf&AspxAutoDetectCookieSupport=1

[31] It is important to note, as per Point 1.1.1 of Annex V of the Article 8 Disclosures Delegated Act: "Credit institutions shall disclose relevant KPIs on the basis of the scope of their prudential consolidation determined in accordance with Regulation (EU) No 575/2013, Title II, Chapter 2, Section 2." The regulation also lists other KPIs for banks, but the GAR (main KPI) is the focus for this section of the paper. The disclo- sure templates for banks are available in Annex VI of Article 8 Disclosures Delegated Act here.

concerning environmentally sustainable economic activities, and specifying the methodology to comply with that disclosure obligation

The Commission Delegated Regulation provides therefore specific key performance indicators and calculation methodologies for financial undertakings. Under this Regulation of 6 July 2021 the main KPIs for financial undertakings relate to the proportion of environmentally sustainable economic activities in their financial activities, such as lending, investment and insurance (see for example: Taxonomy KPIs - investment firms' disclosures).

According to Article 4 of the Delegated Act of 6 July 2021 credit institutions are required to disclose the information as specified in respective Annexes V and XI. Specifically, as regards credit institutions the Delegated Act of 6 July 2021 defines three KPIs:

- a main KPI for on-balance-sheet assets related to financing activities,
- KPIs for off-balance-sheet assets and
- a KPI for commissions and fees related to other activities than financing.

The Recital 5 of the Delegated Act of 6 July 2021 designates the GAR (showing the proportion of exposures related to taxonomy-aligned activities compared to the total assets of those credit institutions) as the main key performance indicator for credit institutions that are subject to the disclosure obligations laid down in Articles 19a and 29a of Directive 2013/34/EU. The GAR should relate to the credit institutions' main lending and investment business, including loans, advances and debt securities, and to their equity holdings to reflect the extent to which those institutions finance taxonomy-aligned activities.

In addition to disclosures concerning their banking book, credit institutions should also disclose separately the overall composition of their total assets, including their trading book, and any trends and limits in terms of climate and environmental risks. Financial undertakings are required to provide for a breakdown in the numerator where applicable (See Article 7 of the Delegated Act of 6 July 2021)

All undertakings will have to start disclosing how their business activities align with:

- the climate objectives (adaptation and mitigation) under the EU Taxonomy Regulation in the course of 2022 (covering financial year 2021) and

- all six environmental objectives in the course of 2023 (covering financial year 2022).

"In view of the entry into force and application of Climate Delegated Act by the end of 2021 and material difficulties for assessing compliance of economic activities in 2022 with technical screening criteria laid down in that Delegated Regulation for the previous reporting year, the application of this Regulation in 2022 should be limited to certain elements and qualitative reporting, with the remaining provisions starting to apply from 1 January 2023 for non-financial undertakings and from 1 January 2024 for financial undertakings. Moreover, the key performance indicators of credit institutions related to their trading book and commission and fees for other commercial services and activities than the provision of financing should apply from 1 January 2026" (Recital 12 of Regulation of 6 July 2021)[32]

After revising the main KPIs proposed by the most important guidelines and regulation (Table 1) the main KPI for banks remains the Green Asset Ratio (GAR)—which shows the proportion of exposures related to Taxonomy-aligned activities compared with the total covered assets of those banks. The **EBA** also proposed requiring complementary, qualitative information disclosures, including, for example: contextual information to aid the understanding of quantitative indicators; details and justifications of variations in institutions' levels of Taxonomy-alignment; and a description of the use of the Taxonomy in an institution's business strategy (Sullivan & Cromwell LLP , 2021).

The EBA's KPI proposals include:

- Green Asset Ratio: the proportion of assets linked to Taxonomy-compliant economic activities as a share of total eligible assets.
- Additional off-balance sheet KPIs:
- Green ratio for financial guarantees (of corporates subject to NFRD disclosure obligations)
- Green ratio for assets under management (AuM)
- Green ratio for fees and commissions

According to the EBA advice to the Commission – Relevant KPIs for credit institutions (EBA Report, 2021) the main KPI showing the overall alignment of

[32]https://www.emissionseuets.com/taxonomy/1923taxonomy/2185taxonomykeyperformance-indicators-kpis

credit institutions' balance sheets with the Taxonomy should be the green asset ratio (GAR), which relates to their lending business, including loans and advances and debt securities, and to their equity holdings. Credit institutions should provide information on the green asset ratio that shows the proportion of taxonomy-aligned exposures (green assets) compared to total eligible exposures.

Credit institutions should disclose their green asset ratio (GAR) to show the extent to which the financing activities in their banking book (including loans and advances, debt securities and equity instruments in the banking book) are associated with economic activities aligned with the EU Taxonomy and are therefore Paris Agreement- and SDG-aligned (EBA, 2021):

- The GAR should cover all exposures in the banking book to financial and non-financial corporates (NFC) including SMEs, households (residential real estate, house renovation loans and motor vehicle loans only) and local governments/municipalities (house financing), including loans and advances, debt securities, equity instruments and repossessed real estate collaterals.
- Exposures to general governments other than municipalities and to central banks should not be considered at this stage in either the numerator or the denominator, due to the lack of an applicable taxonomy or of standard disclosure obligations for these counterparties. The Commission should consider the eligibility of sovereign bonds and/or central bank exposures for the KPI when reliable disclosures or a methodology for deriving the extent of their taxonomy alignment are available.
- Credit institutions with subsidiaries outside the EU: the EBA acknowledges the additional challenges of collecting relevant information for exposures to non-EU counterparties, as the EU Taxonomy and the NFRD apply only at EU level, and a proportionate approach is being proposed. The EBA recommends that these institutions should disclose their GAR at EU level, for exposures to EU counterparties. In addition, given the relevance of their non-EU exposures, they should identify lending and equity exposures in the banking book to non-EU counterparties that pertain to sectors (NACE sectors 4 levels of detail) covered by the taxonomy. Then, proxies should be used to determine, on a best effort basis, estimates and ranges on the part of those exposures aligned with the Taxonomy, and this information should be disclosed separately from the EU GAR with appropriate caveats.

Information on the lending and equity portfolio should include point-in-time information on the stock of loans, to show the level of alignment of the institutions' activities with the Taxonomy; and on flows of new lending to show how they are transitioning towards sustainable economic activities, how they are adapting to new climate change circumstances, and how they are helping their counterparties in the transition and adaptation path.

For their commercial activities, including business and services to corporates that generate fee and commission income, other than lending, equity holdings or asset management, credit institutions should disclose information on the proportion of the institution's fee and commission income derived from those products or services that are associated with economic activities that qualify as environmentally sustainable.

For their off-balance-sheet exposures, credit institutions should disclose a ratio based on the level of alignment with the Taxonomy of the underlying assets of the relevant off-balance-sheet exposures, including financial guarantees and assets under management.

The EBA recommends that assets in the held for trading portfolio are excluded from the computation of the GAR, given their volatile and variable nature and that the purpose of this portfolio is different from that of the banking book. The EBA advises that, alternatively, credit institutions should disclose the following information, taking into account a proportionate approach. In addition, credit institutions should provide separate disclosures for their trading portfolio in terms of overall composition, trends, targets and limits. More granular disclosures are proposed for those institutions with a higher level of trading activity, and whose trading portfolio is above a certain threshold.

Credit institutions should disclose the information required in Article 8 of the Taxonomy Regulation using the KPIs specified in the Anex I- KPIs for credit institutions (Article 8 Taxonomy) and in the rest of this document and not the KPIs proposed under Article 8 of the Taxonomy Regulation for non-financial corporates in terms of turnover, capex and Opex, for the reasons explained in the paragraphs in this section.

In its recent report, EFRAG highlighted that KPI mentioned in different guidelines, framework and standards are numerous and are not granular enough to provide key information to FIs:

- Climate-related KPIs are the most mature ones in terms of definitions, scopes and methodologies. However, when it comes to social, governance or other environmental topics, KPIs are few, with sometimes unclear definitions and methodologies.
- But even on climate-related issues, the definitions and calculation methodologies are not yet mature: many climate indicators coexist, with different calculation methodologies. In addition, the lack of transparency, frequent changes in methodologies and their complexity are a challenging issue for FIs.
- ESG KPIs used by the three main EU regulations shows that there is no convergence

In conclusion, data methodologies are not standardised and not transparent, information is not frequently audited, hence not comparable: nevertheless, high quality, comparable and verifiable disclosure is a prerequisite to enable FIs to correctly assess the risks and opportunities in their investment decision-making process and to respond correctly to current and upcoming EU regulations.[33] *Whether or not, "investor needs cannot be satisfied only by consistent and comparable metrics." (Adams, 2022) who critically examine the call for 'harmonisation' of sustainability reporting frameworks and standards that occurred alongside an increase in ESG investing during the COVID-19 pandemic and identify three myths that have been promulgated in calls for 'harmonisation' that seek to simplify sustainability reporting and ESG analysis*

[33]https://www.efrag.org/Assets/Download?assetUrl=%2Fsites%2Fwebpublishing%2FSiteAssets%2FEFRAG%2520PTF-NFRS_A5_FINAL.pdf&AspxAutoDetectCookieSupport=1

4. The cons of proposed KPIS

4.1. GHG scope 3 emissions

The Task Force's recommendations on climate-related financial disclosures are structured around four thematic areas that represent core elements of how companies operate: governance, strategy, risk management, and metrics and targets. But the Task Force survey on implementation found the Metrics and Targets recommendation "somewhat difficult" or "very difficult" to implement.

Since 2017, Scope 3 GHG emissions, including the Scope 3 investment category, have received increasing attention in both the public and private sectors. Scope 3 GHG emissions are becoming an essential component of climate-related risk analysis in commercial and financial markets. Scope 3 GHG emissions are an important component of overall GHG emissions for several reasons.

Despite increased demand and reporting, the disclosure of Scope 3 GHG emissions faces a number of challenges like methodology, data, boundaries and organizational challenges. Category 15 of the GHG Protocol's Scope 3 Standard relates to investments, which the GHG Protocol notes are a form of Scope 3 GHG emissions "applicable to investors and companies that provide financial services. Investments are categorized as a downstream Scope 3 category because the provision of capital or financing is a service provided by the reporting company." For financial organizations, Scope 3 GHG emissions, especially category 15, are by far the largest component of their total GHG emissions. However, assessing and pricing exposure to climate-related risks within the financial system depends on the effectiveness of the climate-related disclosures of the companies that are financed by banks, asset owners, and asset managers and underwritten by insurance companies. If the disclosures made by organizations with significant direct and indirect GHG emissions do not include sufficient information on Scope 1, Scope 2, and Scope 3 GHG emissions, then the banking and insurance industries' understanding of the concentration of carbon-related assets on their balance sheets may be incomplete and asset owner and asset managers will have limited visibility into risk associated with carbon-intensive issuers. Since the TCFD published its final report in June 2017, a number of initiatives have emerged to improve the disclosure and reporting of financial organizations' GHG emissions. Two of these developments are of particular relevance for the Task

Force's guidance on this topic: (1) the Partnership for Carbon Accounting Financials (PCAF) and (2) the Climate Risk Officer (CRO) Forum methodology on carbon footprinting for the insurance industry.[34]

4.2. Turnover, capital expenses (CapEx) and operational expenses (OpEx)

EBA advice to the Commission on key performance indicators for credit institutions' disclosures KPIs in terms of turnover, capital expenses (CapEx) and operational expenses (OpEx) proposed by Article 8 of the Taxonomy Regulation for non-financial undertakings are not considered appropriate for credit institutions:

- a KPI in terms of turnover is not relevant given the variety of counterparties and economic activities financed by banks, the different sources of income they rely upon and the structure of their profit and loss accounts;
- on the other hand, the main sources of credit institutions' greenhouse gas emissions (GHG) are scope 3 emissions coming from their counterparties, and not scope 1 direct GHG emissions or scope 2 GHG emissions linked to their own consumption of purchased electricity, heat, or steam. Consequently, indicators defined in terms of OpEx or CapEx devoted to investments or maintenance of activities aimed at reducing scope 1 and 2 GHG emissions are not relevant for credit institutions either.

4.3. GAR

A number of challenges are identified by **UNEP FI and EBF (2021)** in case studies used to test the application of the EU Taxonomy to more than 40 transactions and clients (Raux, 2021). While some are generic, others relate to specific banking products. They overlap with some of the above mentioned and could be systematized as follows:

- **Unspecified uses of proceeds** - Loan proceeds means all amounts advanced as part of a loan, whether advanced directly to the borrower or otherwise. Companies often have general credit facilities in the form of

[34] https://assets.bbhub.io/company/sites/60/2021/07/2021-Metrics_Targets_Guidance-1.pdf

general purpose loans or revolving credit facilities (RCFs). These are used by companies to cover diverse corporate expenditures and are not solely related to specific capital investments. This is therefore likely to be the most significant challenge faced by banks in the application of the EU Taxonomy to banking products.

- **Data-related challenges** - It is important to note that, at the time of writing this report, companies were not legally required to disclose information that is specifically aligned to EU Taxonomy requirements. Data available to banks at the time the case studies were conducted was typically data made available by companies on a voluntary basis, either publicly or directly, and data made available by larger companies that fell under the scope of the NFRD. Besides data availability, other challenges include: Quality, comparability, standardisation, relevance, verification, and time to achieve acquisition.[35]
- **Operational challenges** - Together with the challenge of finding relevant data, banks will also face operationa challenges. The operational reality is often more complex than that captured by the EU Taxonomy. Linking the EU Taxonomy classification system to economic activities brings operational challenges for banks. For example, borrowers' activities may be connected to several EU Taxonomy economic activities. In such cases, banks need to perform and store several assessments for a single client, one for each of the economic activities in which they are involved.
- **Documentation, monitoring and time needed to complete transactions** - Another operational issue is the management of increased documentation requirements. Loan documentation records use of proceeds and any information deemed essential to the contract between the bank and the client, and will therefore become an important part of the process in the application of the EU Taxonomy. At this point, standard documentation is insufficient to assess and monitor alignment of client business
- **Testing the application of the EU Taxonomy to core banking products** - Despite the availability of documentation, tracking use of proceeds remains difficult, particularly in complex group structures. Loans may fund several business lines within the group entity that acts as the borrower, or

[35] Specific categories of data-related challenges are the following: Data and information pertaining to SMEs; Data and information pertaining to non-EU based assets; Data and information availability for DNSH, Minimum Social Safeguards and Segmentation by turnover or revenues are limited and patchy

funds may be used for multiple purposes, both equally difficult to track. Increased documentation requirements will impact the time needed to complete transactions, whatever their degree of complexity. In some cases, the EU Taxonomy assessment will take longer to complete – due to the time required to collect relevant information - than the time available to complete a transaction. This could become a competitive disadvantage for banks, especially when clients have the option to use non-EU based banks.

- **The burden on processes must be absorbed by banks' IT infrastructure** - Anticipating the implementation of the EU Taxonomy, most banks cite the challenge of adapting internal information processes and the cost of developing IT tools and support. Adapting new data flows into existing internal processes is very time consuming, and question the extent to which it will be possible to move away from manual handling. This in turn raises the question of associated costs, to both banks and customers. Some banks envisage these costs to be significant enough to affect product viability.
- **Increased complexity and risk of inconsistencies** - Overall, banks will have to cope with more extensive, demanding and complex assessment processes. The EU Taxonomy goes well beyond existing internal taxonomies and Environmental and Social Risk Management (ESRM)/ESG frameworks, particularly when it comes to the depth of criteria and systematic use of thresholds and metrics.
- **Traditional support tools and services are not well suited to support the application of the EU Taxonomy** - The extent to which external validation of compliance with the EU Taxonomy is a viable option remains unclear, as the reliability of data presented by clients cannot be guaranteed. A company's own assessment of its EU Taxonomy alignment would probably benefit from third party verification, though this may precipitate a further challenge, with banks facing differences in data quality that impact the comparability of portfolios. How these issues will eventually be resolved can significantly impact the level of consistency in the application of the EU Taxonomy to core banking products.
- **Segmentation and classification by economic activities may lead to inconsistencies across the industry** - Segmenting alignment with the EU Taxonomy makes it difficult for banks to match the EU Taxonomy classification of economy activities with turnover or revenue figures provided by companies, as these figures are often presented in aggregate. Conversely, where more granular data is available, the segmentation of turnover, revenues, capex and opex figures reflects the legal structure of a

group as opposed to its classification by economic activity as per the EU Taxonomy. Where borrowers do provide more detailed data, it is important that the format is standardised and consistent across different sectors to facilitate comparability, and avoid inconsistencies in how banks' portfolios reflect their alignment with the EU Taxonomy.

- **Uncertainties -** Client preferences (for example for Green Bonds, Green Loans and Sustainability) may not be fully addressed through the EU Taxonomy. Banks see the Green Bond and Green Loan Principles as essential references, because they address international markets in which most of them operate, even when based in the EU. The lack of clarity over how these frameworks will conform to the EU Taxonomy creates some uncertainty as to how banks will be able to support and meet their clients' needs.

The implementation of the EU Taxonomy is likely to be driven by a reporting requirement such as the "green assets ratio" through NFRD and/or Article 8 of the EU Taxonomy Regulation. The implementation of the EU Taxonomy may need to be rolled out across the portion of the balance sheet corresponding to the final requirements. Corporate clients that integrate sustainability into their business strategies may drive application of the EU Taxonomy, because they increasingly demand sustainable financial products that provide preferential terms and/or reputational benefits. If cases such as these become more common, the implementation of the EU Taxonomy would likely be more focused on identifying top performers across a selection of industries, and less on addressing compliance across the eligible client base.

The biggest challenge is data availability according **EBA (2021).** In particular, a lack of clarification and governance of data at the EU level as well as a lack of support for institutions on this matter was stated, creating concerns regarding data comparability, scalability and as to how far this is sustainable. The concern exists in particular for SMEs, the retail portfolio and non-EU exposures, counterparties not covered by the NFRD. Not only was the availability of data stressed, but also counterparties' own ability to assess and disclose information in the first place.

Even in the case of larger corporate customers, one bank stated that third party assessments vary widely and that they would therefore need to approach customers on a bilateral basis. In this context, it was also mentioned that bilateral exchange between banks and counterparties was not efficient at the bank level, the counterparty level or at the level of the system as a whole, as multiple banks would be contacting the same counterparty. In the context of data availability, several respondents raised the need for a data hub organised centrally at EU level.

The timing issue arising from disclosures by counterparties being applicable only from January 2022 and the applicability to financial institutions of disclosing KPIs for the same date, creating further data challenges, and called for a phased-in approach.

Data concerns were followed by challenges relating to IT capacity and capabilities in terms of the average challenge score assigned. An example given for the challenges related to IT capacity was the fact that current systems tend to classify counterparties only by one economic activity, which will need to be changed in order to incorporate and apply the EU Taxonomy. Extensive developments and extensions to IT systems would be necessary, also including the collection and storage of data.

There are identified other challenges like staff availability, training challenges, the lack of a clear methodology as well as regulatory uncertainty. The Taxonomy's complexity was stated, together with insufficient clarity on the taxonomy roadmap, resulting in a focus on the bank's own internal ESG agenda and hence to date no investment in the taxonomy application, in turn implying greater challenges to kick start the taxonomy application (EBA Report, 2021). Uncertainties with regard to regulation and timing were also stated to have so far not shifted the priorities sufficiently towards the Taxonomy and the related investments needed (IT, staff training, timing, etc).

The green asset ratio comes with other limitations, too (**S&P, 2022**). A bank can be making significant progress in helping polluting clients reduce their environmental impact without it conforming to the taxonomy.

Substantial sums of banking assets will not be included in the scope of the upcoming green asset ratio, revealing the metric's shortcomings in accurately comparing European lenders' environmental efforts. But the ratio may be of limited use to compare the greenness of banks' balance sheets across the board as large parts of assets are out of its scope, according to European banks' latest sustainability reports. For example, assets held for trading and exposures to governments and central banks are excluded from the GAR calculation altogether, while financing to small and medium-sized enterprises or non-EU corporate counterparties can never qualify as green.

European banks have also disclosed the share of assets in the scope of the green asset ratio that are "taxonomy-eligible" and, as such, can qualify to be included in the numerator of the GAR. An activity is considered taxonomy-eligible if it is described in the taxonomy regulation, such as renewable energy or real estate, and therefore has the potential to contribute to one of the EU's environmental objectives. Only in 2024 will EU banks have to assess whether these assets actually meet the performance criteria and can be labeled green and be used to calculate the GAR. At present, taxonomy-eligible assets are largely limited to banks' financing of residential real estate as well as to EU corporates subject to disclosure obligations under the Non-Financial Reporting Directive, or NFRD, a piece of EU disclosure regulation that applies to certain large companies.

Meanwhile, financing to SMEs, non-EU counterparties and sectors not covered by the EU taxonomy will be excluded from the numerator but not the denominator of the GAR. In essence, this means such assets will be assumed to be 0% sustainable in the GAR calculation. This puts banks with large exposures to those segments at a structural disadvantage when seeking to boost their GAR. Even if every single asset in a bank's banking book is environmentally sustainable, its green asset ratio could never exceed the eligibility ratio.

In its proposed framework, the EBA asks banks to release information on everything from exposure to carbon-intensive companies to climate change physical risk. It also proposes a Banking Book Taxonomy Alignment Ratio, or BTAR, which attempts to make up for one of the GAR's shortcomings by extending the numerator to include counterparties not covered by the NFRD. This complementary metric is intended to help give a more complete picture of banks' taxonomy alignment and incentivize lenders to provide green finance to SMEs, even if institutions still face significant data availability challenges and may have to rely on estimates and proxies when calculating the BTAR. The EBA furthermore intends to introduce a measure that can capture ESG risks in banks' trading book at a later stage. This makes it more complex to measure a green asset ratio and raises the risk that banks "window dress" their holdings the day the ratio is calculated.

An EU-wide pilot exercise on climate risk, published by the EBA in May last year, estimated an average GAR of just 7.9% for a sample of 29 EU banks, although it emphasized limitations such as data gaps and variation in approaches used.

According to SEB The EU Taxonomy is an excellent tool, but not broad enough in its current format to cover all relevant sectors and transition metrics. When looking at portfolio level, the EU Taxonomy provides good guidance to approximately 30% of the sector metrics the banks need.

Over time, the scope of the green asset ratio and availability of data will improve to some extent. European corporates are now required by the taxonomy regulation to disclose information on their own eligible activities, which a BNP Paribas spokesperson said will enhance the bank's disclosures from 2023. This year BNP Paribas used NACE codes, the European standard for classifying economic activity, to qualify taxonomy eligibility for corporate clients, which represents an estimate only.

Banks clearly see the opportunity for market practices to be aligned to increase comparability. Developing methodologies for the application of the EU Taxonomy to different products at industry level will be critical to avoid a lack of operational consistency.

However, aligning to the granularity and comprehensive nature of the EU Taxonomy will be a significant challenge from an operational point of view and will require significant efforts on the part of banks.

Pilar Gutierrez, head of unit reporting and transparency at the EBA, recognized that it will be more relevant to compare the green asset ratio of banks with similar business models, in particular those that have a predominantly traditional lending business. The GAR should be assessed together with the range of other disclosure requirements the EBA has introduced into the Pillar 3 framework, and not in isolation. Pillar 3 is part of the global Basel standard for bank prudential regulation that seeks to promote market discipline through regulatory disclosure requirements. (S&P, 2022).

Conclusion

The fact is that over the last decade, sustainability reporting has become increasingly important in the financial industry. There has been an increase in transparency, improvements in standards, reporting frameworks and regulations, and also increased stakeholder involvement in the decision-making process. The first question posed at the beginning was the main reasons why banks adhere to certain regulations and requirements and where to draw the line between voluntariness and obligation for the reporting of environmentally sustainable development.

After review of 70 researches in the field it could be concluded that:

- Banks banks strive for transparent environmental sustainability reporting to meet stakeholder expectations rather than financial benefits.
- Voluntary initiatives should not be voluntary and more regulation should be undertaken by national and regulatory bodies.

Then the aim was to analyze the recent efforts of regulatory authorities and their proposed methods and measures of environmental sustainability, as well as the problems that may arise in their implementation.

European Union (EU) legislation requires large companies to disclose information on social and environmental challenges since 1973. The EU's ambition to maintain its leadership in environmental protection is reflected in its long-term vision for 2050. The most recent regulations for the purpose are NFRD, SFDR, Taxonomy Regulation and changes proposed to Pillar 3 which are the main focus in the research. After their analysis and comparison it could be concluded that:

- The indicators proposed by individual regulations in recent years in the EU to measure environmental sustainability should be synchronized
- It should be carefully assessed whether the proposed environmental indicators are suitable for the relevant sector (banking in our case)

Finally, relevant recommendations for their better application in the future by European banks are considered. Over the last few years, various market and industrial initiatives have focused on the convergence of reporting standards covering climate issues, as well as on bringing and improving the comparability of climate indicators. The recently established working group on "Financial Statements Related to Nature" is expected to provide an evaluation framework by the end of 2022. The financial sector plays a leading role in the development of environmentally friendly financial solutions and investments. In a digital transformation, organizations cannot rely solely on financial and material resources to achieve their goals (Ovcharova, 2019). Environmental problems are undoubtedly a challenge, but they also open up new opportunities for development.

Environmental risk reports should be subject to appropriate internal management processes, such as those used for financial disclosures, and included in the list of key financial documents. Emphasis needs to be placed on quantitative indicators to take account of environmental risk, in particular the disclosure of indicators of the financial impact of risks related to climate change and environmental protection. Banks should provide the necessary data on climate change and the impact that the environment will have on activities such as pricing, credit risk and customer relationship management. Lack of data should not be an obstacle to action.

Regardless of the differences in the nuances of the implemented policies, the bank management should assess the growing importance of the ecological responsibility and the ways of adaptation to the changing environment. Incorporating environmental considerations into key banking activities can contribute to sustainable development.

Table 2. Appendix B. Advantages and disadvantages of environmental indicators

	Characteristic	Application	Advantages	Disadvantages
GHG accounting	Cross-sectoral assessment of greenhouse gas consumption by investors	• Linking the dots between portfolios and climate change • Screening of project financing • Real estate energy efficiency measures • Commitment to reducing corporate emissions in the short term • Building portfolios for issued shares ideally together with green / brown indicators • Public communication and reporting	• Wide awareness of the intensity of carbon emissions in individual sectors • Significance among corporate clients and experience • The standardization of corporate reporting in various sectors, which allows reporting at the portfolio level	• High uncertainty related to financial asset data • Incomplete coverage • Lack of an accounting standard • Data variability related to external factors
Green/ Brown metrics	Sectoral indicators that distinguish between activities and technologies such as solutions (green) and climate problems (brown)	• Negative / positive screening for project funding • Negative screening and environmental targets for corporate bonds (eg green bonds) • Building portfolios for issued shares together with carbon indicators • Investments in various technologies	• Quantitative indicator with high data transparency • Relevant indicator for corporate governance	• Applicable only for key sectors • Problems in distinguishing climate friendliness into categories • There is no standardized format for summarizing data from individual sectors

ESG scores	Indicators based on quantitative and qualitative measures of climate, including carbon and green / brown exposure.	• Commitment to corporate strategies of companies • Engaging on climate issues along with non-climate issues	• Summarized indicators covering a number of factors • Well-established frameworks	• Black box • Risk of greenwashing • Not directly related to a specific strategy

Table 3. Appendix C. Climate indicators examples by category

Category	Sample unit	Sample indicators
GHG emissions Range 1, 2 and 3; emission intensity	MT (metric tones)	• Absolute band 1, band 2 and band 3 GHG emissions • Funded issues by asset classes • Weighted average carbon intensity • Greenhouse gas emissions per MWh of electricity produced • Gross global greenhouse gas emissions from scope 1 covered by emission control regulations
Risks of transition Amount and degree of assets or business activities vulnerable to transition risks	Amount or percentage	• Volume of real estate collateral, highly exposed to the risk of transition • Concentration of credit exposure to carbon-related assets • Percentage of revenues from coal mining • Percentage of revenue in passenger-kilometers not covered by the Compensation and Reduction Scheme Carbon Offsetting and Reduction Scheme for International Aviation (CORSIA)
Physical risks Amount and degree of assets or business	Amount or percentage	• Number and value of mortgage loans in 100-year flood zones • Wastewater treatment capacity located in 100-year flood zones

activities vulnerable to physical risks		• Revenues related to abstracted and consumed water in regions with high or extremely high source water stress • Proportion of property, infrastructure or other alternative asset portfolios in an area subject to flooding, heat stress or water stress • Proportion of real assets exposed to climate hazards 1: 100 or 1: 200
Climate opportunities Share of revenue, assets or other business activities related to climate opportunities	Amount or percentage	• Written net premiums related to energy efficiency and low carbon technologies • Number of (1) zero-emission (ZEV) vehicles sold, (2) hybrid vehicles and (3) hybrid vehicles • Revenues from products or services that support the transition to a low-carbon economy • Share of delivered homes certified according to the green building standard
Capital expenditures Amount of capital expenditures, financing or investments to climate risks and opportunities	Reporting currency	• Percentage of annual revenues invested in research and development of low-carbon products / services • Investment in climate adaptation measures (eg soil health, irrigation, technology) • Internal price of carbon
Carbon prices Price per tonne of greenhouse gas emissions used by the organization itself	Price in reporting currency, for MT CO2e	• The price of carbon in the shadows, by geographical area • Part of the employee's annual discretionary bonus related to investments in climate-related products
Remuneration Share of executive management remuneration related to climate	Percentage, weight, description or amount in the reporting currency	• Integrate climate goals into long-term incentive cards for CEOs • Weighing the effectiveness against the objectives of the operational issues for the remuneration assessment card

4. Appendix D. Studies on the evolution of sustainable reporting

Author	Period	Aim of the study	Conclusions
Sobhani (2011)	2000-2009	Sustainability reporting practices	The level of disclosure increased over the period under review, except for energy, environment and human rights issues
Harun, Rashid (2013)	2012	Determining the quality of sustainability reporting	Disclosure of some sustainability information in low-quality bank reports
Araya (2014)	2000-2013	Sustainability reporting	
Rogošić (2014)	2013	Determining the factors of corporate social reporting	Very few Croatian banks publish CSR reports
Pulejo и Rappazzo (2015)	2000-2014	Exploring the voluntary nature of reporting	Many ethical banks do not use standards and guidelines in their sustainability reports mainly due to the voluntary nature of reporting in Europe
Hummel и Festl-Pel (2015)	2013	Sustainability disclosure in the context of greenwashing	There is selective disclosure of information about sustainability issues Comparing environmental disclosure by systemically important banks Banks show wide variation in quality and quantity of disclosure
Carè (2017)	2011-2015	Comparing environmental disclosure by systemically important banks	Banks show wide variation in quality and quantity of disclosure
Masud, Bae и Kim (2017)	2010-2014	Environmental accounting	Environmental disclosures mostly concern the green banking and renewable energy categories and less

			the environment and waste management categories
Nwobu, Owolabi (2017)	2010-2014	Sustainability reporting	Emphasizes economic and social indicators more than environmental ones
Akter,Siddik (2018)	2014-2016	Environmental Finance Reporting Disclosures are not clear and classified.	Banks emphasize social and economic indicators more than environmental ones
Lundbergи Ek (2018)	2012-2016	Sustainability reporting trends	Environmental reporting is improving significantly
Korzeb и Medina (2019)	2015-2017	Analysis of reporting through multivariate assessment	During the period under review, sustainability support was not one of the priorities of the Polish banking sector

Table 5. Appendix E. Studies on the negative relationship between sustainability and financial performance of banks

Author	Period	Aim of the study	Conclusions
Soana (2011)	2004	An analysis of the relationship between CSR and CFP for 37 Italian banks.	There is no relationship between the variables in the short run
Abeysinghe and Basnayake (2015)	2009-2013	Determining the relationship between CSR disclosures and financial performance of commercial banks	There is a negative relationship between CSR disclosures and financial performance of selected local commercial banks
Okiro and Omoro (2013)	2006-2010	To establish the relationship between CSR investment and sustainable growth of banks in Kenya.	CSR generates potential long-term benefits

Wu and Shen (2013)	2003-2009	They examine the relationship between CSR and financial performance and discuss banks' motivations for CSR	CSR is negatively related to non-performing loans
Folajin et al. (2014)	2006-2012	To find out the impact of CSR on the profitability of the United African Bank	CSR expenditure has a negative effect on net profit in the short term, but in the long term it provides better returns
Taskin (2015)	2013	An Analysis of Turkish Banks' CSR Practices and Their Financial Performance	The results show that ROA and ROE have no relationship with CSR
Tijani and Adeoye (2017)	1992-2014	Analysis of the relationship between CSR and CFP of African banks Insignificant relationship between CSR and financial performance.	It is recommended that bank management consider CSR as a business opportunity that is beneficial in the long run
Mravlija (2017)	2002-2015	Analysis of the relationship between CSR and CFP in the banking sector in the short- and long-term perspective	The results show that the implementation of CSR activities has long-term financial effects
Nobanee and Ellili (2017)	2013	Investigating the effect of banks' economic, environmental and social disclosure on their financial performance	Sustainability disclosure does not have a significant impact on bank performance.
Bimha and Nhamo (2017)	2011-2014	Constructing an index to assess the effectiveness of environmental management and determining its relationship with operational efficiency indicators of banks	The results show a significant negative correlation between the constructed index and operational efficiency in most banks

Nguyen (2018)	201-2016	Examining the relationship between CSR disclosure and bank financial performance	There is a significant negative relationship between sustainability disclosure and financial performance of the banks studied
Fijałkowska and Garsztka (2018)	2012-2016	Analysis of CSR results and the financial performance of state-owned banks from Central and Eastern Europe	Corporate social and environmental results do not affect the financial performance of banks from Central and Eastern Europe
Mohamud (2018)	2010-2016	A Study on the Impact of CSR on Financial Performance in East African Banks	The result showed that there is a negative relationship between CSR and ROE
Deutsch and Pintér (2018)	2006-2013	To determine the relationship between CSR and financial performance of banks in the Hungarian banking sector	CSR activities lead to negative returns in short-term analysis, but they can provide returns in the long-term
Cuervo-Cazurra (2018)		The evolution of corporate social responsibility of business groups	Long-term analysis of CSR investments is required, not a survey of short-term reports
Sung Kim and Oh (2019).	2010-2015	An Analysis of the Relationship between CSR and CFP for Indian Companies	Empirical results show that improving CSR actions does not always lead to higher profitability

Table 6. Appendix F. Studies on the positive relationship between sustainability and financial performance of banks

Author	Period	Aim of the study	Conclusions
Carnevale and Mazzuca (2014)	To 2014	1) The direct effects of the sustainability report on the share price of European banks 2) Indirect effects on financial indicators 3) The value of their sustainability reports in different countries	Sustainability reports differ across European countries in line with the hypothesis of different institutional contexts
Wangari (2014)	2008-2013	Examining the Impact of Voluntary Disclosure on Financial Performance	Correlation analysis results show a positive relationship between ROE and voluntary disclosure
Achoki, Kule and Shukla (2016)	2011-2015	Investigating the effect of voluntary disclosure on financial performance	There is a strong relationship between voluntary disclosure, size and financial performance of banks
Guan, Hu and Ren (2017)	2007-2014	Study the impact of carbon intensity of loans on non-performing loans	Carbon intensity of loans has a positive effect on the ratio of non-performing loans of banks
Matuszak and Rozanska (2017)	2008-2015	Exploring the relationship between CSR reporting and financial performance.	The results show a positive relationship between bank sustainability disclosures and their profitability as measured by ROA and ROE, but the relationship between disclosures and NIM is negative
Chowdhury (2018)	2012-2016	Investigating the correlation between sustainability and bank financial performance	The results show that the integration of sustainability in the banking sector has a significant impact on total assets, ROA and ROE

Oyewumi, Ogunmeru and Oboh (2018)	2010-2014	Examining the effects of CSR investment disclosure on corporate financial performance	Disclosure of commitment to environmental sustainability enhances reputation and has a positive impact on financial performance
Gitahi, Nasieku and Memba (2018)	2010-2015	Analysis of CSR disclosure in annual reports	Sustainability information has a significant positive relationship with average market price per share (MPS)
Buallay (2019)	2007–2016	Investigating the relationship between ESG and operational (return on assets), financial (return on equity) and market performance	Empirical results show that there is a significant positive impact of ESG on bank performance. Specifically, environmental reporting also positively affects ROA and TQ (Tobin's q coefficient)

Table 7. Appendix G. Researches on the impact of Voluntary Sustainability Reporting on Banks

Author	Period	Aim of the study	Conclusions
Weber (2015)		Risk assessment, sustainable finance, voluntary initiatives and regulations in the banking sector	Despite criticism of their low impact, they help to integrate sustainability into the core business of banks and put pressure on those who do not adopt these codes of conduct
Oyegunle (2016)	To 2015	A study of sustainability reporting regulations in the banking sector of developing countries	Voluntary initiatives focused on the financial sector and the environment have been successfully implemented in developed economies, but the same cannot be said for developing economies.

Adeyini (2016)	2016	Analysis of voluntary codes in the financial sector to determine the differences between their members and other banks	There is a significant difference between the two groups of banks
Novokmet and Rogošić (2016)	2014	Analysis of the sustainability report of UniCredit Group in accordance with the GRI-G4 framework	The study report shows shortcomings in the reporting of environmental indicators by the bank
Mahmud and Islam (2017)	2011-2015	Analysis of sustainability reports according to the GRI framework	Only 8 banks out of 30 published a sustainability report from 2011 to 2015 according to the GRI framework. In most cases, information on sustainability reporting does not meet the GRI guidelines
Islam, Jain and Thomson (2016)	2005-2012	A review of sustainability disclosures in the Asia-Pacific region under the GRI framework	Evidence of a significantly higher level of sustainability reporting by GRI members than non-members. There is also a significant difference in disclosure levels before and after GRI members join
Mar Miralles-Quiros (2018)	2001-2013	Analysis of GRI Sustainability Reports of 75 European Public Banks	European stock markets value this type of information significantly positively. The findings show that the financial crisis does not change investors' preferences for this type of information
Weber and Laronde (2018)	2013-2014	Environmental reporting by banks	Environmental reporting in the financial industry is still in its infancy

Basic (2016)	2013	Exploring the relationship between financial performance and EP compliance	Financial institutions that adopt the principles are larger and perform significantly better in terms of liquidity and total shareholder return
Finger and Gavious (2017)		Study of the effect of the adoption of EP on the performance of banks	In developed (developing) countries, the adoption of EP is associated with an increase (decrease) in financing activity, as well as the share of interest income
Chen (2018)	2003-2010	Research adoption of EP on bank liquidity	EPFIs generally have higher liquidity than non-EPFIs

Reporting of ecological sustainability of banks

Sevgi Mertkan

Sevgi Mertkan, "Varna Free University "Chernorizets Hrabar", Department of Economics, Varna 9007, Bulgaria

Abstract

The increased interest in measuring sustainable development stems from studies that highlight the difficulties in measuring non-financial information and offer guidelines for developing common evaluation frameworks. There are a large number of studies that offer different reporting measures. The reporting of environmental information is currently often underestimated and lags behind the information on financial, economic and social indicators due to the indirect impact of the banking sector on climate change. The current research concept is focused on clarifying the key aspects of the environmental determinants of sustainable development in banks and developing an effective framework for their quantification. This concept proposes the development of a modified model for reporting on the environmental banking performance. Specific indicators are also proposed for the operational reporting of the environmental performance of banks, which are becoming increasingly important along with strategic decisions for sustainable development.

Keywords: sustainability, ecological indicators, banks, financial sector

Introduction

The fact is that over the last decade, sustainability reporting has become increasingly important in the financial industry. There has been an increase in transparency, improvements in standards and reporting frameworks, and increased stakeholder involvement in the decision-making process. Of particular importance for banks is the choice to participate in voluntary sustainability initiatives in the short and long term, which require adequate and transparent reporting.

The aim of the study is to analyze the most common methods of reporting on sustainable development by banks. After the literature review, as well as the recommendations of the sustainable development initiatives, the most frequently used methodologies and indicators for operational reporting are presented. In addition, a modified framework for assessing banks' reporting of environmental sustainability has also been proposed. The framework includes an analysis of banks' reports (including financial, CSR, sustainability), as well as any other publicly available information on environmental protection related to the particular bank. As a result of the analysis, a numerical / value assessment is formed for the effectiveness of the bank's reporting of environmental sustainability.

Unlike financial statements, where investors are the main users of information, sustainability reporting has many stakeholders who have different expectations about the subject of reporting. Moreover, each group of stakeholders has their own views on correct reporting, which will allow them to make the right decisions. However, the banking industry still lacks a consensus on pursuing a generally accepted and coherent strategy to counter the financial risks posed by climate change. Even if we only hypothetically assume that all bank customers consider the risks associated with environmental protection in a transparent and standardized way, the banks themselves still do not have developed comprehensive strategies further developed into tactical plans at the operational level to manage these risks. The aim of this study is to analyze the ways of transparent disclosure of environmental information in the financial industry, the most commonly used environmental indicators of banks and the necessary database for this purpose.

Nomenclature

CDP	Carbon Disclousure Project
CDSB	Climate Disclosure Standards Board
COP	Conference of the Parties
CSR	Corporate Social Responsibility
DJSI	Dow Jones Sustaiability Index
EAP	Environmental Action Program
EBIT	Earnings Before Interest and Taxes
ECB	European Central Bank
EEFIG	The Energy Efficiency Financial Institutions Group
EMP	Environmental Management Performance
EOP	Environmental Operational Performance
ER	Environmental Rating
ESG	Environmental, Social, Governance
ESI	Environmental Status Indicator
EU	European Union
FRSF	Financial Reporting Standards Foundation
GBP	Green Bond Principles
GFANZ	Glasgow Financial Alliance for Net Zero
GHG	Greenhouse gas
GRI	Global Reporting Initiative
IEA	International Energy Agency
IFRS	International Financial Reporting Standards
IIRC	International Integrated Reporting Council
KPI	Key Performance Indicators
MPI	Management Performance Indicator
NFRD	Non-Financial Reporting Directive
OPI	Operational Performance Indicator
PCAF	Partnership for Carbon Accounting Financials
SASB	Sustainability Accounting Standards Board
SEI	Sustainable Energy Investment
UNFCCC	United Nations Framework Convention on Climate Change
UNGC	United Nations Global Compact
UNPRI	United Nations Principles for Responsible Investment

1. Government environmental measures and initiatives

Climate change and environmental protection are among the most significant challenges of our time to achieve sustainable development. The global importance of sustainability is reflected in changing consumer expectations, as well as in national and international regulations.

The First United Nations Summit on the Earth (Stockholm, Sweden, 5-16 June 1972) adopted a declaration setting out the principles for the protection and improvement of the environment and an action plan containing recommendations for international environmental action. She called on world governments to "anticipate and prevent possible man-made climate change that could be detrimental to human well-being." This event is of interest to many experts and researchers, which is why environmental issues are on the agenda of many international conferences on climate change (see Annex 1).

A key point in the climate debate is the adoption of the United Nations Framework Convention on Climate Change (UNFCCC). It is followed by a series of annual conferences of the Parties, held annually by the Conference of the Parties (COP), the decision-making body responsible for monitoring and reviewing the implementation of the United Nations Framework Convention on Climate Change.

The Kyoto Protocol, adopted in December 1997, supplementing the United Nations Framework Convention on Climate Change (UNFCCC), also highlights the international community's approach to the problem. It did not enter into force until 16 February 2005, as Australia and the United States refused to ratify it, and its adoption by Russia proved key to its entry into force (Zhelyazkova, 2013).It is an extremely important document to ensure that the signatories not only support voluntary initiatives, but also take specific legally established targets to reduce their greenhouse gas emissions. More than 1,300 multilateral and more than 2,200 bilateral environmental agreements (International Environmental Agreements Database Project) have been signed so far. They are further evidence of the growing concern of companies in all sectors for environmental issues and attempts to harmonize environmental policies at the international level - "Global warming is a weapon of mass destruction" and is the most serious problem facing everyone is facing today, even more serious than the threat of terrorism" (Forsyth 2011).

The last most significant global initiative is the so-called Glasgow Climate Pact, which aims to turn the 2020s into a decade of climate action and support. The 197 participating countries are committed to providing $ 100 billion a year from developed to developing countries, reducing emissions so that the average global temperature increase is limited to 1.5 degrees, and eliminating inefficient fossil fuel subsidies.

With the rapid development of the economy, Chinese banks are not left out of the debate and are becoming an emerging force on the international financial scene. However, some of their solutions lead to irreversible environmental problems, as a result of which China is beginning to "green" banking policies to promote sustainable development (Bal, 2014). Nevertheless, the European Union remains the most active party in the debate.

In November 1973, the First Environmental Action Program was approved. Since 1973, the EU has adopted six Environmental Action Programs (EAPs). In 2001, the EU launched its Sustainable Development Strategy, which complements the Lisbon Strategy for Promoting Growth and Jobs with an Environmental Dimension. In line with these strands, the Europe 2020 strategy[36] aims to deliver "smart, inclusive and sustainable growth". The "Resource Efficient Flagship Initiative in Europe"[37] identifies the path to sustainable growth and supports the transition to a resource-efficient, low-carbon economy.

The EU's ambition to maintain its leadership in environmental protection is reflected in its long-term vision for 2050. Europe to be the first climate-neutral continent. The Community is introducing new key climate and energy measures to stimulate the "contribution" of clean energy to zero net greenhouse gas emissions in Europe by 2050 (Gercheva, 2020).

---

[36] In 2013, the Council and the Parliament of Europe adopted the Seventh Environment Action Program for 2020, entitled "Living well within our planet". Based on the Program, it also emphasizes the need for better implementation of EU legislation in the field of environment, state-of-the-art science, investment and the integration of environmental aspects into other policies. The Europe 2020 strategy is the EU's agenda for growth and jobs for the current decade. It emphasizes smart, sustainable and inclusive growth as a way to address structural weaknesses in the European economy, increase its competitiveness and productivity, and maintain a sustainable social market economy (Europe 2020 strategy).

[37] Europe's resource efficiency strategy is part of the Europe 2020 strategy - the EU's growth strategy for a smart, inclusive and sustainable economy. It supports the transition to sustainable growth through resource efficiency and a low-carbon economy.

The ECB presents 13 supervisory expectations for 112 banking institutions in formulating and implementing their business strategy, their risk management frameworks and improving their environmental risk disclosures. It considers climate and environmental risks (C&E risks) as the main risk drivers / drivers for existing categories such as credit, market and operational risk. The ECB first assessed the state of environmental risk management in the banking sector in November 2020, and then published its Guide to Managing These Risks. The Guide describes how institutions should take environmental risks into account when formulating and implementing their business strategy and their risk management frameworks, including stress tests. The ECB further expects the institutions to become more transparent by improving the disclosure of these risks. The latter requirement can be met through the use of qualitative and quantitative indicators.

European Union (EU) legislation requires large companies to disclose information on social and environmental challenges. The Non-Financial Reporting Directive (NFRD)[38] sets out the rules for disclosing non-financial information by large companies. According to this directive, large companies, including financial institutions, must publish reports on the policies they implement with regard to environmental protection, as well as disclose their risk profile in detail. At present, the financial market suffers from a number of information gaps: information on the sustainability of financial products, if available, is inconsistent and largely incomparable.

In this context, the EU institutions have reached a political agreement to develop a uniform classification of environmentally sustainable economic activities.[39] "Only if investors have clear and reliable information about the impact of their investments can they make financial decisions in accordance with their own sustainability preferences and confidently balance their portfolios with sustainable assets. (ECB, 2020).

---

[38] According to Directive 2014/95 / EU, institutions are required to disclose information on climate and environmental risks. In addition, Article 432 of the Capital Requirements Regulation further clarifies that environmental information is considered essential. Moreover, when an institution decides not to disclose this information, it must clearly state the reason.

[39] The taxonomy was published on 22 June 2020 and entered into force on 12 July 2020. The Taxonomy Regulation instructs the Commission to establish a valid list of environmentally sustainable activities by setting technical screening criteria for each environmental objective. These criteria will be established by means of delegated acts in 2021 and 2022 and will improve the quantity and quality of available climate and environmental disclosures.

In April 2020, CRO Forum, a group of chief venture directors from large multinational insurance companies, announced the methodology for insurers to calculate weighted average carbon intensity. In November 2020, the Partnership for Carbon Accounting Financials (PCAF) launched the Global Standard for Greenhouse Gas Accounting and Reporting for the Financial Industry, which outlines methodologies for measuring funded emissions for specific asset classes in accordance with Greenhouse Gas Protocol. The Financial Sector Science-Based Targets Guidance (TCFD, 2021) encourages financial institutions to use this global PCAF GHG reporting standard to measure funded emissions. In December 2020, the group of Carbon Disclousure Project (CDP), Climate Disclosure Standards Board (CDSB), Global Reporting Initiative (GRI), International Integrated Reporting Council (IIRC), and Sustainability Accounting Standards Board (SASB), called the Alliance - published a prototype of a standard for climate-related financial disclosure. The prototype outlines a vision that integrates both financial accounting and sustainability disclosure. In February 2021, the International Financial Reporting Standards Foundation (IFRS) announced plans to establish a Sustainability Standards Board. To this end, a working group was set up in March 2021 to accelerate the convergence of global sustainability standards. In April 2021, the United Nations launched the Glasgow Financial Alliance for Net Zero (GFANZ) to bring together various financial sector initiatives focused on zero net GHG emissions targets by the middle of the century.

The importance of the banking sector in the implementation of sustainable development strategies suggests that in the coming years the topics related to "green" banking will gain increasing popularity and public importance. Investments for sustainable development of banks affect not only their reputation, but also have a direct bearing on the quantitative measures of banking performance.

Undoubtedly, the status and potential of *Bulgarian banks* have a significant impact on the general state of the economy of the Republic of Bulgaria. This requires responsible behavior on the part of all banks operating within our country, although at present the notion of corporate social responsibility within Bulgaria is formed mainly as a consequence of the initiatives undertaken by large banks and the results of their projects. This fact requires the encouragement of energy and support from banks with more modest resources in order to further stimulate competitiveness and economic development. (Marinov, 2015). There are some serious misconceptions in Bulgaria about the exact nature of CSR.

Examples are Bulgarian companies, for which CSR is mostly expressed in compliance with legal norms and restrictions. Looking through Carroll's CSR pyramid, it turns out that most companies equate CSR with legal liability - the second level of the pyramid. Another problem for Bulgarian companies (including banks) is the fact that CSR is treated as a general interest in the welfare of employees. Most companies do not see CSR as a multidimensional strategy with a long-term impact and simply focus on its social aspect. Often companies participate in certain CSR activities only to present themselves as socially responsible or to respond to public pressure. The quick review of CSR activities of the major Bulgarian banks gives the impression that they are rather philanthropic activities in the form of various initiatives for culture, education, sports, donations, ie. as a form of grant funding. There are no forms of financing projects or other investments that bring economic benefits both to the bank itself and to society as a whole. No Bulgarian bank mentions the strategic positioning of sustainable development or its environmental aspect.

2. Measuring sustainable development

The reporting of environmental information is currently often underestimated and lags behind the information on financial, economic and social indicators due to the indirect influence of the banking sector on climate change. Environmental care reporting has the potential to improve the results of sustainable development measures and corporate social responsibility (CSR), but there are still many untapped reserves to achieve the desired results for banks. The current research concept is focused on clarifying the key aspects of the environmental determinants of sustainable development in banks and developing an effective framework for their quantification.

In the light of the EU's Climate Neutrality Plan, measuring and reporting on environmental performance is becoming a top priority for any business. The reason for the importance of measurement is also given by Harrington (1987) - “If you can't measure it, you can't understand it; if you can't understand it, you can't control it; if you can't control it, you can't improve it." Braun (1996) argues that measurement shows whether companies achieve their goals or not. According to Simmons (2000), measurement helps companies periodically set their business goals (in the short and long term) and provides managers with valuable information about progress toward sustainable development. Caroll (2000) emphasizes the subjectivity of measuring resilience. Graafland et al. (2004) point out the advantages that come from measuring and benchmarking sustainability - transparency and accountability in the company's actions, a systematic approach and a more objective view.

Increased interest in measuring sustainable development stems from studies that highlight difficulties in measuring nonfinancial information and offer guidelines for developing common evaluation frameworks (Mitchell, 1996; Jollands, 2006; Aravossis et al., 2006; Graafland et al., 2003; Graafland et al., 2004; Sachs et al., 2006; Kovačič, 2007; Turker, 2008; Carroll, 2000). There is no widely accepted methodology to assess and rank a company's social responsibility and consensus on the criteria to be measured and evaluated. The results of sustainable development activities cannot be measured by a single approach. Many studies test different reporting measures, but because the concept of sustainable development is too broad and complex, it could not include all possible dimensions in a common framework. Therefore, the question arises as to whether its individual parts are quantifiable and suitable for aggregation (Grigoris, 2016).

Lastly, another very important reason for the transparent reporting of sustainability is because of its positive link with the financial performance of banks, as well as other aspects of banking. The following are the latest studies in this regard. The study results of Al-Dhaimesh (2019) revealed that there is a statistically significant effect of sustainability accounting disclosure on the financial performance and that the banks operating in Jordan give more priority to the economic dimension disclosure, than to the social and environmental dimensions.

Adam (2020) found that improvement in energy efficiency (i.e., lower energy intensity) drives the profitability of commercial banks upward. Commercial banks should include the energy utilization behavior of their clients in their credit valuation. This could help the banks design tailor-specific interest rates to deal with the different risk profiles of their clients. On the borrowers' side, such an initiative by the bank can lead to more informed decisions on energy efficiency investment. Certainly, promoting energy efficiency alone cannot be the panacea to raise the profitability of commercial banks. As revealed in this study, bank-specific and external factors play significant roles in explaining banks' profitability. To increase profit, credit risk policies and operational efficiency should be pursued aggressively by banks.

The final report of EEFIG working group on risk assessment (2021) demonstrates that the benefits of attaching energy performance data to mortgage records to better manage credit risks. All financial institutions are recommended to research how to include energy performance data for all buildings collateral in their customer data management systems. It also conclude that there is a statistically significant correlation between the energy performance of building collateral and mortgage credit performance.

Bătae (2021) collected data from the Refinitiv database for 39 European banks, for the period 2010–2019. The results show a positive relationship between emission reductions and financial performance. However, the findings show market investors do not value a bank's involvement in social responsibility initiatives and do not endorse the adoption of best governance practices that could reduce the riskiness of a bank's portfolio. These findings have practical implications for bank managers and company boards in selecting and disclosing ESG policies and initiatives.

The overall results of the study of Tawfik (2021) showed a moderate positive relationship between all sustainability variables (including environmental) and financial performance of commercial banks operating Oman, United Arab Emirates, and Jordan for the period 2008-2018.

Munjal (2021) contribute significantly for policy makers in Indian banking sector to establish mandatory environmental legislations for reporting on environmental practices in order to improve non-financial disclosure and financial performance in Indian banking sector.

The opposite direction of the link has also been studies. Amuakwa-Mensah (2022) conclude that an improvement in banking performance based on our five banking performance indicators (return on asset, market capitalisation, asset quality, managerial efficiency and financial stability)is associated with an increase renewable energy consumption for our global sample.

Feridun and Gungor (2022) the article concludes that the major regulatory and supervisory expectations can be categorized into four key areas: (i) board-level attention to climate risks and integrating them into internal governance frameworks, (ii) embedding climate risks into strategies and overall risk management frameworks, (iii) identifying climate-related material exposures and disclosure of relevant key metrics, and (iv) assessing capital impact from climate risk through scenario analysis and stress testing. The article also presents a number of implications for banks and banking regulators in other jurisdictions to help them identify the actions required to address climate change risks in the banking sector.

Caby (2022) empirically examines the influence of climate change management on banks' profitability using panel data of a sample of 137 banks from 36 emerging and developed countries during the period 2011–2019. The empirical evidence shows that, although banks seem to be aware of the consequences of climate change on their business, to the point of making it a strategic topic worthy of the board of directors, they remain very timid in terms of operational implementation. It leads to a positive impact on profitability limited to the overall quality of climate change management and disclosure and an ex-post justification of the topic's relevance to the board. The foreseeable introduction of new banking regulations and the current weak relationship between climate change managerial practices and financial performance should encourage banks to pay greater attention to these practices to preserve their future returns.

The German CSR Forum shares the generally accepted view of the importance of the systematic presentation and evaluation of sustainability reporting tools. The rapid spread of sustainable development ideas and trends in the transition from voluntary to greater formalization and legalization of sustainability necessitate the development of stricter standards and reliable verification schemes. The second conclusion of the forum is the complementarity and interdependence of the tools. Pioneering instruments such as the UN Global Compact are now combined with reporting frameworks to enhance their capacity to provide greater accountability. General instruments are complemented by specific ones that correspond to specific sectoral, geographical regions or stakeholders.

In order to properly assess threats and opportunities, banks need to have a comprehensive *vision, mission and strategy* for environmental performance and environmental risk management, which is in line with their main strategic goal. A number of financial sector regulators conduct "strategic reviews" of industrial practices to ensure that financial institutions manage environmental risk sources in an appropriate way. *Stress tests* serve as a tool to assess the resilience of banks to adverse conditions and shocks. They are designed primarily to assess operational risk, but banks also use them as a tool to measure their exposure to credit, liquidity and market risks. The development of stress tests after the global financial crisis logically leads to the need to apply them in a similar way to environmental risks.

The TCFD recommendations provide both corporates and financial institutions with a consistent, high-level guidance to assessing and disclosing climate-related risks and opportunities (UNEP FI, 2018). They require banks to adopt a forward-looking, scenario-based approach to climate impact assessments, extending their horizons decades into the future. It is expected that implementing the recommendations will generate new sources of information for market actors and policymakers, influence the allocation of capital, and facilitate the transition to a more sustainable, low-carbon economy.

While comparisons can be made with macro-economic stress testing commonly employed by banks, climate scenario analysis or "stress testing" has a somewhat different application. Macro-economic stress testing, generally defined as comprehensive, firm-wide scenario analysis, is intended to estimate capital needs and manage capital over one to five years. A climate transition response, however, will evolve over decades. Banks can address the major challenges inherent to modelling transition risk:

- Transition scenarios provide plausible views of how transition risk might evolve across sectors over the next few decades
- Borrower-level calibration allows each bank to tailor the approach and overcome a lack of empirical data to estimate changes in credit outcomes
- Portfolio impact assessment, together with the scenarios, provides a structured analytical framework that makes the approach repeatable, systematic, and consistent and helps coordinate and integrate analysis and judgment across a bank

Scenario analysis and stress tests are expected to become crucial tools to assist banks in drawing up assessments of sustainable and environmentally sound investments. There are some major challenges for applying a stress testing approach to environmental risks.[40] Despite similarities, the assessment of transition risk presents unique challenges compared to traditional risk evaluation. To develop a comprehensive methodology for assessing climate-related transition risk, banks have to overcome six key challenges.

First, limited empirical data exists to measure the strength of the climate-credit risk relationship. Banks lack historical data with which they can assess the impact of climate risk on credit losses.

Second, long time horizons for transition impacts challenge the way banks usually manage risk. Transition impacts will likely be experienced over intergenerational time horizons: transition scenarios often project impacts over 30–100 years. Specific transition risks may not materialize over the one- to five-year periods that banks typically use to conduct business planning and stress testing exercises.

Third, transition risks vary across sectors, both in terms of how, and how much, they impact specific industries. Such differences make scenario information at an

[40] First, stress tests cover a short-term time horizon (up to 1-2 years), which, however, is incompatible with the time of manifestation of the consequences of climate risks. Second, stress tests are designed to measure shock and cyclical shocks, while environmental risks may be more prolonged and non-cyclical. At this stage, these mechanisms are still underdeveloped and further research is needed to fully integrate climate risks into banks' traditional stress test methodologies.

aggregate, economy-wide level insufficient for informing transition risk analysis. To make the exercise tractable and accurate, banks require a methodology that can be both used flexibly across sectors while capturing major differences in sector risk.

Fourth, the methodology needs to be systematic, repeatable, and consistent in order to be useful for disclosure. The approach used by banks should follow an organized, systematic analytical structure and should yield results that can be compared across banks along a variety of dimensions, including sectors, geographies, and scenarios.

Fifth, banks need to tailor transition risk assessments to their own organizations. A purely generic, top-down analysis of transition risk is fundamentally inadequate. Top-down analysis may neither capture bank-specific portfolio considerations, nor banks' own assessment of the magnitude and nature of these risks. Transition risk assessment should reflect the knowledge of institutional experts to foster ownership and mainstream adoption of these analyses. Further, risk materiality often varies substantially from bank to bank due to portfolio exposures. Customization at an institutional level must play a role in a transition risk methodology.

Finally, conducting quality scenario analysis requires major coordination across the organization. Transition risk analysis requires a range of industry, credit risk, and sustainability experts from across the bank. The approach should make the work required by banks manageable, with clearly defined inputs and outputs, in order to facilitate execution across complex organizations.

However, the concept of sustainable development, in addition to corporate governance, should be implemented throughout the banking organization - and especially at the operational level. In carrying out these complex and complex tasks, the actions of the banking management can be assisted by specialized teams for environmental sustainability such as compliance teams, as well as by bank employees at the operational level. Moreover, the environmental performance itself can be characterized by providing green training to employees (including operational) on energy and paper conservation, as well as reducing energy consumption and carbon emissions from banking. (Zhang, Wang, 2022).

The environmental performance can be presented as a set of: environmental management performance (EMP); (2) environmental operational performance

(EOP) and (3) environmental rating (ER) assessment. The last element (ER) reflects the assessment of specialized rating agencies.

Environmental Management Performance (EMP) is the result of strategic banking decisions for environmental management such as participation in environmental initiatives, standards, environmental policy, environmental risk management and more. The developed modified Scholtens framework can be used for this indicator.

The Environmental Operational Performance (EOP) is formed on the basis of quantifiable environmental indicators. Climate-relevant indicators are primarily nonfinancial metrics that can be complemented by financial metrics such as business segmentation data.

The importance of reporting non-financial information has been clarified so far. The difficulties associated with this process related to the lack of quantitative measures of sustainability standards are analyzed. Next, after a thorough analysis of existing practices, a specific method is proposed, focused only on the operational reporting of environmental norms and standards.

What are the most commonly used approaches in research to measure resilience? According to Djalilov, Vasylieva and Lyeonov (2015) these are:

3. Operational measuring of sustainability

What are the most commonly used approaches in research to measure resilience? According to Djalilov, Vasylieva and Lyeonov (2015) these are:

- the investment approach, which is used in the presence of detailed reports on the individual sustainability initiatives of banks
- indexing method - uses international indices such as: KLD 400 Social Index, Asset4-ESG, GRI, etc.;
- binary method - takes into account the presence (1) or absence (0) of certain sustainability criteria in the bank statements.

3.1. Sustainability reports

Stakeholders put banking management under pressure to provide environmental information in their annual reports, with different stakeholders interested in different environmental indicators. Thus, reporting on environmental issues has a wide range - at the corporate, national and international levels, which includes qualitative and quantitative, positive and negative or neutral information about the environment. According to the European Commission, green finance includes investment solutions with environmental, social and managerial aspects that ensure customer and public satisfaction. The environmental performance of banks is described from Mikolajczyk (2017) as "the impact of the banking business on the environment."

Internal carbon pricing

The concept of carbon pricing serves to construct a price for a good or an attribute that is currently not appropriately reflected in the pricing of goods or services. Carbon pricing relates to valuation of GHG emissions to allow for the inclusion of the negative externality created by this environmental product into economic analyses.

On the one hand, the financial industry is reacting to carbon pricing regulations, which exposes investments in fossil-fuel companies and other carbon-intensive industries to previously unforeseen costs. On the other hand, the recognition that physical climate change impacts are becoming a systemic risk across the broader economy makes powerful stakeholder groups, risk departments and valuation teams more attentive to the link between a changing climate and asset value. Finally, the need to disclose climate change related risks by corporates is also being advocated or required by regulators, encouraged by the Financial Stability Board's Task Force on Climate-related Financial Disclosures.[41]

In theory, there are generally two approaches to determine the value of carbon. The first is based on the cost to society, while the other is based on the cost to reduce. The approach to valuation of a carbon price is dependent on the purpose of its application. The theoretical elements, including regulatory pricing, marginal abatement cost pricing, social pricing, and peer pricing, are relevant to guide the methodological approach to define an internal carbon price within a financial institution.

Climate finance tracking

Over the past years climate finance tracking in banks has gained a lot of ground. This interest has emerged from the international context of developed country pledges to mobilise USD 100 billion in climate finance, per year, by 2020. Spurred on by the emphasis given to climate finance tracking by the international climate negotiations and a variety of public banks, commercial banks are increasingly aware of benefits from building a robust climate finance tracking framework. Climate finance tracking builds on a growing recognition that the measurement of financial flows to mitigation and adaptation projects and

[41] Under a mandate from the G20, the Financial Stability Board set up the Task Force on Climate-related Financial Disclosures to "undertake a coordinated assessment of what constitutes efficient and effective disclosure and design a set of recommendations for voluntary company financial disclosures of climate-related risks that are responsive to the needs of lenders, insurers, investors, and other users of disclosures". The purpose of the Task The Task Force provides guidance on the overlap between different reporting initiatives and becomes the 'umbrella' disclosure-reporting framework for banks. Hereby ensuring alignment with all key disclosure frameworks, including the G20/OECD Principles of Corporate Governance, the CDP Climate Change Questionnaire and the Global Reporting Initiative G4 Sustainability Reporting Guidelines.

programmes forms an elemental part of a broader sustainability, or low-carbon, strategy of a financial institution.

The Paris Agreement strongly increases the global need to set up uniform processes to track climate finance flows internationally. Requirements and expectations from this international level of governance will ultimately also trickle down to commercial banks, although with some delay. At the same time, a bank's approach on climate finance tracking should recognise that the measurement of financial flows to mitigation and adaptation projects and programmes forms an elemental part of a broader sustainability-, or low-carbon-strategy of a financial institution.

There are a variety of reasons for a financial institution to track climate finance. In addition to tracking for purposes of disclosure to a variety of stakeholders, three key reasons can be identified; growth, access to capital and value risk.

3.2. Indexing method

In terms of sustainability, there are very few independent rating agencies that evaluate companies in terms of their CSR policies and database on resource use and emissions. The academic literature acknowledges the disadvantages of using this data (Garcia-Castro et al., 2010; Semenova and Hassel, 2015; Dorfleitner et al., 2015). In particular, ratings do not inform about sustainability and focus on policies instead of results. So far, however, there is no alternative (Sholtens, Klooster, 2019). Therefore, a number of studies rely on specialized rating agencies. The overall rating is a balanced assessment of environmental, social and corporate responsibility. The environmental pillar consists of categories such as reducing emissions, product innovation and reducing the use of limited resources. Providers of sustainability assessments have different theories about its content and measure effectiveness in different ways. It can be concluded that the measurement process is highly subjective. Using different estimates to account for sustainability may lead research to different conclusions. Further studies are needed to address the constructive validity of the assessments provided by MSCI, ASSET4 and Sustainalytics, and others. (Bouten and Cho, 2017).

This category of indicators consists of qualitative scores given to companies based on climate-related issues. These scores are usually embedded in broader ESG (environmental, social, governance) scores. For investors interested in climate issues, climate-related indicators used to feed the broader scoring can be isolated to find the climaterelated qualitative score for a company (Dupre, 2015).

Several providers systematically evaluate companies on a variety of ESG criteria. They assign weighted scores to each company (and sector) on criteria relevant to the company's ESG impacts, and translate these scores into ratings. These scores are based primarily on qualitative data and benchmarking against industry practices. The overall score / rating of a company can be used to assess the sustainability of a portfolio. Providers typically rely on public data sources, including the companies themselves, media, NGOs, and other stakeholders, for the information needed for their ratings.

Given its intangible nature, a standardized definition of ESG has not been established. As a result, different entities use different interpretations and different weightings for their criteria. This is reflected in the range and types of indicators used by ratings providers to determine their ratings.

Climate is a subcomponent of the environmental set of ESG considerations. Ratings providers can disentangle climate issues from a company's ESG ratings. Only a limited number of ESG providers offer this service through a specific toolkit that focuses exclusively on climate issues. Other ratings providers can offer bespoke analysis on climate change as part of their ESG services. Climate scores usually focus on a company's public climaterelated targets and strategies, together with its actual climate friendliness, assessed on the basis of carbon footprinting and / or green / brown exposure metrics.

Climate scores integrate both quantitative and qualitative indicators. Examples of each are:

1) Quantitative metrics: Carbon footprint, GHG emissions reduction target (quantitative), electricity generation mix, carbon reserves, sales of climate-related technologies; 2) Qualitative metrics: GHG emissions reduction target (qualitative), climate mitigation strategy, disclosure practices related to climate impact, stakeholder responses.

Climate scoring is an effective summary indicator that can offer a comprehensive overview of indicators. A climate rating together with the underlying analysis can provide a comprehensive picture of the climate performance of a company compared with the other indicators discussed in this report.

On the other hand, Climate scores are generally subsumed in a broader ESG score and that nd ESG scores usually adopt a best-in class logic within sectors. While climate scoring (like other indicators) can be only as good as its inputs its score is subjective, introduced by qualitative metrics and weighting. Subjectivity always introduces a risk for validity of the indicator, a concern that exists less for carbon footprinting and green / brown exposure metrics. In this way, climate scores represent a black box. Climate (ESG) scores alone have only limited applicability alone, but they have significant applicability as a complementary metric.

Four providers offer toolkits to separate climate metrics from other ESG metrics.

- EIRIS's Climate Change Toolkit.
- CDP's Climate Performance Leadership Index.
- South Pole Group's Climate Impact Assessment.
- MSCI's Global Climate Index.

EIRIS's Climate Change Toolkit includes a carbon profile, a carbon risk factor, and a carbon engager, which serve to highlight how companies are addressing climate change combined with their climate change impacts. The carbon profile calculates the climate impacts of companies and the carbon risk factor assesses management responses to climate change.

CDP collects metrics focused on corporate disclosure related to climate change and climate change mitigation targets. It then creates a scoring scheme based on this data. It provides comparative information on a company's management of its carbon footprint, climate change strategy, and risk management processes. The results are published in its annual Climate Performance Leadership Index. CDP analysis is often used by other agencies to assess companies' climate strategies.

South Pole Group's Climate Impact Assessment is a forwardlooking toolkit conducted jointly with the CDP. It combines South Pole Group's carbon footprinting and financed emissions methodology with CDP's assessment of corporations' climate mitigation strategies. The assessment provides concrete advice on engagement issues related to corporate targets and strategies, as well carbon footprinting.

MSCI develops specific climate ratings for companies as part of its ESG research. The MSCI Global Climate Index is built on these ratings. Company ratings are based on three themes: renewable energy, clean technology and efficiency, and future fuels.

In summary, on the one hand, the number of ratings and sustainability indices is growing. On the other hand, there is no consensus on the exact definition of sustainable development, corporate sustainability and the set of measurable indicators.

3.3. Binary method

One of the most commonly used approaches to measuring sustainable development is the so-called content analysis, in which binary variables ("0" and "1") are assigned to companies on individual aspects of sustainability. If several of its dimensions are evaluated, a binary result can be assigned to each dimension, after which they are aggregated. The key advantage of this method is flexibility. The researcher can focus only on a single dimension of sustainability that is of interest to him, collect the necessary data and use it further in statistical analysis. The main weaknesses stem from the subjectivity that is present at every stage of the analysis - from data collection, through their interpretation to the assignment of an assessment. Another significant problem is the voluntary nature of sustainability reporting. As this reporting is not necessarily there is a potential for deviation from the selection. Socially responsible companies are more likely to report their achievements than less socially responsible companies. Moreover, the activities reported and those actually performed may differ (Galant and Cadez, 2017).

The Content Analysis method, according to some authors, is the most suitable for extracting information on sustainable development (Horuckova and Baudassé, 2017). Social and environmental policies, environmental and social management systems, banking products and services (such as various loans, mortgages, funds, asset management, bonds, microfinance, project financing, savings and investment banking) are analyzed. A value of 1 is determined when companies apply an appropriate environmental or social system of products, services, policies or management system. If they do not apply / do not meet the given criterion, they are given a value of 0. After assigning the individual values, the sum of all indicators is calculated. The application of the binary evaluation method aims to prevent subjectivity in ranking efficiency, thus increasing the reliability of evaluation (Chowdhury, 2018). It has also been used by popular rating and ESG rating systems such as the Thomson Reuters Asset4 ESG, the MSCI-KLD Score, and in numerous previous academic studies (Weber, 2017;

Weber at. Al., 2008; Scholtens, 2008; Kempf and Osthoff, 2007; Griffin and Mahon, 1997; Whittaker, 2012).

The binary method has also been used to measure resilience in the framework of Scholtens (2008), which deserves special attention due to the fact that it is increasingly used in studies (Relano - Paulet 2012; Laidroo – Sokolova, 2015). Its model also makes it possible to compare the sustainable practices of companies that are not included in ethical ratings, as the assessment of the framework is determined on the basis of publicly available bank data. Previous studies, such as Simpson and Kohers (2002) and Wu and Shen (2013), examined the overall effectiveness of CSR in the banking industry using published estimates. Wu and Shen (2013) refer to the weakness of this approach to measuring CSR, citing Chatterji and Levine (2008) and Chatterji et al. (2010), according to which "these indicators are often invalid and can mislead stakeholders" (Wu and Shen, 2013). They call for research that focuses on specific aspects of CSR - environmental, social or managerial (Finger, 2018). The social and environmental performance of Hungarian banks based on the framework is measured in two ways. First, using 29 indicators from the Scholtens framework (CSP1). Second, through the modified framework model, in which the basic and sub-criteria of the basic model are changed to eliminate some shortcomings (Deutsch and Pintér, 2018).

There is a common perception that there are many examples of inadequate consideration of sustainable development leading to different types of standards and frameworks that can confuse stakeholder stakeholders. The current research concept includes a framework with selected indicators for sustainable development, which can be used as an additional tool to traditional financial statements. It includes a structured list of activities divided according to the categories of green transition. Ratings in the form of 0 or 1 are assigned according to the individual environmental criteria. The number of criteria met or the sum of all units is in fact the environmental assessment of the company.

However, the quantitative method used to assess a qualitative indicator may limit the validity of the results. Conclusions based solely on numerical data on sustainability as one of the "soft" success factors pose a risk.

Scholtens (2008) made the first attempts to develop its own framework for quantifying sustainable banking behavior. To create a more transparent method than that of rating agencies, he is developing a framework that combines different elements. Its main advantage is that it can also be used by those who do not have access to expensive patented information, as it relies on publicly available data, including the websites of various banks (Verkerk, 2014).

The Scholtens framework includes four sets of indicators for banks' social responsibility: (1) codes of ethics, sustainability reporting and environmental management systems; (2) environmental management; (3) responsible financial products; (4) social behavior. They reflect the different areas relevant to the sustainable development of institutions. The emergence of more and more new initiatives and tools for sustainability reporting requires an update of the Scholtens framework. It is too broad and extends to all aspects of CSR. In this respect, the application of a modified version could be of greater benefit to stakeholders if it focuses only on the environmental pillar of sustainable development. The current research concept advocates the need to narrow the scope of the existing framework and at the same time "upgrade" it with new, additional indicators.

The concept of sustainable development is very complex, complex and includes various indicators in the measurement framework. The difficulties stem mainly from the nature of the results obtained, which are difficult to quantify, as well as the lack of a standardized disclosure procedure. It is certainly true that the category of "sustainable development" is difficult not only to define but also to quantify. Therefore, the research concept proposes the development of a modified model for accounting for environmental banking performance. It is based on the original Scholtens framework, but builds on and complements the indicative groups so that they correspond more closely to the environmental focus of the concept of sustainable development.

The first group of the framework "Codes of Ethics, Sustainability Reporting and Environmental Management Systems" examines the compliance of banking with certain principles, standards and other sustainability reporting initiatives. In the modified version, the number and composition of the principles included are different. The Who cares wins initiative does not appear in the modified framework because it covers the period 2004-2008 and is no longer relevant. This group is complemented by GRI standards, UNPRI, Green Bond Principles.

GRI currently provides the most widely used sustainability standards worldwide (Skouloudis et al., 2009; Tsang et al., 2009; Brown et al., 2009; Levy et al., 2010; Roca and Saercy, 2012; Marimon et al. al., 2012; Rodríguez-Gutiérrez, 2013). It is also the most widely accepted sustainability reporting framework according to the Boston College Center for Corporate Citizenship (2013) and Perez (2016). In addition, GRI standards are the most commonly adopted standards for accounting for sustainability in the banking sector (Monte, 2009; Araya, 2014), which is why it is necessary for banks to receive an assessment of their adoption and implementation.

Addressing the principles of responsible investment in the new framework is important due to the growing demand for ethical or socially responsible investment (SRI). Supporters are expected to contribute to the development of a more sustainable global financial system by adhering to the principles.

Green Bond Principles are present in the modified version, as they are designed specifically for banks and address precisely the research problem of climate change. The second group in the modified framework includes environmental management systems, and there are no new additions to the original framework.

The third group includes the responsible financial products and services of banks, for which there are also additional fields - offering project financing, carbon trading, participation in climate markets and microfinance. This group is complemented by the latest environmental determinants of bank performance - GHG, Brown / Green indicators and sector-based energy / carbon indicators.

The group of indicators of social behavior (within the framework of Sholtens) leads to a possible assessment of the internal (attitude to the workforce) and external social commitment of the bank (its attitude and behavior towards society through community engagement, volunteering, sponsorship). outside the research concept. The focus of this concept is on the assessment of banks' environmental performance, while the Sholtens framework also includes an assessment of social indicators.

The modified framework focuses on the proactive environmental responsibility of institutions or what is voluntary. Therefore, the fourth group for the assessment of social behavior is completely outside the scope of the forthcoming analysis and is therefore missing from the modified framework.

In order to have a benchmark for the results, lastly, the new framework re-examines whether banks are included in the so-called sustainable indices, selecting only DJSI and FTSE4Good, which are global indices. Due to the conflicting opinions about these indices, only these two were selected. Moreover, it is precisely because of the shortcomings of such rating agencies, such as difficult access, lower transparency, their focus on corporate governance and regulation, etc., that the Scholtens framework has been developed. The comparative profile of the Scholtens frame and the modified variant are presented in Table 1:

Table 1. Modifies Framework of Sholtens

Original Framework of Sholtens	Modified (Environmental) Framework of Sholtens
1. Group of Codes of Ethics, Sustainability Reporting and Environmental Management Systems	
• Sustainability report • UNEP FI • Equatorial principles • UN Global Compact • Who Cares Wins • Certified OS management system (ISO 14001)	• Global Reporting Framework (GRI) • UN Principles for Responsible Investment (UNPRI) • Certified ISO management system (ISO 140001) • UNEP Financial Initiative (UNEPFI) • Carbon Principles (CDP) • Green Bond Principles
2. Environmental Management	
• Environmental policy • Supply chain management • Quantitative objectives for environmental management • Transparency of implementation • Risk management for credit lending • Exclusion of certain sectors • World Bank Guidelines • OECD Guidelines	• Sustainability report • Environmental policy • Supply chain management • Quantitative objectives for environmental management • Risk management for credit lending • Exclusion of certain sectors
3. Responsible Financial Products	
• Socially responsible investments • Socially responsible savings • Sustainable investment • Microcredit • Environmental consulting services • Air conditioning products • Other sustainable products	• Socially responsible investments • Investment in renewable energy technologies • Participation in climate markets • Microfinance • GHG accounting • Brown / Green metrics • Sector-specific indicators
4. Social Behavior Group	
• Sponsorship • Community participation • Training and education • Diversity and opportunities • Feedback from employees • Business Ethics	
5. Sustainability indices	
• DJSI • FTSE4Good	• DJSI • FTSE4Good

Thus structured, the modified framework examines bank reporting through the prism of modern applied principles, frameworks and tools for sustainable development. Unlike Scholtens' version, the emphasis here is on environmental issues and the active participation of banks in reducing the negative impact of economic activity on the environment. Below is an example application of the framework for 2 banks - one from a developed European country and the other from a developing country.

Table 2. Demontration of the Modified Framework of Sholtens

	UniCredit Spa	National Bank of Egypt
Strategic initiatives		
GRI	1	1
UN PRI	1	0
ISO 14001	1	0
CDP	1	0
GBP	1	0
Management level		
Sustainability report	0	1
Environmental policy	1	1
Quantitative objectives for	1	0
environmental management	1	1
Risk management for credit lending	1	1
Exclusion of certain sectors		
Operational level		
Socially responsible investments	1	1
Investment in renewable	1	1
technologies	1	0
Participation in climate markets	1	1
Microfinance	1	1
GHG accounting	1	0
Brown/ Green metrics	1	0
Sector-specific metrics		
Assestrment of rating agencies		
DJSI	1	0
FTSE4Good	1	0
TOTAL:	**19**	**9**

The framework can be applied for individual years for comparison, as well as adding or removing certain criteria. By its design, the modified model could be presented as an environmental framework for sustainable development. This framework is more specialized in the field of environmental protection. It has also been updated in accordance with the latest requirements and programs for environmental CSR, which makes it suitable for effective assessment of the measures taken by banks to protect the environment.

4. Environmental indicators

Key Performance Indicators (KPIs), both financial and non-financial, are an important component of the information needed to track companies' progress towards these goals for all types of quality information and reporting (PricewaterhouseCoopers, 2007). These need to be closely aligned with strategic objectives and are often used to assess difficult-to-measure activities (Balasundaram, 2009).

"Environmental indicators" are the results of the management of the environmental aspects of the organization (EC, 2001). They include all or some of the following aspects: energy consumption and related greenhouse gas emissions; water consumption; waste generation and management; and any other impact on the environment resulting from the use or operation of premises or buildings. A number of studies use a diverse set of environmental indicators. James (1994) groups them by processes, resource consumption, emissions and waste, efficiency, risk, environmental impact, consumer perception and financial impact measures. Bartolomeo (1995) develops a more pragmatic approach, separating performance indicators from impact indicators. Performance indicators are based on processes (efficient use of raw materials) and systems (efficiency in achieving environmental efficiency goals) or refer to the financial dimension (economic efficiency in the implementation of environmental programs). Impact indicators assess environmental impacts in physical and monetary terms. Ilinic et al. (1998) distinguish between internal system measures (EPs that strengthen organizational processes), external measures for stakeholder relations (interactions between the company and its external electoral groups), external impact measures (negative external factors) and finally, internal compliance measures compliance with laws and regulations). ISO 14031 distinguishes three main types of environmental indicators:

1) Management Performance Indicator (MPI) - an environmental performance indicator that provides information about management-level efforts that affect an organization's environmental performance.

2) Operational Performance Indicator (OPI) - an indicator of environmental performance that provides information on the environmental performance of the

organization. Such an indicator is, for example, the energy used per unit of product per year.

3) Environmental Status Indicator (ECI) - a specific indicator that provides information on local, regional, national or global environmental status.

An innovative method was proposed by Dr. Bishawjit Chandra Deb (2020), which uses various indicators to report on environmental practices such as green investment, participation in green initiatives and management of green activities by the Environmental Risk Management Committee.

As stated in the report of the Task Force on Climate-Related Financial Disclosures (TCFD, 2020), each organization must clearly disclose how to measure climate risks and opportunities). Access to the indicators and objectives used by the banks allows investors and other stakeholders to better assess the organization's risk-adjusted return, ability to meet financial obligations, overall exposure to climate risks, and progress in management or adapting to these risks. Therefore, they should consider the use of climate indicators in their disclosures, such as GHG emissions from 1, 2 and 3, as well as other key performance indicators (Annex 4).

Banking institutions are increasingly integrating climate risk into their risk appetite reports by using more qualitative and / or quantitative indicators. Qualitative ones usually include goals or guidelines for the institution's readiness to take certain risks, while the second group of risk indicators is developed on the basis of (partly) quantitative methodology. The methodology and data used to develop quantitative indicators must be transparently defined. An approach to creating a climate risk reporting framework has been developed, consisting of three components, namely 1) data gap analysis, 2) data collection strategy and 3) data management and reporting framework. The Eurosystem considers that data gaps currently hinder the development of appropriate risk assessment and risk monitoring frameworks for the financial sector.

Types of data. Three types of information--primary data, secondary data, and performance data—are used in climate metrics. Each type of data has financial components and nonfinancial components and is collected by three sources: companies as the owners of physical assets, public sector agencies directly at the physical asset level (e.g. government controls of mining sites), and university or commercial data providers who aggregate and sometimes sell data.

Accessing data from companies. Investors access company data primarily through annual reports, either directly or through data providers that aggregate annual report information. The scope of these disclosures is usually regulated. In the European Union for example, reporting of nonfinancial data is regulated by a European Directive on nonfinancial and diversity information, although the climate-related disclosure requirements in this directive are relatively underdeveloped and not standardized. A number of key climate indicators are usually not reported by companies, notably the breakdown of capital expenditure by energy technology and the nature of R&D investment. Companies justify this disclosure gap by arguing that it involves propriety information that could affect competitiveness.

Accessing public data. Investors can access public data either directly or through data providers. This data may be relevant for assessing specific companies (e.g., fuel efficiency of cars by manufacturer) or for benchmarking companies relative to national indicators (e.g., annual electricity generation).

Accessing data from data providers. Data providers aggregate (and usually sell) data from physical assets, companies, reporting mechanisms, and public agencies. Data providers also provide tertiary performance data, such as qualitative scores, or ESG scores, developed by applying weights to a dataset.

Financial vs. nonfinancial data. Both financial and nonfinancial data can be relevant for climate-related investment activities. Regulatory and market standards usually result in financial data that is reported in a standardized fashion (e.g., earnings before interest and taxes). Nonfinancial data, in contrast, is largely nonstandardized and thus needs to be harmonized, although there are exceptions (e.g., proved oil & gas reserves).

Primary data is directly provided by companies through surveys or annual reports. Primary data may also be collected by public agencies or data providers at the physical asset or corporate level. (Sales, EBITDA, net profits, debt levels, Proved reserves, CO2 emissions (incomplete), reporting on climate change strategy / risk)

Secondary data includes data and metrics collected, aggregated, harmonized, and estimated by data and metrics providers using annual reports, public data sources, and analysis of physical assets. (Geography of sales, tax, cost of capital, harmonization of business segmentation, Installed capacity, breakdown of capital expenditure, estimates of CO2 emissions)

Performance data (subjective or objective) developed by data and metrics providers, including scoring, benchmarking, and ratios (P/E ratio, EV/EBITDA, ESG scores, risk metrics related to climate change)

UNEP FI`s report from 2015 areport groups nonfinancial climate indicators into three categories: 1) Carbon Footprint; 2) Green and brown indicators; 3) Climate ESG scores;

The Portfolio Carbon Initiative (2018) examines the disclosure of climate indicators by 14 development banks and 21 commercial banks (mostly large universal banks) and assesses those that can be used to assess the contribution of the banking sector to solving environmental problems. Exemplary climate indicators are presented in Appendix 2. They are systematized also into the following three groups (Weber and Chris, 2018):

- GHG accounting / GHG emissions
- Green and brown indicators
- Sector-specific energy and carbon indicators

GHG accounting is an estimate of the greenhouse gas emissions of investors, which can be distributed proportionally to investors and lenders through their share in the "financed GHG emissions"[42]. The concept of funded emissions has been actively developed in both the investment and banking sectors since 2005. However, it gained considerable popularity in the preparation of COP 21 in November 2015 and is a reporting of greenhouse gas emissions of companies from which the bank borrows or invests its capital. This concept differs significantly from the traditional corporate reporting of greenhouse gas emissions by banks, which applies only to the operational emissions of the banking institution (for example, related to its buildings, IT systems, etc.). This type of reporting is outside the scope of GHG accounting. Development banks and commercial banks that apply the Equatorial Principles use GHG accounting to measure greenhouse gas emissions related to a specific project activity.

Carbon emissions data are the only type of data that allows comparisons of intensity between different sectors. In addition, although there is a significant degree of error at the individual level, this error is relatively low at the portfolio level. Another advantage is that the costs of this type of data are relatively low for

[42] Allocation of the emissions of the main enterprise, activity or portfolio to the investors holding a financial share.

institutional investors. These measures, as well as the other 2 groups, suffer from some imperfections - there are problems with reporting, inaccuracy of emissions in the 1 and 2 emissions, data uncertainty, possible subsequent problems in their use in combination with financial data (UNEPFI, 2015). The accounting of funded emissions uses CO2 emissions as an indicator at the portfolio level. On the other hand, the aggregation process leads to a lower level of transparency than, for example, sector-specific indicators.

Indicators measuring GHG emissions associated with financial assets and their underlying entities are called carbon metrics, or carbon footprinting. Across sectors and asset classes, carbon footprinting acts as a "heatmap" to highlight a portfolios' overall exposure to key high-carbon sectors. (UNEP FI,2015)

The key question for financial institutions is the carbon footprint of the portfolio, called the "financed emissions." The 2° Investing Initiative reviewed the state of the art of such financed emissions methods in 2013 with a focus on listed equities (due to both the size of typical equity portfolios and data availability for listed companies). Carbon footprinting data is, at its core, a measure of the GHG emissions of an underlying company allocated to its investors. Thus, it represents an absolute value (annual GHG emissions) that needs to be normalized to be comparable across companies, sectors, or portfolios. Data can be normalized in terms of revenue, sales, market capitalization, products, or employees. Normalizing by market capitalization allows for a comparison across sectors, but may create biases if market capitalization changes. Normalizing by sales is a challenge given differences in currencies and prices (e.g., two cars sold can have very different prices). Both allow however for a comparison of GHG emissions across sectors, an advantage in terms of a portfolio indicator.

Carbon footprinting data is arguably the only type of data that enables a relevant comparison of climate intensity across sectors. Moreover, although there is a significant margin of error for data at an individual security level, this error is relatively low at the portfolio level. Moreover, the costs of implementing carbon footprinting is relatively low for institutional investors and may decrease as more data providers become available.

Several key accounting issues arise when using carbon footprinting

Problems with reporting. The first challenge presented by the accuracy of carbon footprinting and associated methodologies has to do with reporting issues. While reporting to the CDP has increased significantly in recent years, it is still mainly limited to listed companies. Given the voluntary nature of GHG reporting outside of countries with mandatory corporate reporting, there are major concerns about the quality of reported data, particularly its accuracy and completeness. A 2015 study found that the scope 3 emissions reported by companies are probably less than 30% of their actual scope 3 emissions. Given the significant share of scope 3 emissions in many high-carbon sectors, this can be a concern.

Another challenge with carbon reporting data is that investors can use three different consolidation approaches (equity share, financial control, or operational control) to calculate their scope 1, 2, and 3 emissions. Using different consolidation approaches can result in different results because GHG emissions are allocated to different investors. Uncertainty around scope 1 and 2 emissions. In most cases, carbon data provided by reporting companies for scope 1 and 2 are secondary (estimated) data based on the application of emission factors to primary energy, raw material consumption, and electricity purchases. The uncertainty of the related emission factors ranges from 5% (oil, gas, and coal) to 10-15% (electricity), though until recently no standard existed for how to report electricity purchases. Generally, it is assumed that the quality of scope 1 and scope 2 emissions data is sufficient to distinguish among different companies. Research by Liesen and others (2011) suggests that this may not be the case. Of course, it is likely that data quality has improved since this study and further research is needed.

Uncertainty around physical data. Recent developments in GHG accounting, such as science-based target setting, have advocated for normalization by physical output (e.g., tons of steel, kilowatt hours). For these sector-specific metrics the level of uncertainty varies greatly among products and industries. In many cases, the precision of activity data reported necessitates the use of industry averages rather than process-specific factors, which in turn leads to additional uncertainties (in some industries differences between old and innovative processes can be as high as 100% compared to the benchmark). Implications for use. How does the significant uncertainty around GHG emissions data impact investors' ability to use this data effectively in combination with financial data? Estimates suggest that uncertainty of the data drops significantly at a portfolio level. The question is whether alternative metrics are better suited or may be complementary.

Green/brown metrics measure exposure to or investment in green or brown technologies, industries, or sectors. Unlike carbon footprinting, these metrics are generally sector-specific and measure a breakdown of exposure to green or brown technologies at either the company or the portfolio level. (UNEP FI,2015).

The second group of indicators determines which financial activities are solutions and which problems are related to climate change. "Brown" funding includes financial flows to activities and technologies that significantly increase greenhouse gas emissions. "Green" refers to financial flows for zero or low carbon assets or activities (such as green bonds that can support climate or water activities, environmental protection and other related activities). The practicality of green and brown measures is significantly higher than that of greenhouse gases or other indicators, as tracking them requires only financial information for the portfolio in question: financial data as opposed to others that require financial and non-financial data (e.g. emission intensity, etc.)

These metrics support the process of constructing portfolios for project financing, for the issuance of shares and bonds, private equity and securities, as well as for investor positioning. Green and brown reporting cover a range of indicators across different sectors, not all of which are available to investors. The main challenges facing this group are access to data and the difficulty of categorizing climate impact. Sectors are sector-specific and cannot be easily aggregated or compared.

The measures used to account for the climate contribution are used much more frequently than those used to account for climate change. In other words, banks focus almost entirely on green finance, limiting the reporting of information on brown finance. It is also difficult to determine whether controversial technologies such as natural gas, nuclear energy and bio fuels are green or brown. However, if green and brown exposures are reported transparently by banks, this will improve the understanding of climate progress in the financial sector (Cummis, 2018).

This category includes two main types of metrics: (1) ratios of exposure to different technologies or business lines and (2) sector-specific energy or emissions intensity/efficiency metrics. Investors primarily access green / brown exposure metrics through ESG data providers. As discussed, data can also be accessed through bespoke databases. Examples of core data providers include Wood Mackenzie (recently acquired by Verisk Analytics) on the oil, gas, & coal sector, ThomsonReuters and Infrastructure Journal on project finance, and GlobalData for the power sector. Some data is publicly available; for example, the U.S. Energy Information Administration makes its data available for free. At a high level, green /brown metrics can be used as follows:

- Portfolio construction – project finance. Projects can be distinguished as green or brown through taxonomies, and investors can use these metrics to set minimumgreen targets or screen brown projects.
- Portfolio construction – bonds. Data on green / brown exposure is limited in the bond space, but financial data on business segmentation by sector can be used (c.f. p. 50). In addition, there is a growing universe of labeled green bonds.
- Portfolio construction – listed equities. Investors can construct indices using green / brown exposure metrics in addition to carbon footprinting for key high-carbon sectors. Beyond technology-specific metrics used for tilting, indices can be constructed on the basis of labeling companies green or brown based on shares of revenues derived from a certain technology. South Pole Group and Trucost have developed metrics on the fraction of revenues derived from coal.
- Engagement – private equity and listed equity. Investors can engage with companies on corporate capital allocation decisions, specifically on capital expenditure using green/brown taxonomies and sector-specific intensity metrics.
- Investor positioning. Investors can partially aggregate green/brown exposure metrics for public reporting. Portfolio-level indicators are currently being developed by several data providers including MSCI and the Financial Times Stock Exchange. Key challenges are access to data and the extent to which green / brown categories distinguish between climate impact within categories (e.g. between gas and coal).

Green/ brown metrics are currently limited to specific sectors, and cannot be easily aggregated or compared across providers.

Financial data can help inform nonfinancial activity data. Investors can use financial data to track the capital expenditure intensity or share in indices, the value of fixed assets, or sectorspecific data such as installed capacity. However, these data to not necessarily inform on the extent to which a capital expenditure is climate friendly. They can be used as a proxy, however, for climate friendliness. These data, together with data like EBIT and rate of return, are also relevant from a risk perspective. From an engagement perspective, it may also be interesting to look at climate and financial data in combination with the structure of financing. These data can show the extent to which investors can influence internal sources of capital.

Sector-specific energy and carbon indicators are the quality indicators provided by specialized analysts of ESG (Environmental, Social, Governance), which were discussed above. Climate environmental, social, and governance (ESG) scores are qualitative indicators given to companies based on climate-related issues. Such scores are usually embedded in broader ESG scores used primarily for screening portfolios. Such scores generally focus on risk but integrate elements related to climate friendliness as well.

They are used less frequently and include the reporting of specific energy and / or emission indicators in absolute terms (eg saved kWh, megawatts MW) or ratios (eg CO2 / kWh). Such indicators are very useful, as a key performance indicator (CPI) can be derived for each sector or technology in an appropriate way. There is currently no standardized definition of ESG. This is reflected in the scope and type of indicators used by the various agencies in determining their indicators and ratings. Another limitation is that ESG results usually take a best-in-class[43] approach in individual sectors. A problem is the subjectivity of the results in determining the quality indicators and in the weighing, which always creates a risk for the validity of the indicator. Therefore, climate assessments are still identified with a "black box"[44]. The disadvantage of sector-specific energy and carbon indicators is that they require efforts by the bank to generate non-financial (energy, carbon, technology) sector-specific information, which in most cases is missing (Weber and Chris, 2018). Finally, climate assessments (ESGs) are in themselves of limited applicability.

In general, the most appropriate choice of indicator is a function of the purpose of the analysis (Thomä and Dupré, 2018). The advantages and disadvantages of the different groups are presented in Annex 3. Different metrics are more appropriate for different investor climate strategies. The most commonly used metric—carbon footprinting—has significant advantages in public signaling and cross-sectoral

[43] "Best investment grade" refers to the composition of portfolios through active selection only of those companies that meet certain environmental, social and management criteria.

[44] It is not clear what data is included in the analyzes leading to the respective ratings / ratings of the companies provided by the ESG rating agencies. In the absence of such information, it is not certain that the analysis is complete or objective

exposure assessment, but is not equipped to inform investment decisionsл Thus it should be complemented by other metrics including sector-specific green/brown metrics and ESG carbon ratings, which include a qualitative (though subjective) assessment of the company's business strategy and can capture forward looking aspects like R&D and capex strategies. Although there is no single perfect indicator, investors can take meaningful action by using a combination of metrics tailored to the appropriate asset class to inform their strategy, while continuously integrating new indicators as they are developed.

While considering target setting and performance tracking, it is also crucial for investors to track and engage with projects developing new and improved metrics.

Avoided GHG emissions. Carbon metrics are currently almost exclusively brown metrics. However, several data providers and institutions are developing methods to track emissions reductions or "avoided emissions" at project and company levels.

Locked-in GHG emissions. A key weakness of current carbon footprinting methods is the inability to account for future emissions and the lock-in effect of physical assetsл While there are significant questions around these types of metrics (Annex 1), simple proxies can already be applied.

Specific issues related to carbon footprinting. Issues such as consistency in allocation and double counting challenge the consistency of carbon footprinting across methods and data providers

Defining green and brown. Taxonomies around green and brown are still poorly developed, but the Climate Bonds Initiative is developing taxonomies for a number of sectors. A process has also been launched by the German G7 presidency. In terms of brown metrics, work by the Carbon Tracker Initiative and others is helping to define which types of high-carbon investments may be aligned with 2° C roadmaps and which investments are misaligned.

Tracking capital expenditure. A key shortcoming of current data frameworks is the extent to which capital expenditure data by energchnology is missing. Some companies do disclose such data but reporting is far from universal. The biggest challenges relate partly to corporate reporting and, in the major climate-related sectors to data aggregation by data providers.

Setting targets. Climate scenarios do not enable setting GHG reduction or investment targets for each sector or company. Two international research efforts, both based on the IEA scenarios – the Sectoral Decarbonization Approachat company level and the Sustainable Energy Investment (SEI) Metrics Research Consortium at portfolio level are currently addressing this issue.

The main results of analysis of the reporting of sustainability in the banking sector confirms that:

- Environmental reporting should be carried out at at least 2 levels - strategic and operational.
- All government and voluntary initiatives unite around the need for operational environmental risk assessment.
- The analysis of the most frequently used indicators at the operational level for the environment in the bank statements highlights the reporting of greenhouse gas emissions, brown-green indicators, sector-specific energy indicators.
- The study contributes with a modified framework for assessing the environmental sustainability of banks, which is a combination of both strategic initiatives of banks for environmental protection and measures taken at the management and operational levels.
- There are some serious misconceptions in Bulgaria about the exact nature of CSR and sustainability – it is mostly expressed in compliance with legal norms and restrictions or philantropic voluntary activities.

Conclusion

Over the last few years, various market and industrial initiatives have focused on the convergence of reporting standards covering climate issues, as well as on bringing and improving the comparability of climate indicators. These efforts include work to harmonize greenhouse gas (GHG) reporting methods to allow banking organizations to measure funded greenhouse gas emissions through their loans and investments.

The recently established working group on "Financial Statements Related to Nature" is expected to provide an evaluation framework by the end of 2022. The financial sector plays a leading role in the development of environmentally friendly financial solutions and investments. In a digital transformation, organizations cannot rely solely on financial and material resources to achieve their goals. (Ovcharova, 2019) Environmental problems are undoubtedly a challenge, but they also open up new opportunities for development.

Accounting for carbon emissions, setting adequate targets and incentives and disclosing transparent information to investors allows us to track progress in environmental risk management and the need for corrective action. For theeffectiveness of the measures taken, it is important to introduce specific indicators to measure the results of the efforts made. At the operational level, it could be recommended that all banks provide information on direct and in particular indirect GHG emissions in Scope 1 and Scope 2 and, where appropriate, GHG emissions in Scope 3 and associated risks.

Environmental risk reports should be subject to appropriate internal management processes, such as those used for financial disclosures, and included in the list of key financial documents. Emphasis needs to be placed on quantitative indicators to take account of environmental risk, in particular the disclosure of indicators of the financial impact of risks related to climate change and environmental protection. Banks should provide the necessary data on climate change and the impact that the environment will have on activities such as pricing, credit risk and customer relationship management. Lack of data should not be an obstacle to action.

Regardless of the differences in the nuances of the implemented policies, the bank management should assess the growing importance of the ecological corporate responsibility and the ways of adaptation to the changing environment. Incorporating environmental considerations into key banking activities can contribute to sustainable development. A forward-looking corporate leadership of a sustainable banking organization should integrate the concepts of environmental sustainability and CSR into its strategy to achieve better financial and non-financial results.

Appendix A. International initiatives for environmental protection

Year	Measures taken and international conferences related to climate change	Related Documents
1979	First World Conference on Climate Change, Geneva. Calls on all peoples to strongly support the proposed program and strategies to help countries make better use of climate information in planning social and economic development.	PROCEEDINGS OF THE WORLD CLIMATE CONFERENCE, A CONFERENCE OF EXPERTS ON CLIMATE AND MANKIND, GENEVA, 12-23 FEBRUARY 1979 https://library.wmo.int/pmb_ged/wmo_537_en.pdf
1987	Montreal Protocol. It is designed to protect the ozone layer by gradually eliminating the production of numerous substances that cause ozone depletion.	The Montreal Protocol, https://ec.europa.eu/clima/sites/clima/files/docs/montreal_prot_en.pdf
1988	The Intergovernmental Panel on Climate Change (IPCC) has been established. It is widely accepted by its sponsors, governments and the competent bodies of the UN Framework Convention as an authoritative source of information on climate change.	PRINCIPLES GOVERNING IPCC WORK https://www.ipcc.ch/pdf/ipccprinciples/ipccprinciples.pdf
1988	Conference in Toronto. Emphasizes the need to "reduce CO2 emissions by around 20% from 1988 to 2005." The 20% figure continues to be used as a benchmark by environmental non-governmental organizations (NGOs) and some nations.	The Changing Atmosphere: Implications For Global Security http://cmosarchives.ca/History/ChangingAtmosphere1988e.pdf
1989	Conference in Ottawa. Includes new elements in a framework convention for the protection of the atmosphere.	Ottawa Meeting (1989) Meeting statement of the International Meeting if Legal and HJlicy Experts

		on the Protection if the Atmosphere, Ottawa, Canada
1989	A conference in Tata that defines global warming as the greatest crisis facing humanity. The first international meeting on climate change, addressing the concerns of developing countries.	Tata Conference Statement (1989) International Conference on Global Warming and Climate Change: Perspectives from Developing Countries, Tokyo Conference (1989).
1989	The Hague Conference, at which the signatories agree to promote the creation of a new institutional authority to combat global warming.	The Hague Declaration on the Environment, https://www.jstor.org/stable/20693363?seq=1#page_scan_tab_contents
1990	Second World Climate Conference in Geneva. It is the most comprehensive call for joint international action on climate change.	Director-General of the United Nations Educational, Scientific and Cultural Organization (UNESCO) at the closure of the Second World Climate Conference https://www.dgvn.de/fileadmin/user_upload/DOKUMENTE/WCC-3/Declaration_WCC2.pdf
1990	Conference in Bergen. Specifies the specific measures needed to combat climate change	Bergen Declaration https://www.regjeringen.no/globalassets/upload/kilde/md/rap/2002/0002/ddd/pdfv/156076-engelsk.pdf
1992	The United Nations Framework Convention on Climate Change (UNFCCC) has been signed together with the UN Convention on Biological Diversity and the UN Convention to Combat Desertification.	United Nations Framework Convention On Climate Change https://unfccc.int/resource/docs/convkp/conveng.pdf
1994	UNFCCC enters into force. Its aim is to "stabilize greenhouse gas concentrations in the atmosphere at a level	https://treaties.un.org/doc/Publication/CN/2016/CN.735.2016-Eng.pdf

	that would prevent dangerous anthropogenic interference in the climate system"	
1995	The first COP 1 conference is held in Berlin. An agreement has been reached on the first joint measures in the framework of international action on climate change.	DOCUMENTS OF THE CONFERENCE OF THE PARTIES AT ITS FIRST SESSION (COP1) http://unfccc.int/cop5/resource/cop1.html
1996	COP 2 is being held in Geneva, Switzerland. Accepts the scientific findings on climate change proposed by the Intergovernmental Panel on Climate Change (IPCC). Rejects uniform "harmonized policies" and calls for legally binding medium-term goals.	DOCUMENTS OF THE CONFERENCE OF THE PARTIES, AT ITS SECOND SESSION (COP2) http://unfccc.int/cop5/resource/cop2.html
1997	The Kyoto Protocol - formally adopted in December at COP 3. The Protocol legally binds countries to emission reduction targets.	SESSIONS, COP3 https://unfccc.int/processandmeetings/conferences /past-conferences/kyotoclimatechangeconference-december-1997/cop-3
1998	COP 4 is taking place in Buenos Aires, Argentina, where Member States are adopting a two-year Action Plan to develop mechanisms for implementing the Kyoto Protocol.	SESSIONS, COP4 https://unfccc.int/processandmeetings/conferences /pastconferences/buenosairesclimatechangeconferencenovember1998/cop-4
1999	COP 5 is being held in Bonn, Germany. It is a technical meeting and does not come to conclusions.	SESSIONS, COP5 https://unfccc.int/processandmeetings/conferences /past-conferences/bonn-climatechangeconference-october-1999/cop-5
2000	COP 6, Part I, takes place in The Hague, the Netherlands, at which the parties agree to meet again. COP 6, Part II takes place in Bonn, Germany, and the Bonn Agreements are signed. All countries except the United States agree to implement the mechanisms of the Kyoto Protocol	SESSIONS, COP6 https://unfccc.int/processandmeetings/conferences /past-conferences/the-hague-climate-conference-november-2000/cop-6

		https://unfccc.int/processandmeetings/conferences/past-conferences/bonn-climatechangeconference-july-2001/cop-6-2
2001	COP 7's Marrakesh agreements have been signed, detailing the rules for implementing the Kyoto Protocol, creating new funding and planning tools and a technology transfer framework	SESSIONS, COP7 https://unfccc.int/processandmeetings/conferences/pastconferences/marrakechclimatechangeconference-october-2001/cop-7
2002	COP 8 is being held in Delhi, India. The countries adopted the Delhi Ministerial Declaration, which called on developed countries to transfer technology to developing countries.	SESSIONS, COP8 https://unfccc.int/processandmeetings/conferences/pastconferences/newdelhiclimatechangeconference-october-2002/cop-8
2003	COP 9 is being held in Milan, Italy. New guidelines for reporting emissions are being adopted based on IPCC recommendations. The Special Climate Change Fund (SCCF) and the Least Developed Countries Fund (LDCF) have been introduced.	SESSIONS, COP9 https://unfccc.int/processandmeetings/conferences/pastconferences/milanclimate-changeconference-december-2003/cop-9
2004	COP 10 is being held in Buenos Aires, Argentina. The progress made since their first conference 10 years ago and future challenges are discussed, with a special focus on climate change mitigation and adaptation. The Buenos Aires Action Plan is being adopted to promote better adaptation of developing countries to climate change.	SESSIONS, COP10 https://unfccc.int/process/conferences/pastconferences/buenosairesclimatechangeconferencedecember-2004/cop-10
2005	COP 11 / CMP 1 is being held in Montreal, Canada. This conference is the first since the entry into force of the Kyoto Protocol. The Annual Meeting of the Parties (COP) is complemented by the first annual meeting of the Parties to the Kyoto Protocol (CMP). Countries that ratify the	SESSIONS, COP11 https://unfccc.int/process/conferences/pastconferences/montreal-climatechangeconferencedecember-2005/cop-11

	UNFCCC but do not accept the Kyoto Protocol have observer status.	
2006	COP 12 / CMP 2 is being held in Nairobi, Kenya. A five-year plan is being adopted for developing countries to support adaptation to climate change.	SESSIONS, COP12 https://unfccc.int/process/conferences/past-conferences/nairobi-climate-change-conference-november-2006/cop-12
2007	COP 13 / CMP 3 is being held in Bali. The Parties agree on a Bali Action Plan, which provides for measures to mitigate greenhouse gas emissions following the expiry of the Kyoto Protocol in 2012. The Bali Action Plan does not require binding greenhouse gas emission targets for developing countries.	SESSIONS, COP13 https://unfccc.int/process/conferences/past-conferences/bali-climate-change-conference-december-2007/cop-13
2008	COP 14 / CMP 4 is being held in Poznań, Poland. The countries are starting negotiations on the funding mechanism to help poor countries adapt to the effects of climate change.	SESSIONS, COP14 https://unfccc.int/process/conferences/pastconferences/poznan-climate-change-conferencedecember-2008/cop-14
2009	The COP 15 agreement in Copenhagen to reduce emissions and mitigate the effects of climate change has been signed, and this agreement is non-binding.	SESSIONS, COP15 https://unfccc.int/process/conferences/pastconferences/copenhagenclimatechangeconferencedecember-2009/cop-15
2010	The Cancun agreements, prepared by the Conference of the Parties to COP 16, have been adopted and are the greatest collective effort to reduce emissions in a mutually responsible way.	SESSIONS, COP16 https://unfccc.int/process/conferences/pastconferences/cancun-climate-changeconferencenovember-2010/cop-16
2011	The Durban Platform for Enhanced Action, drawn up and adopted at COP 17, has been introduced, recognizing the need for a post-2020 climate change plan.	SESSIONS, COP17

		https://unfccc.int/process/conferences/pastconferences/durban-climate-change-conferencenovember-2011/cop-17
2012	COP 18 is taking place in Doha. The Doha amendment to the Kyoto Protocol has been adopted. The amendment includes: new commitments for the parties to the Kyoto Protocol; a revised list of greenhouse gases to be reported by the parties and amendments to several articles of the Kyoto Protocol.	SESSIONS, COP18 https://unfccc.int/process/conferences/pastconferences/doha-climate-change-conference-november-2012/cop-18
2013	The key decisions of COP 19 / CMP 9, which include the further development of the Durban Platform, the Green Climate Fund and long-term finance, the Warsaw Framework for REDD Plus and the Warsaw International Loss and Damage Mechanism.	SESSIONS, COP19 https://unfccc.int/processandmeetings/conferences/pastconferences/warsawclimatechangeconference-november-2013/cop-19
2014	COP 20 is being held in Lima, Peru, in December. The main goal of the conference is to reduce greenhouse gas (GHG) emissions in order to limit the increase in global temperature to 2 degrees Celsius above current levels.	SESSIONS, COP20 https://unfccc.int/process/conferences/pastconferences/lima-climate-change-conference-december-2014/cop-20
2015	The COP 21 is taking place in Paris and the Paris Agreement is adopted on 12 December, which regulates measures to reduce climate change from 2020. The agreement provides for a global action plan for climate change, limiting global warming to well below 2 ° C and is signed by 195 countries	SESSIONS, COP21 https://unfccc.int/processandmeetings/conferences/past-conferences/paris-climatechangeconference-november-2015/cop-21
2016	COP 22 is being held in Marrakech, the North African country of Morocco. The main problem is water scarcity,	SESSIONS, COP22

	water purity and water-related sustainability in the developing world, including many African countries.	https://unfccc.int/processandmeetings/conferences/pastconferences/marrakechclimatechangeconference-november-2016/cop-22
2017	COP 23 is taking place (November 6-17) in Bonn, Germany. It ends with the so-called Fiji's implementation requirement, which sets out the steps needed to implement the Paris Agreement in 2020. This is the first COP conference since President Donald Trump announced that the United States would withdraw from the agreement.	SESSIONS, COP23 https://unfccc.int/processandmeetings/conferences/unclimatechangeconferencenovember2017/sessions-of-negotiating-bodies/cop-23
2018	COP24 was held between 2 and 15 December 2018 in Katowice, Poland. The conference agreed on rules for implementing the Paris Agreement - how governments can measure and report on their efforts to reduce emissions.	SESSIONS, COP24 https://unfccc.int/processandmeetings/conferences/pastconferences/katowiceclimatechangeconference-december2018/sessionsofnegotiatingbodies/cop-24
2019	COP 25 (2-13 December 2019) was chaired by the Government of Chile. The conference was designed to take the next important steps in the UN climate change process.	SESSIONS, COP25 https://unfccc.int/abouttheunclimatechangeconference-december-2019
2021	COP26 took place in Glasgow, Scotland, United Kingdom, from 31 October to 13 November 2021. The 197 participating countries signed the Glasgow Climate Pact, aimed at preventing dangerous climate change.	The GLASGOW CLIMATE PACT, https://unfccc.int/process-and-meetings/the-paris-agreement/the-glasgow-climate-pactkeyoutcomes-from-cop26

Appendix B. Advantages and disadvantages of environmental indicators

	Characteristic	Application	Advantages	Disadvantages
GHG accounting	Cross-sectoral assessment of greenhouse gas consumption by investors	• Linking the dots between portfolios and climate change • Screening of project financing • Real estate energy efficiency measures • Commitment to reducing corporate emissions in the short term • Building portfolios for issued shares ideally together with green / brown indicators • Public communication and reporting	• Wide awareness of the intensity of carbon emissions in individual sectors • Significance among corporate clients and experience • The standardization of corporate reporting in various sectors, which allows reporting at the portfolio level	• High uncertainty related to financial asset data • Incomplete coverage • Lack of an accounting standard • Data variability related to external factors
Green/ Brown metrics	Sectoral indicators that distinguish between activities and technologies such as solutions (green) and climate problems (brown)	• Negative / positive screening for project funding • Negative screening and environmental targets for corporate bonds (eg green bonds)	• Quantitative indicator with high data transparency • Relevant indicator for corporate governance	• Applicable only for key sectors • Problems in distinguishing climate friendliness into categories • There is no standardized format for summarizing

		• Building portfolios for issued shares together with carbon indicators • Investments in various technologies		data from individual sectors
ESG scores	Indicators based on quantitative and qualitative measures of climate, including carbon and green / brown exposure.	• Commitment to corporate strategies of companies • Engaging on climate issues along with non-climate issues	• Summarized indicators covering a number of factors • Well-established frameworks	• Black box • Risk of greenwashing • Not directly related to a specific strategy

Appendix C. Climate indicators examples by category

Category	Sample unit	Sample indicators
GHG emissions Range 1, 2 and 3; emission intensity	MT (metric tones)	• Absolute band 1, band 2 and band 3 GHG emissions • Funded issues by asset classes • Weighted average carbon intensity • Greenhouse gas emissions per MWh of electricity produced • Gross global greenhouse gas emissions from scope 1 covered by emission control regulations
Risks of transition Amount and degree of assets or business activities vulnerable to transition risks	Amount or percentage	• Volume of real estate collateral, highly exposed to the risk of transition • Concentration of credit exposure to carbon-related assets • Percentage of revenues from coal mining • Percentage of revenue in passenger-kilometers not covered by the Compensation and Reduction Scheme Carbon Offsetting and Reduction Scheme for International Aviation (CORSIA)
Physical risks Amount and degree of assets or business activities vulnerable to physical risks	Amount or percentage	• Number and value of mortgage loans in 100-year flood zones • Wastewater treatment capacity located in 100-year flood zones • Revenues related to abstracted and consumed water in regions with high or extremely high source water stress • Proportion of property, infrastructure or other alternative asset portfolios in an area subject to flooding, heat stress or water stress • Proportion of real assets exposed to climate hazards 1: 100 or 1: 200

Climate opportunities Share of revenue, assets or other business activities related to climate opportunities	mount or percentage	• Written net premiums related to energy efficiency and low carbon technologies • Number of (1) zero-emission (ZEV) vehicles sold, (2) hybrid vehicles and (3) hybrid vehicles • Revenues from products or services that support the transition to a low-carbon economy • Share of delivered homes certified according to the green building standard
Capital expenditures Amount of capital expenditures, financing or investments to climate risks and opportunities	Reporting currency	• Percentage of annual revenues invested in research and development of low-carbon products / services • Investment in climate adaptation measures (eg soil health, irrigation, technology) • Internal price of carbon
Carbon prices Price per tonne of greenhouse gas emissions used by the organization itself	Price in reporting currency, for MT CO_2e	• The price of carbon in the shadows, by geographical area • Part of the employee's annual discretionary bonus related to investments in climate-related products
Remuneration Share of executive management remuneration related to climate	Percentage, weight, description or amount in the reporting currency	• Integrate climate goals into long-term incentive cards for CEOs • Weighing the effectiveness against the objectives of the operational issues for the remuneration assessment card

References

1. Zhelyazkova, V. (2013). Climate Change and Environmental Risk Managmenet in the Activities of Financial Institutions. Sofia: Publishing House Sveti Grigorii Bogoslov.
2. Adom, PK (2020) Degree of financialization and energy efficiency in Sub-Saharan Africa: Do institutions matter? https://www.econstor.eu/bitstream/10419/237214/1/1735636924.pdf
3. Al-Dhaimesh, O. H. (2019). The effect of sustainability accounting disclosures on financial performance: an empirical study on the Jordanian banking sector. *Banks and Bank Systems*, *14*(2), 1.
4. Amuakwa-Mensah, F. (2022) Role of banking sector performance in renewable energy consumption, https://www.sciencedirect.com/science/article/pii/S0306261921013222
5. Araya, H. M. B., Mas, E. S., Garrido, F. P. (2014). Sustainability reporting in European cooperative banks: An exploratory analysis. In: REVESCO. Revista de Estudios Cooperativos, Vol. 115, pp. 30-56. Universidad Complutense de Madrid
6. Bal, Y., Faure, M., & Liu, J. (2014). The role of China's banking sector in providing green finance. Duke Envtl. L. & Pol'y F., 24, 89
7. Balasundaram, N. (2009). Determinants of Key Performance Indicators (KPIS) of Private Sector Banks in Sri Lanka. In: The Annals of The" Ştefan cel Mare" University of Suceava. Fascicle of The Faculty of Economics and Public Administration, 9(2), p. 10.
8. Bătae, O. M., Dragomir, V. D., & Feleagă, L. (2021). The relationship between environmental, social, and financial performance in the banking sector: A European study. Journal of Cleaner Production, 290, 125791.
9. Bouten, L. et. al. (2017). CSR Performance Proxies in Large-Sample Studies:'Umbrella Advocates', Construct Clarity and the'Validity Police'. Construct Clarity and the'Validity Police'(August 2017).
10. ECB, Banking Authority (2020) ECB report on institutions' climate-related and environmental risk disclosures, https://www.bankingsupervision.europa.eu/ecb/pub/pdf/ssm.ecbreportinstitutionsclimaterelatedenvironmentalriskdisclosures202011~e8e2ad20f6.en.pdf

11.Caby, J., Ziane, Y., & Lamarque, E. (2022). The impact of climate change management on banks profitability. Journal of Business Research, 142, 412-422.

12.Chenet, H., Thomä, J., Janci, D., Dupre, S., Hubert, R., Robins, N., Cruickshank, P. (2015). Financial risk and the transition to a low-carbon economy. Towards a carbon stress testing framework. Franse: INIS

13.Chowdhury, R. K. (2018). Corporate Sustainability and Financial Performance of Bangladeshi Banks (Master's thesis, University of Waterloo).

14.Djalilov, K. et. al. (2015). Corporate social responsibility and bank performance in transition countries. In: Corporate Ownership and Control, Vol. 13(1CONT8), pp. 879-888.

15.Dr. Bishawjit Chandra Deb, Shuvabrata Saha, Md. Mominur Rahman. (2020). "DOES GREEN ACCOUNTING PRACTICE AFFECT BANK PERFORMANCE? A STUDY ON LISTED BANKS OF DHAKA STOCK EXCHANGE IN BANGLADESH". PalArch's Journal of Archaeology of Egypt / Egyptology, 17(9), 7225 - 7247. Retrieved from https://archives.palarch.nl/index.php/jae/article/view/5460

16.EEFIG WORKING GROUP ON RISK ASSESSMENT – FINAL REPORT (2021) https://op.europa.eu/o/opportalservice/downloadhandler?identifier=32387875b94b11ecb6f401aa75ed71a1&format=PDF&language=en&productionSystem=cellar

17.Feridun, M., Güngör, H. (2022) Climate-Related Prudential Risks in the Banking Sector: A Review of the Emerging Regulatory and Supervisory Practices, https://mdpi-res.com/d_attachment/sustainability/sustainability-12-05325/article_deploy/sustainability-1205325.pdf?version=1593598730

18.Forsyth, T. (2011). Global Environmental Problems & Politics. London: University of London (https://london.ac.uk/sites/default/files/study-guides/dv3166-global-environmental-problems-politics-study-guide.pdf, 25.08.2017).

19.Galant, A., Cadez, S. (2017). Corporate social responsibility and financial performance relationship: a review of measurement approaches. In: Economic research-Ekonomska istraživanja, Vol. 30(1), pp.676-693.

20.Gercheva, S. (2020). Tax or Trade: Community Energy Taxation in the Context of Climate Neutrality. Izvestia Journal of the Union of Scientists - Varna. Economic Sciences Series, 9(1), pp.170-173. DOI: https://doi.org/10.36997/IJUSV-ESS/2020.9.1.168.

21. Grigoris, G. (2016). The challenges of corporate social responsibility assessment methodologies. In: International Journal of Economics & Business Administration (IJEBA), Vol. 4(1), pp. 39-55.
22. Horuckova, M., Baudassé, T. (2017). Content analysis applied to social and environmental reporting. In: Acta academica karviniensia, Vol. 17(4), pp. 32-45.
23. Marinov, IS (2015) CORPORATE SOCIAL RESPONSIBILITY OF BULGARIAN BANKING SECTOR – MISSION AND BUSINESS PRACTICE, Dialoge- E Journal, https://www.ceeol.com/search/article-detail?id=468996
24. Monte, T. (2009). Application of Global Reporting Initiative (GRI) in the sustainability reporting of financial services (Master's thesis).
25. Munjal, P., & Malarvizhi, P. (2021). Impact of Environmental Performance on Financial Performance: Empirical Evidence from Indian Banking Sector. Journal of Technology Management for Growing Economies, 12(1), 13-24.
26. Snezhanka Ovcharova, 2019. "Management Of Creativityâ€"A Factor For Sustainable Competitive Development," International scientific and practical conference "human resource management", University of Economics - Varna, number y:2019:i:1:p:176-187, December.
27. TAWFIK, O. I., KAMAR, S. H., & BILAL, Z. O. (2021). The effect of sustainable dimensions on the financial performance of commercial banks: A comparative study in emerging markets. *The Journal of Asian Finance, Economics and Business*, *8*(3), 1121-1133.
28. Perez, O. (2016). The Green Economy Paradox: A Critical Inquiry into Sustainability Indexes. In: Minn. JL Sci. & Tech., Vol. 17, p. 153.Scholtens, B., van't Klooster, S (2019) Sustainability and bank risk. Palgrave Commun 5, 105, https://doi.org/10.1057/s41599-019-0315-9
29. Stan Dupré, Jakob Thomä and Sophie Dejonckheere (2015) CLIMATE STRATEGIES AND METRICSм EXPLORING OPTIONS FOR INSTITUTIONAL INVESTORSp WRI, UNEP-FI AND 2° INVESTING INITIATIVE PORTFOLIO CARBON INITIATIVE, https://www.unepfi.org/publications/climatechangepublications/portfolio-carbon-initiative-publications/climate-strategies-and-metrics-2/
30. Szymon Mikolajczyk, Egbert Liese, Kristian Brüning Nicolette Bartlett, Gediz Kaya (2017) Internal Carbon Pricing and Climate Finance Tracking for Banks: Implementation Guidance Report,

https://www.climatefocus.com/publications/internal-carbon-pricing-and-climate-finance-tracking-banks-implementation-guidance

31. TCFD (2021) Guidance on Metrics, Targets, and Transition Plans, https://www.fsb-tcfd.org/publications/
32. UNEP FI, WRI. (2015). Climate Strategies and Metrics: Exploring Options for Institutional Investors
33. UNEP FI (2018) Extending our horizonts, Assessing credit risk and opportunity in a changing climate: Outputs of a working group of 16 banks piloting the TCFD Recommendations, https://www.unepfi.org/wordpress/wpcontent/uploads/2018/04/EXTENDING-OUR-HORIZONS.pdf
34. Weber, Ch. (2018). Exploring Metrics to Measure the Climate Progress of Bankis, Portfolio Carbon Initiative (https://ghgprotocol.org/sites/default/files/standards/Exploring%20Metrics%20to%20Measure%20the%20Climate%20Progress%20of%20Banks.pdf, 25.08.2017).
35. Weber, O. (2015). The Banking Sector's Contribution to Sustainable Growth–Risk Assessment, Sustainable Finance, Voluntary Initiatives and Regulations. Canada
36. Weber, O. (2017). Corporate sustainability and financial performance of Chinese banks. Waterloo University, In: Sustainability Accounting, Management and Policy Journal.
37. VELITCHKOV, D. K. (2013). CSR: THE CASE OF EUROPEAN MNC SUBSIDIARIES OPERATING IN THE CONTEXT OF BULGARIA AS AN EMERGING ECONOMY.
38. Verkerk, D. (2014). Corporate social responsible behaviour in the financial industry (Doctoral dissertation, NSBE-UNL).
39. Zhang, X.; Wang, Z.; Zhong, X.; Yang, S.; Siddik, A.B. Do Green Banking Activities Improve the Banks' Environmental Performance? The Mediating Effect of Green Financing. Sustainability 2022, 14, 989. https://doi.org/10.3390/su14020989

Shari'ah compliance

In a european banking context

Sevgi Osman

Varna Free University "Chernorizets Hrabar" ORCID 0000-0002-5108-5476

Nedyalko Valkanov

University of Economics - Varna

Abstract

Compliance rules existed even before the earliest modern financial and banking regulations. This paper aims to compare compliance systems in terms of the principles of Islamic finance with those of conventional finance and to determine whether they can exist "under one roof". It focuses on the importance of Shari'ah compliance in Islamic corporate governance and the main body for its assurance – the Shari'ah Supervisory board, which takes various shapes in different legal and regulatory systems. Using the content analysis method, Shari'ah compliance among European Islamic banks (or Islamic windows) was investigated and on this basis the conclusion was drawn that, with the help of internal and external efforts, an effective framework for Shari'ah compliance can be ensured even in traditional financial institutions. Such a framework is needed mostly for the clarification of Shari'ah rules and norms in societies with a vested interest in Islamic financial markets and products.

Key words: compliance; Islamic banks; Islamic windows; European regulations

Introduction

Islamic banking has entered into an increasing number of non-majority Muslim countries. This upward trend should not be overlooked given the oil wealth of majority Muslim countries. Indeed, Islamic financial markets in Gulf Cooperation Countries (GCC) and Southeast Asia will continue to accumulate wealth, and that is why Western nations should make ready different ways to attract international investors. However, in spite of the last several years' rapid financial growth, many regulatory authorities and practitioners can not define the process by which Islamic banks could be introduced into a conventional system.

Islamic finance is based on "Shari'ah" principles established by rulings, known as *fatwas*, of qualified Muslim scholars. Some of the issues covered by these rulings can indeed be quite confusing, as a result of which the respective institutions often seek the assistance of experts in this field. Such issues have led to a common practice among Islamic banks to appoint their own boards of Shari'ah scholars.

Islamic banking relies on the support of regulatory authorities and legal provisions to a greater extent than in traditional banking compliance with Shari'ah law being paramount. To this end, Islamic banks have established robust corporate governance structures to oversee compliance with Shari'ah principles (Bouheni & Ammi, 2015).

These guidelines should not favour the progress of Islamic financial operations nor hinder their development; they should create prerequisites for the parallel existence and even effective competition of both conventional and Islamic forms of banking.

However, this does not mean putting an equal sign between them. When regulating Islamic banking institutions, regulators have to add over the existing traditional regulation practices.

Separation of Conventional and Islamic Banking – Emergence of Islamic Windows

According to Benaissa (2007), a regulator can determine how much can be divided between Islamic and conventional banking. Regulatory practices all around the world range from not allowing Islamic Financial Institutions (IFIs) to a fully Shari'ah- compliant banking sector. In the middle is a dual framework which encourages the development of Islamic banks by protecting them from their competition with conventional analogues offering Islamic products. Whether using one form or another, regulators must take into account the potential consequences this decision may have.

More and more, an effective structure called "Islamic windows" can be seen on the financial landscape. The Islamic bank window is a department of a conventional bank offering Islamic or Shari'ah-compatible financial products and services. In fact, the interconnection goes in two directions: this form could introduce conventional finance activities in Islamic markets or, by contrast, Islamic financial operations could be established in non-Muslim markets, e.g., in Europe. An Islamic bank window is valid only if it complies with the requirements set by the AAOIFI, the Accounting and Auditing Organization for Islamic Financial Institutions (Yaquby, 2005):

- Complete segregation of funds;
- Existence of a Shari'ah supervisory board (SSB);
- Management based fully on Islamic concepts;
- Safeguarding of Muslim investors' funds against negligence, trespass, and fraud;
- Compliance with AAOIFI standards.

The bulk of Islamic countries' regulators either do not favour the Islamic bank window or impose the separation of Islamic from conventional banks for two main reasons:

- to prevent the mixing of conventional and Islamic banking activities, which is "impermissible" under Shari'ah principles (International Monetary Fund, 2017);

- to mitigate different regulatory frameworks, the result of which is referred to as "regulatory arbitrage" risk (Hasan & Risfandy, 2021).

Despite the contradictions regarding these "windows", Islamic banks could benefit from the long-lived conservative operations of conventional banks. On the other hand, Islamic windows could enhance the competition on Islamic banking markets, which would reduce the cost of Islamic financial products. In addition, Islamic bank windows may contribute to the financial inclusion of Islamic banking in Western or other non- Muslim countries with a low demand for Islamic bank services (International Monetary Fund, 2017). Ratnasari (2021) has also found that Islamic windows were more efficient than full-fledged Islamic banks.

Islamic windows are more stable than fully Islamic banks because they rely on their counterparts' assets, operating in parallel under one roof with conventional banking institutions (Salami & Adeyemi, 2015). However, they are reported separately with their reports being consolidated within the main financial statements of parent banks. These banks have committees or other similar structures, which will be discussed a little later, that monitor the compliance of their operations with Shari'ah principles (Abdul Majid et al., 2011b).

Islamic finance windows of conventional financial institutions have become a notable trend as the Islamic finance industry continues to develop. With their wide- ranging acceptance and increased visibility, Islamic finance windows play a crucial rôle in expanding the availability of financial products and services compliant with Shari'ah principles and rules. However, having Islamic finance windows (versus full- fledged IFIs) results in additional risk factors for the Islamic finance industry as a whole, due to potentially weak Shari'ah governance and / or compliance and certain other risks unique to the windows model. It is of utmost importance to apply Shari'ah governance principles to Islamic finance windows in a holistic manner to ensure that their operations maintain integrity and Shari'ah compliance while fulfilling their fiduciary responsibilities towards all stakeholders in a fair and transparent manner.

Conventional vs Shari'ah Non-compliance Risk

Against this background, an attempt could be made to compare compliance systems in terms of the principles of Islamic finance described above with those of the conventional financial sector. Before that, a brief overview will be made of the emergence and evolution of regulatory compliance functions practiced by financial institutions. In its most general sense, compliance is the adherence to a pre- established set of norms and rules regarding business conduct. It should be noted that such practices existed even before the first modern financial and banking regulations. In this respect, the prototype of such activities can be traced back to the dawn of economic relations. The laws of King Hammurabi of Babylon (18th century BC) prescribing norms of good conduct in trade, the scriptures of the major religions (especially regarding interest), and the strict rules regarding the secrecy and quality of crafts practiced by medieval guilds are but a few illustrations of rules and standards of conduct resembling today's compliance (Valkanov, 2019).

In modern history, the emergence of practices with strict adherence to certain standards in business can be dated back to the introduction of mass production in the early 20th century. The resulting industrial and manufacturing corporations imposed their own systems to provide internal institutional tools to ensure compliance. A pioneer in this respect was the Toyota Motor Company, which in 1963 also formalised specific compliance requirements within the scope of its updated quality policy within the *total-quality-management* (TQM) framework. After the 1980s, compliance issues gradually entered the banking sector. Specific preconditions for this were several scandals related to improper securities transactions carried out by investment banks in the USA (particularly Salomon Brothers, Inc. and Kidder, Peabody & Co.). This was followed by the creation of specialised internal regulatory control units in both banks: a prototype of the modern regulatory compliance units present in the structures of any modern financial institution today. In 1993, again as a result of previous misconduct, the Swiss Schweizerische Bankverein (SBV) introduced a comprehensive compliance organisation.

These cases of misconduct have been accompanied by other major procurement abuses and corporate scandals in the USA, leading to the creation of relevant specialised legislation. An example in this regard is the US Foreign Corrupt

Practices Act (FCPA) of 1977, considered the first piece of legislation to institutionalise issues of compliance. For example, after the famous Enron scandal, the Sarbanes–Oxley Act of 2002 introduced a number of requirements to increase financial transparency within publicly-held companies. Alongside this, the introduction of standards for ethical behaviour in large corporations and government institutions is gaining popularity.

In a European context, the UK was the first country to introduce a detailed corporate governance "code" and was also the first to include the "comply or explain" concept with the *Cadbury Report*, which contained the framework for a new set of rules. The code was fully launched in 1992 and has been copied in other national codes since. Other major regulatory initiatives introducing corporate governance principles and best practices for public companies are the French *Vienot Report* of 1995 (updated in 1999) and AFEP-MEDEF Code of 2023, the Spanish *Olivencia Code* of 1998 and Unified Good Governance Code of 2006, the Italian *Preda Code* of 1999, the German Corporate Governance Code of 2002, known as the *Cromme Code*, the Dutch Corporate Governance Code (*Tabaksblat Code*) of 2003, etc.

As a general incentive for the introduction of such regulatory initiatives, one can point to a number of cases of misconduct and significant corporate scandals involving large public companies like Enron (2001) and Parmalat (2003). The discussion remains why, despite the existence of such a regulatory framework, misconduct continues among large public companies, such as the UK GlaxoSmithKline bribery scandal of 2013 and Tesco Accounting Scandal of 2014, German Volkswagen Dieselgate of 2015 and Wirecard fraud of 2020, and Switzerland's Credit Suisse collapse of 2023 – with numerous cases of illegal activities like money laundering, tax evasion, and corporate espionage.

In evolutionary terms, six stages can be noted in the advent of compliance within the operational activities of financial institutions. The *introduction stage* went from the late 1980s to 1990s and mainly involved investment banks and the securities trading units of large banking groups. Internal compliance units like these were usually established in the aftermath of corporate scandals, fraud, and other misconduct. Prior to that time, compliance activities were still treated as ancillary to those of business ethics. These include professional ethical standards and codes of conduct, whistleblowing systems, the articulation of corporate social responsibility values, etc.

The *second stage* covers the period after the end of the 1990s and the first years of the new millennium. Compliance activities then entered the banking industry en masse and ethical compliance became unified with the compliance sphere. The war against terrorism also necessitated a fundamentally new look at the rules for identifying the customers of financial institutions and monitoring their transactions. Of key significance was the introduction of the United States' Patriot Act (2001), on the basis of which these policies became virtually mandatory both for domestic financial institutions and for all those linked to the US financial system.

In the *third stage*, compliance left the banking segment and became part of the structures of other financial institutions. There has been full integration of all anti-money laundering (AML) / countering the financing of terrorism (CFT) activities into the scope of compliance. The growing importance of money laundering issues and the active integration of the financial sector (mainly through the banking system) in the various preventive initiatives have made compliance activities a key countermeasure mechanism to be implemented through dedicated internal units within the structures of financial institutions.

The fo*urth phase* of compliance development included its regulatory institutionalisation through the introduction of key national and international regulatory standards formalising compliance as a stand-alone policy (US Sarbanes–Oxley Act of 2002; COSO standards, 2004; BCBS, 2005; IOSCO, 2006). Alongside this, an understanding of the importance of the compliance function was being formulated. At the organisational level, the first compliance committees were formalised; where they did not exist, compliance was positioned within risk or internal audit committees.

The *fifth stage* in the evolutionary development of compliance followed the global financial crisis of 2007–2008. The numerous cases of misconduct observed during that period, both at the individual and institutional level, prove that effective compliance in the financial sector is an absolute necessity. The many instances of various misconduct by financial institutions, followed by multi-billion-dollar fines and compensation awards, attest to the critical need for effectively enforced compliance policies within organisations.

The explosion of the latest technological innovations in informatics marks the *sixth stage* in the evolution of financial compliance. After the emergence of FinTech, the Regulatory Technology segment (RegTech) quickly stood out. The opportunity to share regulatory expertise to some extent has relieved the regulatory burden borne by the financial sector as a result of post-crisis regulatory changes. Technologies using artificial intelligence, big data, and even blockchain also have found their application in compliance practices.

In 2005, the Basel Committee on Banking Supervision published the paper *Compliance and the Compliance Function in Banks*, in which compliance is seen as a top-level activity that achieves its highest effectiveness within a corporate culture where the board of directors and senior management meet standards of honesty and integrity (BCBS, 2005: 7). Once more, *compliance risk* is defined as "the risk of legal or regulatory sanctions, material financial loss, or loss to reputation a bank may suffer as a result of its failure to comply with laws, regulations, rules, related self-regulatory organisation standards, and codes of conduct applicable to its banking activities" (ibid.). This broad definition implies moving compliance beyond its basic definition solely with the purely normative context. What is more, it would be fair to say that compliance is essentially a broad category (often illustrated as an "umbrella term"), encompassing both regular activities and those outside the purely legal framework.

In this respect, the following illustrative systematisation of banking operational activities relevant to compliance can be given (Valkanov, 2019, pp. 141–148): normative compliance activities; product compliance; AML (antimoney laundering) and sanctions compliance activities; control activities; risk identification; reporting activities; coordinating compliance activities; business and personal ethics; technological activities.

On first reading, no parallel should be drawn between the Shari'ah-based principles of Islamic finance and traditional compliance policies, insofar as the former are based on canonically set principles and restrictions, while the latter facilitate the application of formalised legal norms and business regulations. On a more detailed rereading, however, more than one or two points of contact can be found that might serve for a more thorough comparative analysis.

Adherence to formalised rules. In conventional compliance, their source can be written laws but also uncodified practices (e.g., internal regulations or perceived self- limitations within the financial institution itself). In Islamic finance, we again have a codified source of legal rule, the Shari'ah, and also scholarly interpretations (fatwas[45]).

Institutional subordination. An example of such is the Basel Committee on Banking Supervision's treatment of the compliance function mentioned above. Similar definitions are given by other supranational institutions with quasi-regulatory status (e.g., IOSCO). In Islamic finance, for its part, we can point to the AAOIFI and IFSB standards as examples.

Ethical problems. Perhaps this is the most pronounced point of mutual contact. Insofar as the foundation of Islamic finance rests entirely upon strictly defined norms of conduct (avoidance of excessive risk, prohibition of charging interest, etc.), from the perspective of conventional compliance, aspects relating to the principles of prudent conduct based on codes of conduct and professional ethics can be pointed out.

Self-regulation. On the face of it, self-regulation and compliance are mutually exclusive activities, especially against the backdrop of the major failure of self-regulatory practices in the financial sphere in the context of the recent global financial crisis. However, the implementation of effective compliance policies can also be a path to conscious self- regulation[46]. From the perspective of Islamic financial norms, refracting the perception of risk and rate of return through the prism of a codified moral and ethical worldview is in itself a justification for embedding a permanent functioning self-regulatory mechanism.

On the other hand, Shari'ah compliance means adherence to the rules arising from the Quran (Holy Book), Sunnah (the traditions or known practices of the Prophet Muhammad), Izma (Consensus, Qiyas (Analogy), and the decisions and conclusions of experienced Islamic scholars. Shari'ah is essential for earning and keeping the confidence and loyalty of stakeholders as well as society: thus, it is

[45] Fatwas are legal opinions or rulings based on the teachings of the Quran.

[46] Self-aware regulation in finance is supported by Valkanov (2019). The aforementioned work supports the compliance thesis as an enabler of more effective self-regulation based on internal, individual financial institution-specific self-regulatory incentives and mechanisms. In this regard, the compliance function can also be seen as a softening buffer between the extremes of full self-regulation and total external regulation. Again, it is argued that conscious self-regulation acts as a preventive measure against the burden of over-regulation and constitutes a foundation for achieving qualitative internal self-control (Valkanov, 2019, pp. 219–221).

not by chance that it has been defined by Sarker (2022) as *"the backbone of Islamic banks"*.

An Islamic bank or IFI is recognised as Shari'ah-compliant if only its activities meet the Shari'ah pronouncements/resolutions issued by the respective Shari'ah boards. Therefore Shari'ah compliance is not only set by another type of compliance requirements but a philosophy of behaviour in an Islamic way. In countries whose central bodies like the national Shari'ah board or council have the power to issue such pronouncements/resolutions, IFIs must be compliant with them. These also have binding legal effects on all the IFIs within the concerned jurisdiction. Non-compliance will lead to voiding the underlying contracts of the Islamic bank or IFI and therefore to loss (Sarker, 2022).

Lailiya (2024) defines Shari'ah Non-Compliance Risk (SNCR) as "a risk associated with the inability or failure of Islamic financial institutions to comply with sharia provisions" (Oz et al., 2016). This risk category can be a threat for Islamic financial transactions and revenues (Mustapha et al., 2021) and even can cause the invalidation of contracts designed to be in accordance with Shari'ah principles (Ginena, 2014).

Obviously, Islamic banks are exposed to a very special kind of risk: "Sharia non-compliance risk distinguishes Islamic banks from traditional ones" (Che Azmi, 2021). Shari'ah compliance is a category considered to have higher priority (IBD, 2018) in the risk catalogue of Islamic banks. Shari'ah compliance across all products and services of Fis as well as their functions, activities, processes, roles, and responsibilities is essential (Ali, 2019).

This risk category is closely related to another: reputational risk. Investors and depositors could easily withdraw their funds after losing trust or in light of any doubts about their IFI's Shari'ah -compliance reputation (Basiruddin & Ahmed, 2020).

Academic questions mark the significance of this risk, but researchers still want to "dive deeper" so that all stakeholders, including managers, are aware of its importance. Only in this way it can be effectively managed and minimised (Lailiya, & Kusumaningtias, 2024).

Islamic banking customers continue to pose a major challenge to the industry by asking a highly relevant question, i.e., is the bank labelled as an "Islamic bank" really

Islamic? Consumers continue to have some level of scepticism towards the supposed Shari'ah compliance of Islamic banking businesses. According to Volker Nienhaus (2013, p. 40), the modern practice of Islamic banking is not fully embraced by all Muslims.

The answer to this question has many dimensions: standardising Shari'ah interpretations, forming primary markets of Islamic banks, establishing global Islamic liquidity centres, adding breadth and depth to the range of Islamic banking products, implementation of AAOIFI and IFSB Standards, strengthening the regulatory and legal environment, etc. The Islamic financial industry has tried to take some actions, but measuring Shari'ah non-compliance risk and defining the level of required capital to mitigate or prevent this risk is still limited due to the lack of a standardised Shari'ah risk rating model.

A bank based on Shari'ah ideology is expected to ensure, top-to-bottom and beginning-to-end, compliance which includes its aims, activities, operations, and management. Neglecting even a single stage of the Shari'ah compliance process could endanger the reputation of an Islamic bank. The IFSB defines SNCR as the risk that arises from an IFI's failure to comply with the Shari'ah rules and principles determined by the Shari'ah board of the IFI or the relevant body in the territory in which the IFI operates. Lack of good corporate governance, Shari'ah professionalism, and adequate control mechanisms are the biggest threats to Shari'ah compliance in Islamic banks. A study by Basituddin (2020) examines the link between corporate governance mechanisms and SNCR. The empirical results show that those banks with a smaller board and higher degree of independence are exposed to lessened Shari'ah non-compliance risk. Additionally, it is concluded that frequency of Shari'ah board meetings is negatively correlated with SNCR and banks with stable corporate governance environments have reduced SNCR (Basiruddin & Ahmed, 2020).

If an IFI has an adequate good governance system and means of control, the SNCR could be mitigated (Lailiya, 2024) because implementing Shari'ah governance can encourage trust in Islamic banks (Rahman El-Junusi, 2009), increase their market share (Rosestino & Kusumaningtias, 2022), and possibly be reflected in long-term customer loyalty (El Junusi, 2012). Good Islamic corporate governance is the best way to improve Shari'ah banking performance (Cahya & Kusumaningtias, 2020).

Oz et al. (2016 have categorised Shari'ah noncompliance risk as part of operational risk under the Basel III framework. Many authors are of the view that Shari'ah non- compliance is an additional dimension which is not comparable with the operational risk of conventional banks and should be treated as an additional risk under Pillar II of the Basel III framework (Ling et al., 2022).

Therefore, SNCR is a serious issue to consider as it may affect the sustainability of Islamic banks. The conscious implementation of Shari'ah governance is a good step in this direction.

Shari'ah Corporate Governance

Conventional and Islamic governance systems firstly differ in ideology: key stakeholders in the former are shareholders, while this circle is wider for the latter and includes employees, partners, public institutions, society, etc. In other words, all possible stakeholders could be included. There are ten different types of stakeholders in Islamic financial institutions (IFIs): shareholders, boards of directors, Shari'ah boards, managers, employees, current account holders, investment account holders, partners through *mudarabah* and *musharakah*, regulators, and external auditors (Hassan & Chowdhury, 2010) – all of whom operate within the economic, financial, legal, and accounting systems as well as with banking associations. Moreover, Islamic corporate governance guarantees the compliance of Islamic banks' operations with Shari'ah principles.

The critical importance of Shari'ah compliance in the Islamic corporate governance framework is also evident in the IFSB's "Guiding Principles on Shari'ah Governance Systems for Institutions offering Islamic Financial Services", whose main aim is the harmonisation of Shari'ah governance structures and procedures across different countries and legal systems. In this document, a Shari'ah governance system is defined "as a set of institutional and organisational arrangements through which an institution offering Islamic financial services ensures that there is effective independent oversight of Shari'ah compliance in its activities". According to the same document, good Islamic corporate governance assumes: (1) a series of organisational arrangements which combine effective IFI management with the interests of stakeholders; (2) incentives for governance structures like a board of directors, Shari'ah supervisory board, and management teams; and (3) compliance with Islamic Shari'ah rules and principles.

From the beginning, IFIs have been developing without a clear legislative or regulatory framework with enough legal force to even sanction them if necessary. Doubt and misunderstanding surrounding their conceptualisation, and different Islamic practices are an obstacle for organisations and regulatory authorities to take meaningful initial steps for applying legislation and regulation. That is why many countries have developed their own standards, making efforts at harmonising practices through the Accounting and Auditing Organization for Islamic Financial Institutions (AAOIFI), the Islamic Financial Services Board

(IFSB), the International Islamic Rating Agency (IIRA), the International Islamic Financial Market (IIFM), and the Liquidity Management Center (LMC).

Islamic Shari'ah governance (SG) principles emphasise clear corporate governance (CG) standards and structures, transparency, reporting, and adherence to those principles. No doubt, Islamic SG in banking provides a specific governance structure apart from that of traditional CG with Shari'ah boards on the top and in compliance with additional Shari'ah norms.

SG is as important for IFIs as traditional CG is for conventional financial institutions. The most significant consequence could be damaged reputations and decreased consumer trust in Islamic banks (Zada et al., 2017). Similar conclusions have been made by Chapra and Ahmed (2002) and Hasan (2009). The lack of an effective framework may cause *Shari'ah compliance shocks*, which will cause both financial as well as non-financial losses. Therefore "the Shari'ah tone" must be set from the top, flowing down the entire corporate leadership chain in all functions and operations of the Islamic bank or window. As mentioned above, the IFSB (2009) has defined Shari'ah governance as "a set of overall mechanisms by which IFIs assure Shari'ah compliance from its beginning to the end". Ginena and Hamid (2015) focus on SG's role in implementing Shari'ah principles throughout all organisational structures of IFIs. The SG framework must include guidelines for internal bodies from middle and operational management level.

Wardhany and Arshad (2012) also focus on a well-established SG framework and infrastructure. When IFIs have adequate governance structures and coordination between them, their Shari'ah compliance cannot be challenged. Hasan (2009) and (Hidayah, 2014) assume that pre- and post- Shari'ah compliance increases the trustworthiness, accountability, reliability, and credibility of IFIs.

According to the IFSB, Shari'ah governance must oversee compliance with the following:

(1) the issuance of proper Shari'ah *fatwas*; (2) bringing them to the attention of middle and operational management; (3) an internal Shari'ah process of compliance; and (4) an annual review of Shari'ah compliance.

As mentioned at length already, IFIs have a specific corporate body called the Shari'ah board alternatively, "Shari'ah committee", "Shari'ah supervisory board", or "Shari'ah advisory board" whose main responsibility is to ensure the Shari'ah compliance of all their actions. Shari'ah compliance is a unique characteristic of IFIs and the main dividing line between conventional and Islamic corporate governance. The board of directors usually appoints three experienced scholars as members of the Shari'ah board, which exercises its duties thanks to its right to issue fatwas. However, a more important issue is the interpretation of fatwas, which is essential for providing clear and understandable information to stakeholders, especially Islamic finance investors.

The "Faces" of Shari'ah Boards in Different Legal Systems

It has been made obvious that Shari'ah governance practices in IFIs differ globally due to the lack of a standardised regulative approach to Islamic banking and finance.

The concrete responsibilities and functions of Shari'ah boards as well as the legal enforcement of their fatwas can be mainly understood within the respective regulatory framework. Islamic banking development depends on the suggested solutions of Shari'ah scholars to previously unknown problems. Therefore, there is no one or best interpretation of such problems: their fatwas occur in the course of IFIs' daily activities.

These issues put the following important questions in front of banks' governance: What are the minimum requirements for Shari'ah board members and their independence?[47] What innovation opportunities are being presented by Shari'ah boards? What about competition with conventional banks? Standardised interpretations across countries? These questions, however, still lack clear answers.

In their attempt to answer these questions, regulators have developed three methods: the first is the *regulation of Shari'ah boards*. The regulator itself chooses Shari'ah board scholars based on an assessment of their knowledge and competencies. This approach allows banks' boards the freedom to issue rulings while maintaining oversight. The second approach is *market-based regulation*. Here, the task to develop methods and standards falls on the shoulders of banks or other market participants. Regulators should consider making Shari'ah ratings mandatory. The third approach is the *centralisation of Shari'ah board approvals*, where a central Shari'ah board controls Shari'ah standards (Benaissa et al., 2007) and guarantees permissibility from an Islamic banking perspective.

Great care must be taken when regulators make compliance decisions so as not to limit banks' innovative capabilities. In other words, the golden middle between competition and innovation must be found.

---

[47] Independence is one of the most important AAOIFI standards regarding Shari'ah scholars who serve on different boards because of their deficit.

There is no one regulatorily accepted model for Shari'ah governance systems (Di Mauro, 2013). In the first group of Muslim countries, Shari'ah governance is seriously regulated and a national Shari'ah body has to be established (Malaysia). In the second group of more liberal Muslim countries, IFIs and their internal Shari'ah compliance bodies have some degree of freedom. Finally, there are IFIs operating in non-Muslim countries, whose legal systems are not interested in any aspect of Shari'ah corporate governance.

In Muslim countries with an established regulatory system, the fatwas of Shari'ah boards are usually regarded as legally binding. In Muslim countries with less robust or not fully developed regulatory systems, the legal enforcement of rulings mainly depends on the corporate governance provisions about Shari'ah boards' activities and the validity of their fatwas. Lastly, in the third category of mixed countries with both legal systems functioning – state law and Shari'ah law – Islamic finance case studies are subject to the secular courts' assessment.

In such cases, there may be a conflict between the national legislation of a given country and Shari'ah law. For example, a court in an EU member state may not consider a financial transaction to be illegal, while it may on the other hand be contrary to Shari'ah principles. It is unsurprising that regulations issued in these countries can contradict Shari'ah law; thus, disputes are settled in such a way as to "force" the Islamic bank into Shari'ah non-compliance.

Shari'ah supervisory boards, independent of their internal positioning within the Islamic bank or externally, observe compliance with Islamic religious principles. Each board is able to design, develop, and issue Shari'ah-compliant financial products and instruments. The internal tasks of Shari'ah supervisory boards are supported by reliable Islamic financial organisations such as the IFSB and the AAOIFI (Di Mauro et al., 2013).

There are national, regional, and international organisations whose aim is to develop guidelines for Shari'ah boards. These are envisaged to ensure Shari'ah compliance in transactions but do not specify details about competent bodies. Shari'ah boards are responsible for: *ex-ante Shari'ah auditing* through issuing fatwas; *ex-post Shari'ah auditing* through verification of transactions with those fatwas; *zakat* calculations and payments; and distribution of non-Shari'ah earnings, income, and expenses among current account holders and investment account holders – the main two group shareholders in an Islamic bank. Each

Shari'ah board must also report on the Shari'ah compliance of all its financial transactions (Ben Bouheni & Bellalah, 2012).

A Shari'ah supervisory board (SSB), also known as a Shari'ah committee (SC) or Shari'ah advisory council (SAC), is an important organ in IFI corporate governance (Clode, 2002). Abubakar (2022) states that though the type of Shari'ah committee is not mandated, its role in monitoring IFIs' Shari'ah compliance is always the same.

A key decision to be made is whether to establish a centralised SSB (in addition to SSBs at bank level) to oversee the Shari'ah governance framework within IFIs. A centralised SSB has the advantage of harmonising Shari'ah-rulings, reducing compliance costs for IFIs. A centralised SSB could be set up by the regulator or, as they are encouraged to do, IFIs can collectively establish such a board (Mejia, 2014).

Shari'ah boards can be established at the *micro* or *macro level.*

Shari'ah boards at the micro level have operational responsibilities in product development and structuring activities, reviewing and approving tasks, issuing an annual Shari'ah compliance certification, issuing fatwas, Shari'ah auditing (McMillen, 2006), ensuring the Shari'ah compliance of investment transactions like shares, equities, and *sukuk* (Ayub, 2007), and *zakat* collection. In sum, the roles of a Shari'ah board could be grouped into three main areas: fatwa issuance, supervision, and review (Dusuki, 2011, p. 709).

At the macro level, Shari'ah boards can be part of the central bank or at regulatory authority level. Shari'ah boards at this level play significant regulatory roles and act as the highest Shari'ah authority of IFIs (ibid.: 708). The regulatory authority provides guidelines for IFIs, appoints institutional Shari'ah supervisory boards, and informs the central bank about Shari'ah matters. At the micro level, there can be an internal Shari'ah board, as in Islamic banks, or simply a Shari'ah advisory board.

Noordin and Kassim (2019) and Alam et al. (2021) have also classified Shari'ah governance into three diversified types of models *centralised, laissez-faire,* and *hybrid.* In the centralised structure, there is again a central Shari'ah supervisory board in the central bank with similar responsibilities as those described in the previous classification. This model is considered to be more stable and comprehensive compared to models in Malaysia, Sudan, Brunei, Indonesia, and

Iran. The "laissez-faire" or decentralised SG model developed by individual SSBs of IFIs involves minimal regulator and market interference. In this model, IFIs and their SSBs ensure Shari'ah compliance independently, which may raise concerns about the quality of compliance, services, and fatwa resolutions due to varying interpretations of Shari'ah principles[48]. IFIs in the hybrid structure (e.g., in the UAE and Pakistan) are required to confirm their Shari'ah compliance and simultaneously must report to a central regulatory body (Noordin & Kassim, 2019; Alam et al., 2021).

Regulatory authorities rarely provide corporate governance frameworks especially concerning Islamic banks. Some regulatory frameworks burden the board of directors with additional Shari'ah compliance responsibility, since the board has the utmost authority in advising on Shari'ah matters. According to Song and Oosthuizen (2014), there are two possibilities: *setting up a national/central Shari'ah board* or *setting up a Shari'ah board in banks reporting to the central bank.*

The relationship of this Shari'ah board with the central bank is an advisory one. A Shari'ah board has to ensure coordination with the central bank and has the main responsibility for the Shari'ah compliance, which usually transmits it through clear guidelines to its senior management, who do the same and disseminate this information to operational management. Middle and lower management levels, on the other side, are supposed to ensure Shari'ah compliance in line with the guidance of the superior Shari'ah board on the top level.

The next important question is to which governance authority the Shari'ah board has to report. According to research by Song and Oosthuizen (2014), it could be the board of directors of the bank, the general assembly of the bank, the top management of the Islamic bank, the executive committee of the Islamic bank, or the bank itself. Another challenge is whether or not the Shari'ah board is accountable to the IFI's board of directors. In most cases, it seems that an advisory relationship exists between the banks corporate governance body and the Shari'ah board in order to ensure its independence.

Shari'ah scholars, who are very difficult to find and cultivate, contribute greatly towards the effectiveness of the Shari'ah governance system. Shari'ah boards play

[48] Typical for GCC countries like Saudi Arabia, Kuwait, and Qatar, as well as the UK, Germany, France, South Korea, Hong Kong, and Japan.

a key role in maintaining the reliability of IFIs, which is achieved by following "*collective jihad*" and the subsequently issued fatwas (Dusuki, 2011, p. 707).

Internally, Shari'ah compliance is usually conducted by Shari'ah auditors, which are structures within the Islamic bank. In countries where Shari'ah law is the first legal source (e.g., Iran, Pakistan, Saudi Arabia, and Sudan), including for banking and financial legislation, an Islamic bank's internal auditor has a statutory responsibility to ensure Shari'ah compliance. In others, an Islamic bank has to arrange a Shari'ah auditor or compliance officer, which must be approved by the bank supervisory authority.

The *external auditing process* in relation to Shari'ah compliance also depends on the applicable legal framework. An Islamic bank's external auditor has a statutory responsibility to control Shari'ah compliance in countries where Shari'ah law is the default source of all legislation. Where it is not, the Islamic bank's external auditor has no direct responsibility to assess or verify Shari'ah compliance by the Islamic bank.

Stable corporate governance systems are supported by appropriate arrangements

with regulators and external companies for financial information services. What is more, these public rating agencies could create a positive financial infrastructure for Shari'ah compliance. Sufficient incentives should be found for these agencies which could effectively oversee Islamic banking in accordance with Shari'ah principles. "Islamic rating" has become an exclusive topic for such government-sponsored organisations as the Malaysian Rating Corporation and the International Islamic Rating Agency.[49]

[49] In addition to Shari'ah boards, most Islamic banks have established a Shari'ah review unit.

Standards for Shari'ah Supervisory Boards

There are numerous types of financial activities, but who in the end decides whether those activities are Islamic or not? There are different standards in different countries. There is no unique set of rules that can be used to check if a financial activity is compliant. This may be surprising for non-Muslims, but it is a fact that there are more than 1.5 billion Muslims and yet no single set of Shari'ah rules in the Islamic world. Therefore, the absence of universal standards in the Islamic financial world is quite normal.

An adequate legal and regulatory framework is instrumental for ensuring the sustainable development of Islamic finance, according to Bedoui (2016). To standardise Shari'ah norms, various organisations have been established to develop international standards and guidelines.

The specialised international standard-setting agencies for Islamic finance are as follows[50]:

1. IFSB (Islamic Financial Services Board);
2. AAOIFI (Accounting and Auditing Organization for Islamic Financial Institutions[51]);
3. IIFM (International Islamic Financial Market);
4. IILM (International Islamic Liquidity Management Corporation);
5. IIRA (Islamic International Rating Agency).

The standards of who of these international Shari'ah supervisory bodies (the AAOIFI and IFSB) have been becoming more similar in recent years, and there is some slight overlap between them. Collaboration of the AAOIFI and IFSB with the IMF and World Bank also helps establish unity in terms of standards. Nevertheless, it should be said that both supervisory boards have no power to

[50] In most countries where Islamic banks are present, the conceptual regulatory framework of the Basel Committee on Banking Supervision (BCBS) is the "default framework".

[51] The AAOIFI developed the Governance Standard for Islamic Financial Institutions (GSIFI), which provides guidance on the definition, appointment, composition, and reporting of Shari'ah supervisory boards. When we talk about Islamic windows standards, there is a special draft for them which shall be the same as prescribed in the relevant AAOIFI standards for fully Islamic banks.

impose sanctions when any Islamic institution does not follow those standards. There are many national- and institutional-level boards who can decide whether a financial product is Islamic or not. Transparency plays a crucial role in this case. Transparency attracts not only more capital from the Islamic world but also helps to eliminate the criticism that Islamic finance mimics conventional finance (Sekreter, 2021).

The Executive Board of the International Monetary Fund (IMF) approves the use of the Core Principles for Islamic Finance Regulation (CPIFR), which were developed by the Islamic Financial Services Board (IFSB) with the participation of the Basel Committee Secretariat on banking supervision.

In addition, Basel III standards establishing new capital and liquidity requirements for international banks have been announced, and the IFSB has produced updated standards and guidance specifically for Islamic banks. However, until now, no research has been undertaken on the implementation of the most recent publication, Revised Capital Adequacy Standard for Institutions Offering Islamic Financial Services. Based on the empirical literature of 23 papers published between 2013 and 2022, Ling (2022) suggests that Basel III has had a major impact on the Islamic banking sector's financial risk. It is recommended for future research to be undertaken to investigate current Islamic banking trends and how Basel III could align with Shari'ah standards.

Shari'ah Compliance in European Banks

The offer of European institutions is aimed not only at customers living in countries where Islam is the dominant religion. It is often highlighted that Islamic financial instruments are not exclusively addressed to Muslims but also others, both individual and corporate clients (Pistrui & Fahed-Sreih, 2010; Masiukiewicz, 2014). Islamic funds may also be attractive for retail and corporate investors. Transactions with such instruments are safe, since they are based on assets and offer higher rates of return than traditional deposits or government bonds. Due to the fact that the global population of Muslims was set to grow up to 2.2 billion by 2020making up over one third of the world population, further increased demand for Shari'ah-compliant banking and investments should also be expected (Zielewski, 2017).

The emergence of Islamic financial institutions is not due to pressure by a European Muslim minority; rather, it is a consequence of strategies for financial markets adopted by authorities which include the creation of global financial centres. In addition, an infrastructural and educational supply network for such entities is being developed. In the future, offerings from Islamic financial institutions will probably also become more attractive for those customers who do not know much about and do not follow Shari'ah law but wish to use services from more trustworthy and ethical banks. It is expected for other Islamic banks to be established, the number of Islamic windows in conventional banks to increase, and further development of Islamic investment funds to take place in Europe (Masiukiewicz, 2017).

The existing Shari'ah governance systems vary across countries. Some of them are in favour of more regulative models while others prefer more liberal management. Certainly, one cannot determine which option is better. Perhaps it depends on the complex impact of many other factors such as the legal system, established relations between regulatory authorities, economic conditions, management practices in companies, etc.

A "reactive approach" is more common in non-Muslim regions like Europe and countries such as the United Kingdom and Turkey, where no regulatory measures have been taken regarding the Shari'ah governance framework. IFIs in these countries are regulated in a similar way as their conventional analogues (Hassan, 2009).

Taking into account that there is no specific legislation governing IFIs or any directive specifying a *Shari'ah governance framework*, regulators are supposed to take action only if there is a significant problem that could potentially have industry-wide consequences.

The research methodology used was content analysis[52] of reports and corporate governance statements of the selected banks. The following section will examine practices in European countries towards the Shari'ah compliance of conventional banks offering Islamic financial services (mostly through Islamic windows) and fully Islamic banks, too. For this purpose, the corporate governance models of the largest representatives will be analysed and presented in Table 1 to answer how well they meet the above mentioned criteria and whether Shari'ah compliance in conventional banks is possible.

[52] A method which can be used qualitatively or quantitatively for systematically analysing written, verbal, or visual documentation.

Table 1. Corporate Governance of European Islamic Banks

	European Bank / IFI	Head-quarters	Main Shari'ah compliance authority	Type of bank	Internal Shari'ah compliance	Reporting to the board ofdirectors	Board members' information
1	ADIB UK	UK	Internal Shari'ah supervisory Committee	1	Yes	NI	Yes
2	Al Baraka Turk	Turkey	Unified Shari'ah supervisory board	1	Yes	No	Yes
3	Al Rayan Bank	UK	Shari'ah supervisory committee	1	Yes	No	Yes
4	Arab African International Bank	UK	Boards of directors	1	NI	No	Yes
5	Bahrain Middle East Bank	UK	Board of directors	1	NI	NI	Yes
6	Bank ABC Group	UK	Shari'ah supervisory board	1	Yes	Yes	Yes
7	Bank of London & the Middle East	UK	Shari'ah supervisory board	1	NI	No	Yes
8	Bosna Bank International	Bosnia and Herzegovina	Shari'ah board	1	NI	NI	Yes
9	Dar Al-Maal Al Islami Trust	Switzerland	Religious board at the board of supervisors level	1	NI	Yes	NI
10	EIIB	UK	Shari'ah supervisory board	1	NI	NI	NI

11	FWU AG	Germany	Compliance	1	NI	Yes	NI
12	Gatehouse Bank PLC	UK	Shari'ah supervisory board	1	Yes	Yes	Yes
13	Habib Bank (HBL)	UK	Shari'ah supervisory board	1	Yes	Yes	Yes
14	HSBC	UK	Shari'ah committee	1	No	No	No
15	J. Safra Sarasin	Switzerland	Shari'ah advisory board	1	NI	NI	NI
16	KT Bank AG	Germany	Ethical council	1	Yes	Yes	Yes
17	Munich Re	Germany	Shari'ah advisory board/ Central SSB of Malaysia	1	Yes	No	Yes
18	National Bank of Pakistan UK	UK	Shari'ah board	1	Yes	Yes	Yes
19	QIB UK	UK	Shari'ah board	1	Yes	No	Yes
20	QNB	UK	Shari'ah board	1	NI	NI	NI
21	Riyad Bank	UK	Shari'ah committee	1	NI	No	Yes
22	SAB	UK	Shari'ah committee	1	NI	Yes	Yes
23	Safa Investment	Switzerland	Shariyah Review Bureau	1	NI	No	NI
24	Solidarity Takafol S.A.	Luxemburg	Shari'ah supervisory board	1	NI	Yes	NI
25	Turkiye Finans	Turkey	Advisory committee	1	NI	Yes	Yes
26	Vakif Katilim Bank	Turkey	Advisory committee	1	Yes	Yes	Yes
27	Ziraat Bank	Turkey	Advisory	1	Yes	NI	Yes

			committee				
28	ABC International Bank PLC	UK	Shari'ah supervisory board	2	Yes	No	NI
29	Ahli United Bank PLC	UK	Shari'ah supervisory board	2	Yes	No	NI
30	Bank of Ireland	UK	No Shari'ah compliance body	2	No	No	No
31	Barclays	UK	No Shari'ah compliance body	2	No	No	No
32	Citi Islamic Investment Bank	UK	Shari'ah supervisor board	2	Yes	NI	Yes
33	Deutsche Bank	Germany	Shari'ah custody	2	NI	NI	NI
34	IBJ International London	UK	No Shari'ah compliance body	2	No	No	No
35	J Aron & Co	UK	No Shari'ah compliance authority	2	No	No	No
36	Lloyds	UK	Shari'ah committee	2	No	NI	Yes
37	RBS	UK	Group board	2	No	No	No
38	Standard Chartered	UK	Shari'ah advisory committee	2	Yes	NI	Yes
39	UBS	Switzerland	Board of directors	2	No	No	No
40	United National bank	UK	Board of directors	2	No	No	No

Source: Authors' contribution.

A survey of Shari'ah corporate governance systems in 40 European banks offering Islamic products has been taken based on the "Islamic and Ethical Finance" list of the UK Government and the "Islamic Crowdfunding" website. The country break-down reveals that most Islamic finance is found in Great Britain and Turkey. These 40 banks that were examined belong to two groups: the first are fully Islamic banks and/or branches of banks with headquarters in an Islamic country, and the second are conventional banks offering Islamic financial products.

There is only one bank which ensures its Shari'ah compliance through a centralised external body (Munich Re). In the other banks, Shari'ah boards are situated at management level and are independent from the board of directors in most of them. In some cases, Shari'ah compliance is under the competence of an advisory committee to the board of directors or belongs to an ethical council, religious board, audit committee, etc. Almost half of the banks have internal Shari'ah units for implementing Shari'ah principles at senior management level. Such variety only in the placement and even in the names of the Shari'ah compliance authorities in European banks shows us that there is an urgent need for harmonisation and standardisation of Shari'ah compliance mechanisms at macro level just like in Muslim countries. An internal Shari'ah compliance structure is present in 16 of the total 40, and 11 report to the board of directors – about quarter, which is a small percentage. The question is whether this interferes with their independence, which is one of the most important AAOIFI standards for Shari'ah boards. Only 4 of the 12 banks from the second group have a structural unit for Shari'ah compliance. Most of the banks (nearly half) have provided information about the members of Shari'ah boards or similar structures. Most who have no information about them feature no such authority at all or lack sufficient accountability over their Islamic financial operations.

The other significant conclusion is perhaps that conventional banks offering Islamic financial products through "Islamic windows" unfortunately do not have a clearly defined structure for compliance with Shari'ah norms. The reason may lie in the fact that these large banks are generally organisationally quite complicated, this segment represents a small share of their operations, and/or they do not have a sufficiently cultivated human capital competent to interpret Shari'ah cases.

Conclusion

In summary, current practices for ensuring Shari'ah compliance rely mainly on Shari'ah supervisory boards. These structures struggle with many challenges relating to their independence, information confidentiality, and lack of competent Shari'ah scholars, as well as clear guidelines for their responsibilities. Some countries have sought the help of external institutions. However, this creates other difficulties for IFI groups operating in different legal systems and may be problematic for regulators in non-Islamic countries. Guaranteeing Shari'ah compliance through market mechanisms is in its infancy.

Despite the difficult combination of the two forms of financing, one thing is certain: this new alternative form has a promising future, and it is appropriate to look for ways to include both in traditional financing. After reviewing the literature, it can be concluded that supervisory or management boards are not competent to confirm or deny the Shari'ah compliance of a given financial institution. But this does not prevent them from working in parallel with their peers and complementing each other.

The results of the literature review, not only in the European region but also in the Middle East, confirm that regulations by a specific central authority would be most effective at least in cases of disputes in certain critical situations. At the moment, however, due to the lack of established regulatory legal frameworks at the national or regional level, compliance issues have to be resolved at the corporate management level by the institution itself. The question was whether the Shari'ah board, which is the most common structure for ensuring Shari'ah compliance, should be an independent body or instead be subordinate to a supervisory board with only advisory duties. The answer should depend mainly on the specific form of Islamic financial products and services provided – whether the bank is fully Islamic or these are provided through Islamic windows. In the first case, the Shari'ah board is supposed to have the main role, taking into account the reputational risk if there is a discrepancy with Islamic principles; and in the second case, it is supposed to be in the form of a committee with a consultative role subordinate to the corporate management.

Internal and external actions should begin with determining which synergistic effect could provide an effective framework for ensuring Shari'ah compliance. Such a framework could improve stakeholders' confidence and would enable innovation, leading to introducing some new Shari'ah-oriented products and services. In issuing its fatwas, the SSB must be guided by standardised contracts and practices emerging from international regulatory authorities. The review of transactions would mainly be entrusted to internal review units, which are in unison with Shari'ah principles at a higher management level and which are responsible to determine whether the IFI's activities meet its Shari'ah requirements. If this process is supported by reputable agents, like rating agencies, stock markets, financial media, and researchers who would channel signals to market players, it is expected that such a framework (including structures and processes, internal and external) could enhance public understanding about the requirements of Shari'ah. This process can be accelerated if more categorical frameworks and norms are introduced by the relevant regulatory authorities at the national or regional (e.g., European) level.

Contribution of individual authors

Sevgi Osman investigated Shari'ah compliance and European Islamic banking practices. Nedyalko Valkanov carried out the research about compliance risk.

Conflicts of Interest

The authors have no conflicts of interest to declare.

References

1. AAOIFI. *Governance Standard No. (5) Independence of Shari'ah Supervisory Board*. Available at https://aaoifi.com/aaoifi-gs-5-independence-of-sharia-supervisory-board/? lang=en [Accessed 04.12.2024].
2. Abubakar, Y. S. (2022). Shari'ah Governance: Some Probable Challenges That May Be Faced by Shari'ah Committee (SC) at Islamic Financial Institutions (IFIs). *International Research Journal of Shari'ah, Muamalat and Islam*, 4 (11), 1–9.
3. Alam, M. K., Islam, F. & Runy, M. (2021). Why does Shari'ah governance framework important for Islamic banks? *Asian Journal of Economics and Banking*, 4(2), 158–172. DOI: 10.1108/AJEB-02-2021-0018.
4. Ali, M. & Hassan, F. (2019). The Study of Potential Shari'ah Non-Compliance Risks in Murabahah Along with Their Risk Management. *Journal of Finance & Economics Research*, (4), 4–58, 10.20547/jfer1904104.
5. Aljabrin, S. & Mejia, A. L. (2014). Regulation and supervision of Islamic banks. *IMF Working Paper*, No. 2014/219.
6. Basel Committee on Banking Supervision. (2005). *Compliance and the compliance function in banks*. Basel: Bank for International Settlements.
7. Basiruddin, R. & Ahmed, H. (2020). Corporate governance and Shari'ah non-compliant risk in Islamic banks: evidence from Southeast Asia. *Corporate Governance: The International Journal of Business in Society*, 20 (2), 240–262.
8. Benaissa, N. E., Jopart, X., Maddux, M., Tanrikulu, O. & Whelan, F. (2007). The Impact of Regulation on the Future of Islamic Finance. In: Ali, S. N. (ed.). *Integrating Islamic Finance into the Mainstream: Regulation, Standardization and Transparency*. Cambridge, MA: Harvard University, 13–30.
9. Bouheni, F. B. & Ammi, C. (2015). Banking governance: what's special about Islamic banks? *Journal of Applied Business Research*, 31 (4), 1621.
10. Che Azmi, A., Rosman, R. & Omar, N. (2021). Shari'ah non-compliant income disclosures and the moral legitimacy strategies of Islamic banks. *Journal of Islamic Accounting and Business Research*, 12 (8), 1146–1164. Detailed info on the report and its contents are available on AGEB EDs – SSB Review and Report, https://aaoifi.com/exposure-drafts-3/?lang=en (Accessed 04.12.2024).

11. Di Mauro, F., Caristi, P., Couderc, S., Di Maria, A., Ho, L., Kaur Grewal, B., Masciantonio, S., Ongena, S. & Zaheer, S. (2013). Islamic finance in Europe. *ECB Occasional Paper* 146.
12. Dusuki, A. W. (2011). *Islamic Financial System Principles & Operations.* Malaysia: ISRA.
13. Exposure Draft (AGEB 2/2023) of the AAOIFI Governance Standard (GS). Shari'ah Governance Framework. Available at https://aaoifi.com/wp-content/uploads/2023/12/ED-Shari'ah-Governance-Framework.pdf (Accessed 04.12.2024).
14. Exposure Draft (AGEB 6/2023) of the Application of Shari'ah Governance Principles to Islamic Finance Windows. Available at https://aaoifi.com/announcement/the- aaoifi-governance-and-ethics-board-ageb-issues-six-exposure-drafts-of-governance-standards/?lang=en (Accessed 04.12.2024).
15. Exposure Drafts, AAOIFI. Available at https://aaoifi.com/exposure-drafts-3/?lang=en (Accessed 04.12.2024).
16. Hasan, A. I. & Risfandy, T. (2021). Islamic banks' stability: Full-fledged vs Islamic windows. *Journal of Accounting and Investment*, 22 (1), 192–205.
17. Hasan, Z. B. (2009). Regulatory framework of Shari'ah governance system in Malaysia, GCC Countries and the UK. *Kyoto Bulletin of Islamic Area Studies*, 3 (2).
18. Hassan, M. K. & Chowdhury, M. A. M. (2010). Islamic banking regulations in light of Basel II. *American Journal of Islam and Society*, 27 (1), 74–101.
19. IBD. (2018). *Knowledge Centre Frequently Asked Questions (FAQs).* Islamic Banking Department, State Bank of Pakistan. Retrieved from http://www.sbp.org.pk/IB/ FAQ.asp
20. IMF. (2018). IMF Executive Board Adopts Decisions to Formally Recognize the Core Principles for Islamic Finance Regulation (CPIFR) for Banking. *IMF Press Release* No. 18/193.
21. Islamic Finance in the UK. (2024), *Islamic and Ethical Finance Website.* Available at https://appgief.org.uk/about/islamic-finance-in-the-uk/ (Accessed 04.12.2024).
22. Kammarti, B. (2022). Sociogenesis of Islamic Finance in Europe. *Kyoto Bulletin of Islamic Area Studies*, (15), 49–70.
23. Lailiya, L. & Kusumaningtias, R. (2024). Impact and risk management of sharia non- compliance in islamic banking. In: *Proceeding International*

Conference on Accounting and Finance (January). UII. Yogyakarta, Indonesia, 583–593.

24.Ling, D. X., Haron, R. & Hasan, A. (2022). BASEL III Capital Regulation Framework and Islamic Bank's Risk. *IIUM Law Journal*, 30 (S2), 93–128.

25.List of Islamic Banks in Europe. (2024). *Islamic Crowdfunding website*. Available at https://www.islamic-crowdfunding.com/list-of-islamic-banks-in-europe.html (Accessed 04.12.2024).

26.Malik, R. (2020). *14th Meeting COMCEC Financial Cooperation Working Group, Shari'ah Governance Framework and AAOIFI*. Available at //www.comcec.org/wp- content/uploads/2021/07/4-A.pdf (Accessed 04.12.2024).

27.Masiukiewicz, P. (2017). Expansion of Islamic finance in Europe. *Journal of Intercultural Management*, 9 (2), 31–51.

28.Mejia, A. L., Aljabrin, S., Awad, R., Norat, M. M. & Song, M. I. (2014). *Regulation and supervision of Islamic banks*. International Monetary Fund.

29.Oz, E., Ali, M. M., Khokher, Z. R. & Rosman, R. (2016). Shari'ah Non-Compliance Risk in The Banking Sector: Impact on Adequacy Framework of Islamic Banks. *IFSB Working Paper*, Series WP-05/03/2016. Available at https://www.ifsb.org/wp-content/uploads/2023/10/WP-05_En.pdf (Accessed 04.12.2024).

30.Pellegrini, M. & Grais, W. (2006). Corporate governance and Shari'ah compliance in institutions offering Islamic financial services. *Policy Research Working Paper*, No. WPS4054. World Bank.

31.Ratnasari, N. G., Hati, S. R. H. & Chalid, D. A. (2021). Full-Fledged vs Islamic Bank Windows: Which One Do Muslim Customers Know Better and Prefer More? *Iqtishadia*, 14 (2), 301–311.

32.Salisu, A., Saniff, S. M. & Hassan, S. A. (2020). Sharia Board of Islamic Banks and the Attitude of Fatwa Shopping. *Ikonomika*, 5 (2), 193-204.

33.Sarker, M. A. A. (2022). Shari'ah Non-Compliance Risks in Islamic Banking: Concept, Significance and Management Methodology. *Thoughts on Economics*, 32 (3/4).

34.Sekreter, A. (2021). Islamic Finance: Its Theory, Products and a Brief View of Islamic Finance in Europe, Einstein Visiting Fellow. In: *4th ICBF Conference* (November). Oxford.

35.Solé, J. (2007). Introducing Islamic Banks into Conventional Banking *Systems*. *IMF Working Paper*, No. 2007/175.

36. Song, I. and Oosthuizen, C. L. (2014, December). Islamic Banking Regulation and
37. Supervision: Survey Results and Challenges. *IMF Working Paper* No. 14/220, Available at SSRN: https://ssrn.com/abstract=2561245
38. Valkanov, N. (2019). *Compliance v pomosht na finansovoto regulirane*. Varna: Nauka i Ikonomika PH. [Вълканов, Н. (2019). Compliance в помощ на финансовото регулиране. Варна: Изд. „Наука и икономика"] (*in Bulgarian*).
39. Visser, H. (2016). Islamic Finance in Europe: Regulatory issues. In: *2nd FinConf Conference* (October). Sarajevo.
40. Wardhany, N., & Arshad, S. (2012). The role of Shari'ah board in Islamic banks: A case study of Malaysia, Indonesia and Brunei Darussalam. In: *2nd ISRA Colloquium* (November). Kuala Lumpur.

Sevgi Osman, PhD, is a Chief Assistant Professor at Varna Free University “Chernorizets Hrabar”. ORCID 0000-0002-5108-5476, sevgi.osman@vfu.bg

Nedyalko Valkanov, PhD, is an Associate Professor at University of Economics – Varna, n.valkanov@ue-varna.bg

How to cite this article:

Osman, S., Valkanov, N. (2025). Shari’ah Compliance in a European Banking Context.

Economic Thought Journal, 70 (1), 72–96. https://doi.org/10.56497/etj2570105

www.ingramcontent.com/pod-product-compliance
Lightning Source LLC
LaVergne TN
LVHW052255200926
848481LV00002B/375
9798899660849